A Librarian's Guide to Graphs, Data and the Semantic Web

Chandos
Information Professional Series
Series Editor: Ruth Rikowski
(email: Rikowskigr@aol.com)

Chandos' new series of books is aimed at the busy information professional. They have been specially commissioned to provide the reader with an authoritative view of current thinking. They are designed to provide easy-to-read and (most importantly) practical coverage of topics that are of interest to librarians and other information professionals. If you would like a full listing of current and forthcoming titles, please visit www.chandospublishing.com.

New authors: we are always pleased to receive ideas for new titles; if you would like to write a book for Chandos, please contact Dr Glyn Jones on g.jones.2@elsevier.com or telephone +44 (0) 1865 843000.

A Librarian's Guide to Graphs, Data and the Semantic Web

James Powell and Matthew Hopkins
Los Alamos National Laboratory

AMSTERDAM • BOSTON • HEIDELBERG • LONDON
NEW YORK • OXFORD • PARIS • SAN DIEGO
SAN FRANCISCO • SINGAPORE • SYDNEY • TOKYO

Chandos Publishing is an imprint of Elsevier

Chandos Publishing is an imprint of Elsevier
225 Wyman Street, Waltham, MA 02451, USA
Langford Lane, Kidlington, OX5 1GB, UK

ISBN: 978-1-84334-753-8

British Library Cataloguing-in-Publication Data
A catalogue record for this book is available from the British Library

Library of Congress Control Number: 2015939547

For information on all Chandos Publishing
visit our website at http://store.elsevier.com/

Dedication

To Paul and his mom, "Ms Lenore"

Contents

About the authors

James Powell was born and raised in Virginia. He attended and later worked at Virginia Tech, where he honed his unique aptitude for both computer science and technical communications. About a decade ago, he moved to the southwest for a job at Los Alamos National Laboratory. He is a software developer specializing in information retrieval technologies and has contributed to a diverse array of projects at the Lab including social network applications, search engines, just-in-time information retrieval tools, Semantic Web applications, applied machine learning, and various projects aimed at managing research data for protein structures, infectious disease models, and data from NASA's Kepler mission characterizing variable stars.

Today, James lives and writes from his home in Santa Fe, New Mexico and works as a Research Technologist in the Research Library of Los Alamos National Laboratory.

Matthew Hopkins was born in Richmond, Virginia. He received his undergraduate degree from the University of Virginia and his Masters in Library Science from the University of North Carolina at Chapel Hill.

He lives with his family in Los Alamos, New Mexico, where he works at the Research Library of Los Alamos National Laboratory.

Preface and Acknowledgments

This book is in part an expanded version of a paper published in the ALA journal *Information Technology and Libraries* in December 2011 entitled "Graphs in Libraries: A Primer." This paper was written by myself and Matthew Hopkins, along with Daniel Alcazar, Robert Olendorf, Tamara McMahon, Amber Wu, and Linn Collins. Even though many library services are based upon or derived from network analysis, there weren't a lot of publications about graph theory and its applications in library and information science. This paper provided a good introduction to the topic, but ultimately a 5000 word feature article could do little more than scratch the surface. Several of us decided it might be worth expanding this paper into a book. We approached Chandos Publishing with a proposal and they suggested we also include material about the Semantic Web. This was a tall order, but we also knew it was spot on because the Semantic Web is an application of graph theory to information organization. We knew that if we pulled this off, we would bring together library science and the fledgling field of complexity in a way that would have a direct impact on future library services. Our book would empower librarians to speak the same language – and leverage the same insights – as complexity scientists.

Our first task was to explain where these technologies came from and why they were of interest to the library community. Our next challenge was to introduce graph theory without scaring off our audience, because graph theory is in fact a product of mathematics, and yet it is an accessible topic even for the nonmathematical inclined. Building on that foundation, we introduced many of the core concepts of the Semantic Web, including the triple, RDF graphs, ontologies, various Semantic Web standards, as well as reasoning and search. Then we surveyed the ways graph theory has been used to explore problems in many disciplines. Finally this we explored various ontologies that glue together Semantic Web graphs representing all the data that libraries accumulate about services and collections. The remainder of the book focuses on graph and Semantic Web "tools of the trade" including authoring, visualization, and storage and retrieval systems. The book ends with a pair of case studies, one based on Semantic Web technologies, the other based on pure graph modeling and graph analytic technologies. Our goal was to provide librarians and the technical staff who support them with strong conceptual foundations as well as examples of data models, rules, searches, and simple code that uses graphs and semantic data to support and augment various information retrieval tasks. We think this book has achieved this goal.

Writing a book is a huge undertaking, placing great demands and not a small amount of stress on those of us who attempt it. I couldn't have pulled off this project without my brilliant co-author Matthew Hopkins, nor the support of friends, coworkers, and family. I owe special thanks to Linn Collins, who encouraged us to pursue this project, and if time and circumstances had permitted, would have been one of our coauthors. I worked for Linn for more than 5 years, and she was a brilliant and supportive boss, the kind of person you'll have the chance to work for once or twice in your career, if you're lucky. Linn was the expert user who supplied many requirements for InfoSynth, the Semantic Web system described in one of the case studies in Chapter 23. The other case study is based on a project called EgoSystem. The director of Los Alamos National Laboratory (LANL), Dr. Charles McMillan, engaged the library directly in discussions that lead to the requirements for EgoSystem. That project fell to the Digital Library Research and Prototyping team, which is led by Herbert Van de Sompel. I consider myself doubly fortunate because like Linn Collins, Herbert is another great mentor as well as a very supportive boss. It has been while working for him that I gained the confidence to pursue this book project. For EgoSystem, Herbert assembled a group that included myself, and another member of his team, a software engineer able to master any programming language in a vanishingly short amount of time, Harihar (Harish) Shankar. We also had the especially good fortune to engage a LANL alum well known in the graph community, Marko Rodriguez, on both the design and implementation of EgoSystem. Marko is brilliant and energetic, and he lives and breathes graph theory. What I learned from working with Marko and the rest of the Ego project team greatly influenced this book. The four of us spent countless hours in a chilly conference room in front of a chalk board hashing out a property graph model that would address many practical – and a few novel, – requirements for the system. The LANL Research Library director Dianna (Dee) Magnoni, who joined LANL midway through the EgoSystem project, and became a strong advocate for its continued development. She was also an enthusiastic supporter of this book.

There were other fortuitous happenstances that helped this project along. For more than a year, Linn and I met with colleagues from the University of New Mexico, including Dr. Diana Northrup and Johann van Reenan, at the Santa Fe Institute to discuss methods for managing research data sets related to the study of karst terrain. Perched on a rocky hillside amongst a dwarf forest of junipers, pinyon pines, and a smattering of cacti, the Santa Fe Institute is a small campus consisting of several contemporary southwestern adobe structures that blend into the rusty hills of crumbled granite. This well-hidden think tank overlooks the city of Santa Fe and has expansive views of the Rio Grande valley, the Jemez mountains, and Los Alamos to the west. It was a beautiful, inspiring, and catalyzing half-way point for us to convene. I remember perusing a number of books and papers lining the walls opposite the glass enclosed open air courtyard adjacent to the Institute's small library. That's where I first encountered the mysterious field of complexity science that seemed to concern itself with everything. A few years later, that led to me participating as a student in the Institute's first MOOC-based course, Introduction to Complexity. Although I have never met author and course instructor Melanie Mitchell personally, I feel I owe her a debt of gratitude because it was while taking her course that I came to realize how graph theory fit in the larger context of the study of complex systems. Sometimes all it takes is one class to change your view of the entire world and for me, this was the class.

No doubt most authors experience at least a few uncomfortable moments of that special kind of despair that accompanies the task of writing a book. I found that even with a completed manuscript, the finish line can still be a long way off. And so, I owe a special debt of gratitude to one person in particular who helped me get to that finish line: Joel Sommers. The authors of any book seeking to survey and tutor the reader about a technology frets about completeness and accuracy. But I also wanted this book to be engaging. With that goal in mind, I tried to introduce each chapter with a novel application of graph theory or an interesting anecdote from computer science. Joel provided many razor-sharp edits that were right on target, and he made valuable suggestions for how I could improve some of these narratives with what he called "joyous (if melodramatic) injections of adventurism." I can't thank Joel, nor my colleagues at LANL enough for all their help and encouragement. I also greatly appreciate my coauthor Matthew's willingness to stick with this project. Without your help, this book would definitely not have happened. With your help, this book emerged as much more than the sum of its parts.

James Powell
Santa Fe, New Mexico
February 3, 2015

Introduction

Single file, rarely out of step with one another, a large contingent of ants marches almost as a single pulsing organism. In intimate proximity to one another, they make their way toward the remnants of a careless human's lunch. From above it is hard to see the stream of tiny ants emerging from a crater-like mound of sand.

As individuals, they are not gifted with keen sight. And despite such close quarters, they don't feel crowded, rushed, or claustrophobic. They effortlessly climb obstacles that would at our scale seem to be insurmountable boulders. They build nests, fights off invaders, and lifts massive items many times its own weight all in support of the collective.

Yet they have no leader. The colony is self-organizing. Like a road crew repainting the stripes along a stretch of highway, they constantly refresh the trail that guides their parade until it is no longer needed. Their highway is a forage line, marked by a pheromone trail. Some random ant discovered the food and excitedly established the trail for others to follow. They make quick work of the breadcrumbs and then attend to other matters. Some ants are soldiers, some are harvesters, some are diggers, and others just clean, switching roles as needed. You'll find no multitasking here.

Their behavior may be simple, but the aggregate results are complex. Ants can quickly adapt to the challenges of the local environment, achieving things as a community that would be impossible for a single ant. They do so by following simple rules, playing simple roles, and occasionally submitting to the whims of chance. They are a perfect example of what scientists call a complex system.

Ants endure and thrive in a dynamic world full of unknowns even though they have no hope of comprehending that world in its entirety. Simple rules guide individuals to perform whatever task is most pressing for their collective survival in the moment. An essential ingredient of those rules is randomness. Food foraging starts out as a random, directionless activity. When ants find a food source, they make pheromone trails to the source. The trails dissipate unless they are reinforced. When the food is gone, the pheromone trail fades away, and the ants usually retreat to their nest or move on to another source of food. Randomness takes over again. We used to believe that the universe was deterministic, that if you knew all the initial conditions and all the rules that govern it, then you could know everything that would ever happen. But ants know better. They don't plan, they react.

In our universe, the best models we have come up with to anticipate what can or might happen are based on probabilities. Inherent in probabilities is an element of randomness. Ants do perfectly fine by individually focusing on discrete, simple tasks. They react rather than acting under centralized direction, without anticipating anything. The colony as a whole knows how to survive. But if some ants stray from the colony, the results can be disastrous for them.

The ant mill phenomenon is illustrative of how important it is for individual ants to remain connected to their colony. If a few ants lose track of their forage trail, they begin to follow one another. Pretty soon they form a circle and they will march around and around until they all die. As a collective, ants manifest complex behaviors that ensure their survival. This behavior is more sophisticated than one would assume possible given what is known about an individual component. Emergence is the term for this phenomenon, and it is characteristic of complex systems (Figure I.1).

The study of complex systems is relatively new, and there are many details around the edges that are a bit hazy. Even the precise definition of a complex system is a subject of debate among those who study them. Complex systems exist all around us and they inhabit the space between organized simplicity (simple, recurring patterns) and chaos. Complex doesn't necessarily imply complicated in the sense that the word complicated is often used. An ant isn't a complicated animal, but an ant colony is a complex system. Complicated systems are not necessarily complex. A car is quite complicated under the hood, but the components are highly individualized and play distinct roles for which they were specifically designed. There seems to be a tipping point somewhere between very simple and completely chaotic where complexity is manifest. In other words, an ant and its relationship to other ants is only as complex as it needs to be in order for an ant colony to survive and adapt to its environment.

Why the sudden interest in complex systems? Well, in the twentieth century, science hit a wall. The era when a single individual laboring tirelessly for a lifetime was able to understand and make significant contributions in a field was drawing to a close. For centuries, progress had come from the process of reductionism. Reductionism supposes that a complex phenomenon can ultimately be understood by comprehending its constituent components. But reductionism was reaching its limits. New knowledge increasingly depended on a considerable foundation of existing knowledge within and across disciplines. Some phenomena mysteriously manifested capabilities that were not suggested by an understanding of their parts. A great deal had been achieved without the benefit of modern computing capabilities. But it was inevitable that we'd reach a threshold where it was beyond a single person's ability to move a field forward. Reductionism was yielding lower returns. Scientific advancement began to depend more and more on large data sets, simulations, modeling, statistical analysis, machine learning, and these advancements suggested that there may be some unknown, poorly understood self-organizing principles that played a crucial role in some natural systems. Our ability to study complex systems is due in no small part to the advances in computing over the last few decades. And one of the techniques we use to understand complex systems is to model them as graphs.

In this book we talk a lot about models and modeling. A graph is a type of model. A model is a representation of some other thing. A paper airplane is a model that bears some resemblance to an actual airplane and can even fly. The advantage of a paper airplane is that you can make and fly your own without killing anyone.

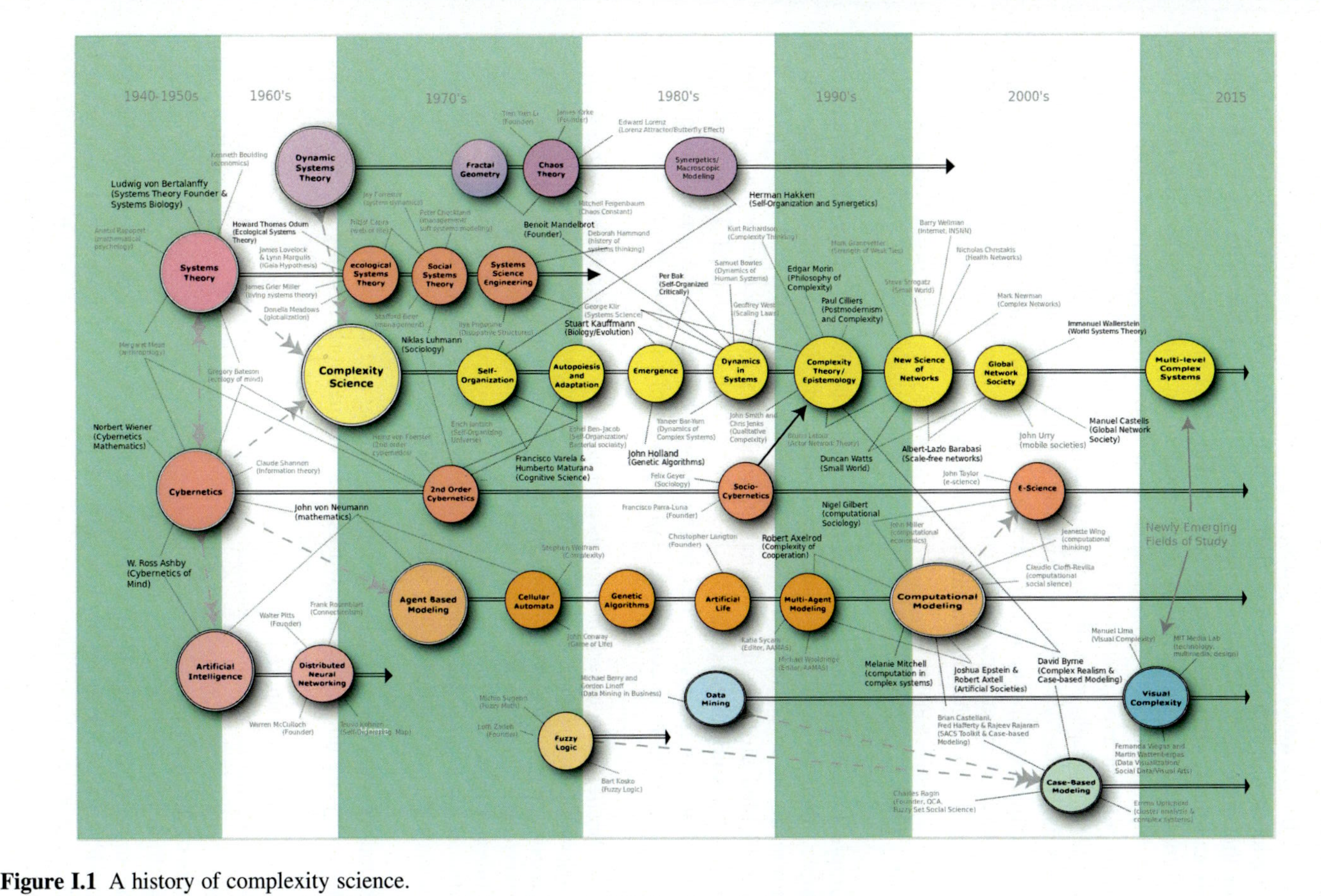

Figure I.1 A history of complexity science.
Source: Castellani, B. (2012). <http://commons.wikimedia.org/wiki/File:Complexity_Map.svg >.

Models are good for exploring aspects of a thing, and for testing ideas about it without doing any harm. Mathematicians often represent their models as formulae and they breathe life into a model by assigning values to its variables.

Graphs are not merely models; they are mathematical models. This type of graph is not the same as a bar or pie chart you're likely familiar with. It is a model of things and their relationships with one another. This model can simultaneously capture complexity and simplicity. A graph model of a complex system can reveal how it has achieved balance within itself without overcompensating, and with its environment, without eventually rendering that environment unlivable.

Visually, a graph is most often represented as a collection of dots with lines between them. The dots are an abstraction for the things that exist in a system, process, or knowledge space, and the lines are relationships among them. Graph theory is the field of mathematics that is concerned with analyzing and exploring graphs. Here is the formula that mathematicians use to describe a graph (Figure I.2):

$$\mathbf{G} = (\mathbf{V}, \mathbf{E})$$

Graphs have been used to gain a better understanding of many phenomena. For example, there was a long-standing mystery in biology regarding the energy requirements of an organism as its size increased. Intuitively, one would guess that if you doubled the size of an animal, it would require twice as much food. But it turns out that's not the case: a 75% increase is all that's required. How can that be? The solution to this mystery lies in the answer to the question: what do a city, a leaf, and a lung have in common? Geoffrey West of the Santa Fe Institute explains:

> *The key lies in the generic mathematical properties of networks. Highly complex self-sustaining systems ... require close integration of many constituent units that require an efficient supply of nutrients and the disposal of waste products. ...this servicing – via, for instance, circulatory systems in organisms, or perhaps transport systems in cities – is accomplished through optimized, space-filling, fractal-like branching networks whose dynamical and geometric constraints are independent of specific evolved organismic design.*

Blood vessels, the vascular system in leaves, and transportation routes to and within a city are not just like networks, they are networks. Nature settled on power-law networks to solve many problems. We're not far behind. The infrastructure that supports our cities, our regional and global transportation systems, and our power grids are networks that have similar properties to evolved network systems. So it should come as no surprise that graph models are useful for understanding many aspects of the natural world.

A graph is a great way to model contacts involved in the spread of disease. The graph starts with patient 0—the first person infected by a disease. From previous research, it may be known that this particular disease has a reproduction number of 2. That means that every infected person infects on average two more people. The incubation period may be on average 4 days before symptoms appear. Patient 0 was

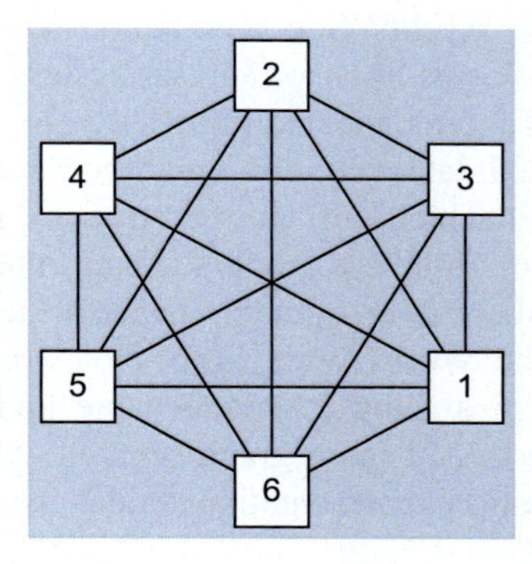

Figure I.2 G = (V,E) says that the graph G is a set of vertices V (labeled 1,2,3,4,5,6) and edges E.

infected 8 weeks ago, and at least 125 people have shown up in area hospitals with the disease over the last 7 weeks. Health care workers begin interviewing patients to determine who had contact with whom. If the contact preceded infection, and only one infected individual is identified, then there's a clear relationship. Pretty soon a tree-like graph emerges that confirms that the reproduction rate has been right around 2. The good news is, as time passes, the graph has more and more nodes with no new connections at all. Quarantine and early treatment are working. The disease seems to be burning itself out. The graph model provides tangible evidence of this. As you might guess from this example, epidemiologists love graphs.

In fact, many disciplines love graphs. Sociologists study communities and communication with graphs. Chemists can study graph representations of compounds before they ever attempt to produce them in the lab. Physicists can study phase transitions and myriad other aspects of matter and energy. Astronomers can study galactic clusters with graphs. Environmental scientists can represent food chains with graphs. Cell biologists can model metabolic processes in a cell and even get some sense for how such a process evolved over time. Economists can study purchasing or investing patterns among consumers. City planners can study traffic patterns to figure out where mass transit might relieve congested roadways. When that transit system is in place, the subway map daily commuters will use is itself a graph. In a connected world, being able to analyze connections is a powerful tool. A portion of this book is devoted to the use of graphs in various fields, and we use these reviews to illustrate various important concepts in graph theory, often building on concepts introduced in earlier chapters.

Tim Berners Lee looked to graph theory for inspiration as he developed a concept for a global network of information. His vision included a democratic model where anyone could encode and share any facts. These facts would be comprehensible by both man and machine. He sometimes even referred to this as the Global Giant Graph. His goal was to push the granularity of information representation down to the level of individual facts. These facts would be shared and interconnected. And like the World Wide Web before it, there would be an ecosystem of standards and technologies upon which this system would be built.

We refer to this Web of interconnected knowledge by various names, including Linked Open Data, the linked data web, or simply the Semantic Web. At the core is a simple information model which defines the structure of a fundamental unit of knowledge called a triple. A triple is a graph segment made up of two nodes and a directed edge between them. These segments reside in a larger knowledge graph. This graph coexists with the World Wide Web. Nodes are represented by unique network identifiers that give a thing a unique name and provide a pointer to it. Identifiers make it possible to add more graph segments that further describe these things. This simple information representation model results in a complex web of knowledge. Sound familiar?

This book is intended to provide an overview of a number of graph-related topics. We have attempted whenever possible to write it so that each chapter can be consulted independently of any other chapter, but there is at times an unavoidable progression of background knowledge that is prerequisite for understanding later chapters.

It is a book of lists. Lists encapsulate and summarize in a way that most everyone finds helpful on some level. Of course when we do start off with a list, we follow up with a narrative that expands the list elements into the things you really need to know about a given topic.

It is a book of examples. To the extent possible, we don't just talk about a given technology, but try to show you examples and explain what it's good for. Standards documents tend to be broad and deep, as they should. We tend to feature vertical slices of a given technology which we hope will give you a good idea of some of the uses for it and an incentive to learn more.

It is a book for people who love books and reading. We try to bring the topics to life with anecdotes from current research papers, other more technical sources, and even historical texts and novels. These are intended to engage, enlighten, and occasionally even entertain.

It is a book that covers more topics at an introductory level, rather than a few topics at a deeper level. You may never need to delve deeply into some topics we cover, but we aim to make sure that if you ever hear about or encounter the topic again, it will be familiar, not foreign.

It is, on occasion, a book of code. Some chapters discuss program code, markup, and information representation languages. If you never plan to write software, you may not need to delve deeply into the handful of chapters that discuss programming and APIs, but we do our best to provide a nontechnical overview before we show you any code. If the code is more detail than you need, skip forward and share the code with a programming friend or colleague. If they are tasked with solving a problem using that particular technology and are new to it, they may thank you profusely, as we strive to introduce concepts from a beginner's perspective.

It is a book to help you get things done. These are big topics. There are more rabbit holes here than in the proverbial briar patch. We steer you clear of the rabbit holes by highlighting solid, widely adopted technologies, not standards and technologies still under development that may or may not come to fruition. We introduce you to things that you can use now. We provide concrete examples throughout and we conclude the book with in-depth case studies of two real-world applications. We believe learning is good, doing is good, but learning while doing is better.

With this book, we will introduce you to some of the finer points of graph theory and the Semantic Web. We hope to provide you with a solid conceptual framework of graph theory, and a comprehensive overview of Semantic Web technologies, which we think makes this book unique in this field. For librarians, it will help you understand how patrons in a variety of fields might be modeling aspects of their field of research, and how you might apply graph theory to some information discovery and retrieval challenges in your library. For information technologists such as software developers, it will give you the background you need to understand how graph theory and the Semantic Web can be leveraged to represent knowledge. There are many open source tools, software libraries, and standards for graph data and for the Semantic Web. We will introduce some specific tools but also give you the knowledge you need to find and evaluate other similar tools.

Although this book is not specifically about complexity science, it is a guidebook to some of the technologies used to model and elucidate aspects of complex systems. There are many excellent books about complexity and complex systems, including "Complexity: a Guided Tour" by Melanie Mitchell, "Deep Simplicity" by John Gribbin, and "Simply Complexity" by Neil Johnson, just to name a few. Any or all of these resources may help you understand the field and its myriad applications.

Libraries are constantly striving to provide new and better ways to find information. We've been doing this for hundreds of years. Graph theory and Semantic Web technologies offer a way for libraries to reinvent themselves and their services, based on relationships. Finding things in libraries used to depend on physical access to those things. Then we introduced layers of abstraction: classification schemes, call number systems, card catalogs, online public access catalogs, and finding aides, to name a few. Yet relationships may be the most natural way for users to find things. Graphs and the Semantic Web are great at modeling and exploring relationships. Libraries can model the relationships among content, topics, creators, and consumers. Rather than mapping all our previous solutions onto the Semantic Web, perhaps it is time to develop a "relationship engine" that can leverage these new technologies to totally reinvent the library experience.

Humans are obviously not ants. But humans can model ant behavior using graphs. We can model the inner processes of an ant's physiology using graphs. We can model an ant colonies' relationship to its environment using graphs. We can model what we know about ants using graphs. Graphs are tools that help us understand complex systems. In a nondeterministic universe, we face myriad unknown and complex challenges, some will be random events, and some will be of our own making. It is contingent upon us to use every means at our disposal to augment our ability to comprehend complexity. Turning our back on complexity is no longer an option. Graph models of complex systems, and the practice of embedding knowledge into graphs, are powerful tools for comprehending complexity—and they enable us to use that understanding to our advantage.

Glossary

graph a set of things and the relationships between them, visually it is often rendered as a collection of dots and lines between them, mathematically a graph represented by the variable G, and is defined a set of vertices and edges {V,E}, thus G = {V,E} is a graph

node an object in a graph, in the mathematical definition of a graph, a node is referred to as a vertex, represented above by the variable V

edge a relationship in a graph, they connect nodes, same in mathematical definition of a graph, represented above by the variable E

property (graph) in a property graph a property is a characteristic of a node or edge, to which a value is assigned, for example, the property name has the value "James"

property (ontology) in a vocabulary a property is a characteristic of a Class, and in RDF it is usually the predicate in a triple. Property names start with a lower case letter and employ camel case, that is, there is no white space in a property name but every distinct word that forms part of the property name is capitalized

class refers to a distinct thing defined in a vocabulary. class names start with an upper case letter

metadata data about data, a collection of predefined terms intended to describe, label, point at or encapsulate other data

instance data this is data that is described by metadata or some element of a vocabulary, for example, an Oak could be considered instance data for a class tree, subclass species, property common name = "Oak"

vocabulary a group of terms that are defined as having some relationship with one another, which describe some thing or some knowledge domain

taxonomy a hierarchical knowledge representation defining a vocabulary

ontology (general) a structured model for representing things that exist in a given domain, their characteristics, and the relationships between them

ontology (Semantic Web) a model representing a vocabulary to describe aspects of and relationships among data

reasoning application of a logical set of decisions to a situation or to data

visualization a pictorial representation of some data, intended to convey details about that data and designed to be viewed on a computer screen or some other form of visually consumed projection

triple a syntactic representation which forms a statement of some information that consists of three distinct components separated in some fashion (e.g., by white space), arranged so that the second (predicate) and third (object) parts of the statement provide information about the first (subject)

URI a uniform, universal resource identifier

namespace a uniform resource identifier that uniquely identifies a vocabulary

vertex for our purposes, a vertex and a node are synonyms

network although network is often used interchangeably with the word graph, a network is a special type of graph that contains weighted (indicating strength of connection), directed edges (indicating direction of relationship)

Graphs in theory

1

Bridging the history

In 1736, partway through Konigsberg, Prussa, the Pregel River split the city into two parallel segments, inscribing an island between the north and south regions of the city. This island itself was also divided by a stream that connected the two forks of the Pregel River. What we know today is that churning somewhere in the river that simultaneously nourished and partitioned Konigsberg, somewhere streaming amid its divisive canals, Graph Theory was about to surface, and it would change everything.

That city, and the inherent problems bestowed by its water-carved enclaves, was the inspiration for a mathematical puzzle, the Seven Bridges of Konigsberg Problem. There were indeed seven bridges in the city, at least at that time. The Pregel River divided the city into north and south. Bridges connected the resulting islands. The western most island had two bridges to the north and two to the south, the eastern island had one bridge each to the north and to the south, and the two islands themselves were connected by a seventh bridge (Figure 1.1).

Mathematicians wondered, could one walk through the city such that he crosses every bridge once and only once?

Leonard Euler solved this puzzle, and in doing so, laid the foundations for graph theory. In considering the problem, he first stripped away the buildings, the roads, the trees—everything but the bridge crossings themselves, the connections between islands. He saw that the answer, whatever it was, could be represented simply by a sequence of these crossings. That is, the answer might be 3, 6, 4, 5, 7, 1, 2. Or 6, 3, 1, 7, 2, 4, 5. It all depended on how one numbered the bridges. But all that mattered was the order in which the bridges were crossed, not the particular route a person took to reach them. In essence, he reduced the problem to a graph.

Graph theory had not been invented at this point. But in his parlance, Euler saw the land masses as vertexes (also called nodes) and the bridges as edges. These are the building blocks of the simplest graphs—a set of nodes connected to each other by edges.

This simplified formulation of the problem made certain features stand out. For instance, Euler understand that for every land mass, one must enter it via a bridge and then leave it via a different bridge. The exception(s) are the starting and ending land masses. But there are at most two of these (one if the walker starts and ends at the same place); the other land masses are intermediate nodes, which must be entered and exited an equal number of times. Each entrance and exit relies on a unique bridge, so the number of bridges connected to one of these intermediate land masses must be even, or else the walk is doomed from the start (Figure 1.2).

Euler discovered that for a graph like this to have a solution, either all the nodes must have an even number of edges or exactly two of them could have an odd

A Librarian's Guide to Graphs, Data and the Semantic Web.

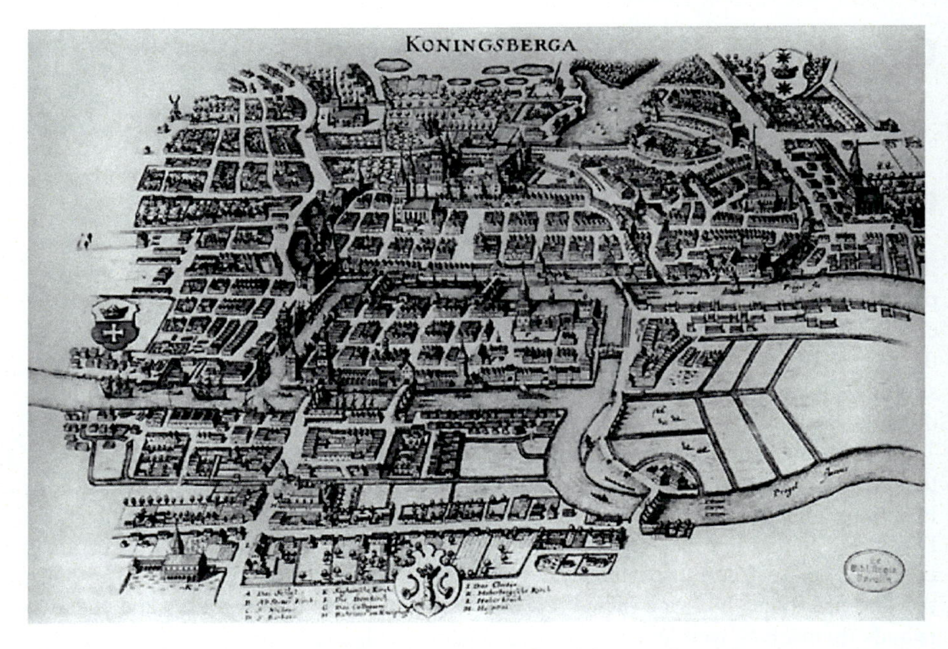

Figure 1.1 A drawing of Konigsberg as it appeared in 1651.
Source: Map by Merian-Erben. <https://commons.wikimedia.org/wiki/File:Image-Koenigsberg,_Map_by_Merian-Erben_1652.jpg>.

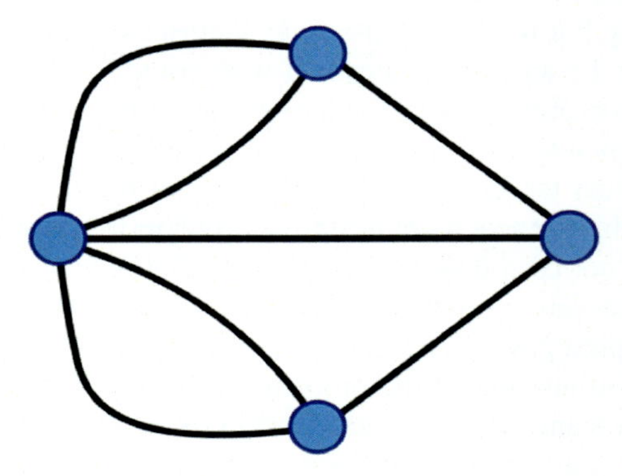

Figure 1.2 Konigsberg bridges as a graph.

number of edges (in which case the successful walker must start at one of these nodes and end at the other). But all the land regions of Konigsberg had an odd number of bridges. Thus, there was no solution. One could not walk a Eulerian path through Konigsberg (as the goal later became called), and certainly not a Eulerian circuit, which is a walk that starts and ends in the same place.

Often in math or science, whimsical problems that are investigated purely to satisfy the curiosity of those doing the investigating can beget solutions that lead to many important findings. This is true even when the solution is that there is no solution at all. (Though with the bombing of two of the bridges of Konigsberg, now called Kaliningrad, during WWII, a Eulerian path is now possible.) In reducing the problem, transforming bridges to edges and land regions to nodes, Euler generalized it. And his findings, and all those that came after, can apply to any problem which involves entities connected to other entities. Connections are everywhere—from the path of infectious diseases through a population to the circulation of money in an economy. These sets of connections, or networks, can be visualized as graphs, and they can be analyzed with graph theory.

Topology

Before we introduce more examples in the history of graph theory, we should note that Euler's solution to the Seven Bridges of Konigsberg problem is also seen as a founding work in the field of topology. A graph can be a generalization of a real world network, like the bridges spanning a city. But while that city has a definite north and south and has varying distances between its land regions, once it is translated into a graph, those distinctions no longer matter. A graph can be twisted around. Its nodes can be big or small or different sizes. Its edges can be long or short or even squiggly. This is a central tenet of topology, in which shapes can be transformed into one another as long as certain key features are maintained. For instance, no matter how you bend a convex polyhedron—like a cube or a pyramid—it is always true that $V - E + F = 2$. This is the Euler characteristic, in which F represents the number of faces of the shape, and V and E represent the vertexes and edges we are already familiar with.

The world is teeming with graphs. When you have this mindset, you see them everywhere. Graphs exist in a city's bridges, in something as small as a pair of dice to something as large as the great Pyramids, and even something as vast and complicated as the internet. (And Google's search engine, which helps tame that complexity, does so in part by exploiting graph theoretics, as we will see in a later chapter.) This book, as part of a bibliographic network, can exist in a graph. You yourself live in a graph. After all, people (nodes) form relationships (edges) with other people (more nodes), so that the whole of human society comprises one large graph of social connections. One might ask, then, what type of graph are we?

Degrees of separation

Yes, there are different types or classes of graphs. Some graphs have many connections, while some have few. Sometimes these connections cluster around certain key nodes, while other times they are spread evenly across all the nodes. One way to characterize a graph is to find the mean path length between its nodes. How many "degrees of separation" exist between any two nodes? In the 1929 story collection *Everything is Different*, Hungarian author Frigyes Karinthy posited the notion that everyone is connected by at most five individuals (hence the term, six degrees of separation). One of his characters posed a game—they should select a random individual, then see how many connections it took to reach him, via their personal networks. Stanley Milgram brought this game to life in his "small world experiments" starting in 1967. (These studies are not to be confused with the Milgram Experiment, which tested a person's willingness to obey authority, even when instructed to deliver seemingly painful shocks to another person, although this too could be graphed.)

Milgram recruited people living in the midwestern United States as starting nodes and had them connect to individuals living in Boston. Note that in a graph, distance has special connotation. The metric distance between two nodes as they are drawn on a sheet of paper is arbitrary. Nodes can be rearranged, shifted closer or farther apart, as long as the connections stay the same. Distance, or path length, refers to the minimum number of edges that must be traveled to go from one node to another within a graph. In Milgram's small world experiment, it is possible, perhaps even likely, that this path length distance is related to the geographical distance separating two nodes—i.e., Boston to Milwaukee. But in a graph of human social connections, the social circles of two nodes may contribute just as much to the path length distance between them. In choosing his start and end points, Milgram hoped to accommodate both geographic and social distance.

Suppose you were selected as one of his starting points. You would receive a packet in the mail. Inside you would find the name and info of a person in Boston. Perhaps you happen to know this target personally. If so, the instructions tell you to send the packet directly to him. More likely you don't know him, so instead you sign the roster and send the packet to someone you do know personally. You choose someone who you think is more likely than you to know the target personally. The experiment was basically a chain letter. And 64 out of 296 packages eventually reached the target, with an average path length between 5 and 6.

Of course, the procedure is not perfect. Any given node who receives the package might give up and never send it on. The longer the chain, the more likely this will happen. Thus, long chains were more likely to die out, thus underestimating the true average path length that connects people. On the other hand, people are only guessing at what the best path might be. They might not find the best chain, and this overestimates the true average path length. Either way, the experiment does tend to confirm out intuition that "it is a small world, after all."

Four color problem

In our next example, we return to maps. This is fitting, as some of the graphs we are most familiar with in our daily lives are subway or train maps. This puzzle, however, concerns cartographic maps. The four color theorem states that any map of connected regions, such as the mainland United States or the countries of Africa, requires no more than four colors such that no two adjacent regions share the same color. Here, adjacency does not include corner-to-corner touching. So in that map of the United States, New Mexico and Colorado are adjacent, but New Mexico and Utah are not.

The theorem can be stated more simply and directly in the language of graph theory. Instead of a map, consider every region a vertex or node. Edges will then connect every pair of nodes which share a boundary segment (but not a boundary point, i.e., a corner). In graph theory parlance, this particular graph is planar. This means that it can be drawn in such a way, with points and lines, that none of the lines cross each other, and they only intersect at end points. We can confirm this by returning to the map configuration. Just draw a dot in the center of each region and then connect adjacent dots with lines. Now we can rephrase the constraint of the problem this way: the nodes must be drawn with at most four colors such that no connected nodes receive the same color. In short, "every planar graph is four colorable" (Figure 1.3).

The similar five-color theorem was proved in 1890 by Percy John Heawood in the midst of correcting an error in an earlier erroneous proof of the four color theorem. In the decades since, there had been many false proofs, or rather, false disproofs, of the theorem. If the theorem were untrue, then the disproof would be a simple matter of creating a map which required more than four colors. Many such potential maps were offered, and all had errors—with a change of the colors of a few regions, or sometimes many regions, they could be four colorable. As no counterexample had been demonstrated, the consensus was that the theorem was likely true; actually proving that was another matter.

Kenneth Appel and Wolfgang Haken proved it in 1976—the first major mathematical proof to use extensive computer assistance. The proof took years to gain acceptance in the mathematical community, for no mathematician could simply check it line by line. But we can describe the general method used, if not the details.

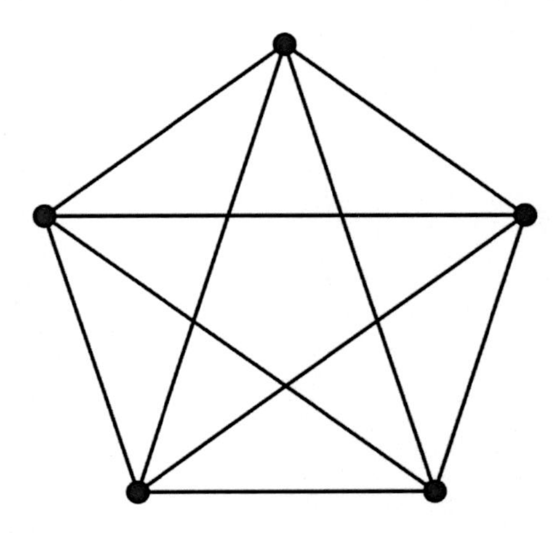

Figure 1.3 A non-planar, completely connected graph.

Imagine that the proof is false. Then there will be some region of a map that requires five colors. Reduce this five-color region to the smallest possible subgraph—i.e., take away any extraneous nodes or edges, leaving just enough so that the remainder still requires five colors. With this imagined minimum subgraph in mind, the proof proceeded this way. On the one hand, Appel and Haken devised a set of 1936 unique maps which are not part of this minimum five-color subgraph (i.e., they are all four colorable). On the other hand, they showed that any potential five-color subgraph contains within it one of those 1936 subgraphs. By the first point, the hypothetical five-color subgraph cannot contain any of those 1936 maps. By the second point, it must contain one of those 1936 graphs. Thus, it cannot exist, and the proof is true.

The De Bruijn-Erdos theorem (1951, preceding the four color proof) can extend the four color theorem from finite planar graphs to infinite planar graphs. It states that a graph can be colored by n colors if and only if every finite subgraph within it can be colored by n colors. Don't worry, we are done with serious math, at least for this chapter. We only bring up this theorem to introduce the mathematician Paul Erdos, a prolific researcher in the field of graph theory, and the subject of the final topic of this chapter. (He is also Hungarian like author Frigyes Karinthy. . .small world!).

Erdos has been honored with the Erdos number, a metric that describes the degree of separation between any researcher and Erdos himself. So someone who collaborated on a paper with Erdos would have an Erdos number of 1. Someone who had never collaborated with him, but had coauthored with one of his coauthors, would have an Erdos number of 2, and so on.

If this sounds familiar, it might be because you are thinking of the Bacon number, which is the degree of separation between a given actor and Kevin Bacon. There is even an Erdos-Bacon number which is the sum of a person's Erdos number and Bacon number, for those who have both published in academia and acted in Hollywood. For instance, the physicist Richard Feynman, who appeared in the film Anti-Clock (1979), has Bacon and Erdos numbers of 3 each, for an Erdos-Bacon number of 6. Natalie Portman also has an Erdos-Bacon number of 6. Graphs are still fun almost 300 years later. But they have also emerged as an important new tool for understanding the world around us.

Graphs and how to make them

2

Space junk and graph theory

Space is vast, and yet we still find ways to fill it. There are tens of thousands of pieces of junk orbiting the Earth. Many travel at incredible speeds. In fact, a discarded screw can cause as much damage as a bowling ball hurled at 300 miles per hour. And the problem is only getting worse, as these objects collide with one another and produce even more pieces of junk.

We don't yet have the ability to track all of this junk or to clean it up. It threatens the lives of astronauts, and even small pieces of debris can do tremendous damage to orbiting satellites. Many of our communication systems depend on those satellites. Over time, these same satellites inevitably fail and become liabilities as they drift from their original orbit or tumble out of control. It may seem like an easy problem to solve, just send up the robotic equivalent of a pool boy, with a net, to scoop up the junk and hurl it into the atmosphere where it will burn up. But its not that easy.

This dangerous game of space billiards seems as though it has very little to do with networks. Yet in a 2009 paper in *Acta Astraunatica* entitled "A new analysis of debris mitigation and removal using networks," researchers developed a theoretical network model for representing orbiting space debris and the interactions among these objects. In their graph model of space debris, the relationship between pieces of debris are interaction represents a collision or the potential for a collision with another object in the future.

The paper spent some time introducing the concept of a graph, and various graph analytic techniques to an audience that had likely not thought about space junk and networks as having any relation to one another. By analyzing this graph of space junk using some of these techniques, they identified a strategy that might help reduce the amount of space junk with minimal effort. Their graph model of debris interactions was vulnerable to what is known as a network attack. In this case, network refers to the Internet. If someone wants to affect the performance of the Internet or limit its access in some fashion, they can use a graph model of the network to identify highly connected points which, if damaged, would significantly affect the performance or availability of Internet services.

It turns out that the debris interaction network is also vulnerable to a network attack, which is obviously a very good thing. In this case, you identify a piece of space junk that is highly connected, that is, it is likely to collide with other debris. The authors suggest that if you can remove that piece of junk, you will have changed the network. And the effect would be greater than if you selected some piece of debris at random.

A Librarian's Guide to Graphs, Data and the Semantic Web.

Graph theory and graph modeling

Graph theory is the name for the discipline concerned with the study of graphs: constructing, exploring, visualizing, and understanding them. Some types of graphs, called networks, can represent the flow of resources, the steps in a process, the relationships among objects (such as space junk) by virtue of the fact that they show the direction of relationships. We intuitively understand graphs and networks because we encounter them in the real world. A family is a hierarchical network, with parents linked to children, siblings, other ancestors, and so on. Trees are a network of leaves or needles, connected to branches, which connect to the trunk, and they invert this form under ground to form roots. A spider's web is a network of filaments spanning the flight path of unsuspecting insects. In winter, whether we know it or not, as the common cold spreads through a school or business, the germs move from person to person in such a way that we can retroactively document the spread and predict their future path (and possibly, how to thwart it) via a directed graph. When we say something went viral, we are paying homage to this contagious behavior. Subway maps, airline hubs, and power grids are all examples of real world networks.

A graph can be used to model many systems, processes, and technologies. Therein lies the challenge, the interesting problem in terms of graph modeling: what part of the system or process to model, and how to represent it as a graph. This is referred to as graph modeling. It may or may not come as good news to you to know that there is almost never one right way to model data in a graph. Modeling usually happens at two levels, first the things and relationships that are immediately apparent in the domain data are mapped into a graph. Then you make another pass where you essentially test the graph model to see if there are important concepts that are lost or ill-represented by edges or as properties. Sometimes these may need to be "promoted" to nodes. Fortunately graph modeling is fairly intuitive and the modeling process can be inclusive, all you need to get started is a white board!

Scientists and researchers studying complex systems often use graph models because it is one of the best abstractions we have for modeling connectedness within a system. Sometimes the apparent network model so closely resembles the actual system that it even becomes tempting to think of the system as a network. As more and more scientists have modeled things using graphs, they have borrowed techniques from one another and developed new ways of exploring these networks. Then other researchers apply these new techniques to their graphs, and often they lead to new insights. Think of it like convergent evolution where animal forms tend to resurface in isolated and only remotely related populations. The tasmanian tiger looked like a dog, even though they are not related. Graph analytic techniques converge on significance despite the differences of what is being modeled. A completely connected graph can represent water molecules in an ice cube or a close-knit family or a group of coauthors who frequently work together.

Graphs are abstract conceptual models for representing some aspect of the world that you can detect, observe, or infer. It is a way of representing things and the relationships between those things. It is understandably easier to think of a graph the way it appears in pictures, as a bunch of circles with lines between them. Visualization tools will draw an image of a graph and try to minimize overlap using various strategies. With some tools, you can move nodes around and change the layout. It is important to keep in mind that a graph visualization is just one way to look at the graph data. No matter how a graph is drawn, the nodes and relationships between them do not change when the layout is changed or manipulated, any more than shuffling a deck of cards changes the contents of the deck.

Nodes, or vertices, and edges are the building blocks of all graphs. Weighted graph use some criteria to assign a numeric value representing the importance, for example, of a node or edge. A directed edge illustrates the direction that information or resources flow between two nodes in a graph. A more generalized graph is the property graph. A property graph associates additional data with each edge and node in the graph. You can think of these properties as a little database associated with each node or edge. Every node and edge has one or more key, value pairs that represent various characteristics of the objects and relationships. You can inspect the properties of a node or edge by first locating it in the graph via a path traversal, graph analysis such as degree metrics, or some type of search, such as a guided or breadth first search. Since every node and edge has a unique identifier, you can use this to get at its properties. If you know the key you are interested in, you can present it, or inspect the keys associated with that node or edge. In property graphs, path traversals, searches, you can make use of node and edge properties as you explore the graph, for example to select particular edges along a path or identify a group of nodes with common characteristics.

A graph representation often necessarily results in a reduction of information about relationships. Here is a trivial example. You have data for a social network that includes people, their friends, and their neighbors. However, you assume that many people don't know their neighbors very well, so you decide to create a graph that only contains friend relationships. This graph contains only a subset of the actors in this relationship. Many graph analytics, such as degree centrality which is counting the number of connections each object in a graph model has, implicitly assume that the objects and relationships in your model are each of a single type. Maybe you have the complete graph of friends and neighbors but you want to extract the friend graph for processing. You can create a subgraph, or a projection of the more complex graph containing friend relationships and the nodes connected to them, and analyze only that subgraph. Subgraphs can also be used to produce simpler visualizations of complex graphs. Large, complex graphs with many nodes and edges can quickly become what we sometimes call "inscrutable hairballs." Visually they are so complex and so tangled that any hope of intuitively learning anything from the visual representation is lost.

Analyzing graphs

There are many possible ways to explore graphs. Researchers sometimes look at graph analytics in different ways. For example, those who use graph models to model actual systems and processes tend to focus on these areas:

1. Network structure
2. Properties of the graph elements
3. How the network evolves over time
4. What kinds of interactions can occur on the network.

In general, graph analytic techniques are used to explore connections, distributions, graph-wide features, and clusters. Connections refer to relationships between objects in a graph (the edges). Some graph analytic techniques are based on counting, that is, identifying some element of a graph and determining quantities related to it. Degree centrality is based on how many edges are attached to a node. Path length is a count of the number of hops between two nodes. In directed graphs, the aspects of the graph that can be quantified can differentiate between in-degree and an out-degree values for a node. These values correspond to the number of incoming and outgoing edges attached to a node. For a graph in which weights have been assigned to edges, degree centrality can be a summation of the weights of all the edges, instead of a count of the edges.

A slightly more complex form of analysis called betweenness centrality is a measure which reveals which nodes are playing a primary role in connecting portions of the graph. In other words, were one to remove a node with high betweenness centrality, portions of the graph could become disconnected or at the very least, the average path length might increase. As we described at the beginning of this chapter, research into space debris as a network found that debris mitigation strategies would be most effective if they identified and eliminated highly connected nodes. Path analysis such as distance between nodes and shortest paths, or identification of particular kinds of paths such as Hamiltonian or Eularian paths, is edge centric means for exploring connections across the graph. Another node measure is cluster coefficient. The local cluster coefficient is a per-node value that is the number of actual connections per node divided by the maximum possible number of connections per node.

Distributions explore global aspects of a graph. Distributions identify statistically significant aspects of the graph, both respect to nodes and edges. This is not unlike the analysis that a researcher might perform on data resulting from a series of observations or experiments. Distribution analysis can incorporate centrality measures, graph density, strength of connections, path analysis, and identification of hubs. From this you can determine the average degree for the graph and identify nodes with the highest and lowest degree values. This type of analysis can also determine if the graph exhibits properties of a particular type of graph such as a small world or scale-free network. Another form of analysis that is the calculation of graph density. This is a comparison of node connectivity in a graph to an abstract graph model where all nodes are interconnected. Since distribution analysis is concerned with global graph characteristics, it often involves comparing a graph with examples of random, small world and scale-free networks to see how closely it resembles one of these graph types.

Commonly occurring and widely studied graph types include:

- Lattices
- Trees
- Random graphs
- Small world graphs
- Regular graphs
- Scale-free graphs.

Cluster analysis is the process of identifying and analyzing clusters. Clusters are groups of nodes that share more connections with one another than with the graph as a whole. As with graphs, there are types of clusters that recur across graphs such as cliques. Cliques are collections of nodes that are highly or completely connected with one another, but sharing only a few connections with the graph as a whole. The cluster coefficient plays a role in identifying clusters since it is a per-node value that indicates how interconnected each node in a graph is with its neighbors. Node betweenness centrality is used to determine which vertices connect clusters to one another or to the graph.

Individual node centrality measures determine the relative importance of a node based on some factor, such as how many edges connect to it, or whether it serves as a bridge between groups of nodes (degree, betweenness centrality). Identification of clusters of nodes looks at the relative number of edges among and between groups of nodes. Graph-wide node-based metrics consider the overall distribution of node degrees, the role that some nodes play in the structure of the graph (degree distribution, hubs), and the characteristic found in some graphs where some aspect of nodes affects their likelihood to be connected in large groups that form partitions (homophily vs. heterogeneity).

Graph matching is a process of evaluating how similar two graphs are, such as whether they share the same types of nodes, whether the edge pattern is similar, and this measure can also take into consideration edge directionality and weights if appropriate. Then there are path measures, which fall into two broad categories. One looks at graph-wide characteristics, such as the graph diameter, whether or not there are cycles, the overall connectedness of the graph, etc. The other considers paths between nodes and measures distance, shortest path, etc. Many of these conceptual categories of graph analysis have been used for a long time. Most of the graph analytic concepts that we will discuss in this book fall into one of these broad categories. Advancements in graph analytics tend to involve refinements to these various approaches, although small world and random graphs, graph matching, and some other computational intense approaches are recent innovations that have emerged with the advancement of computers and software needed to make such analysis practical (Figure 2.1).

A graph model can tell you many things about the system or process it represents. In the last decade or so, much has been made of graph-wide metrics. Graph

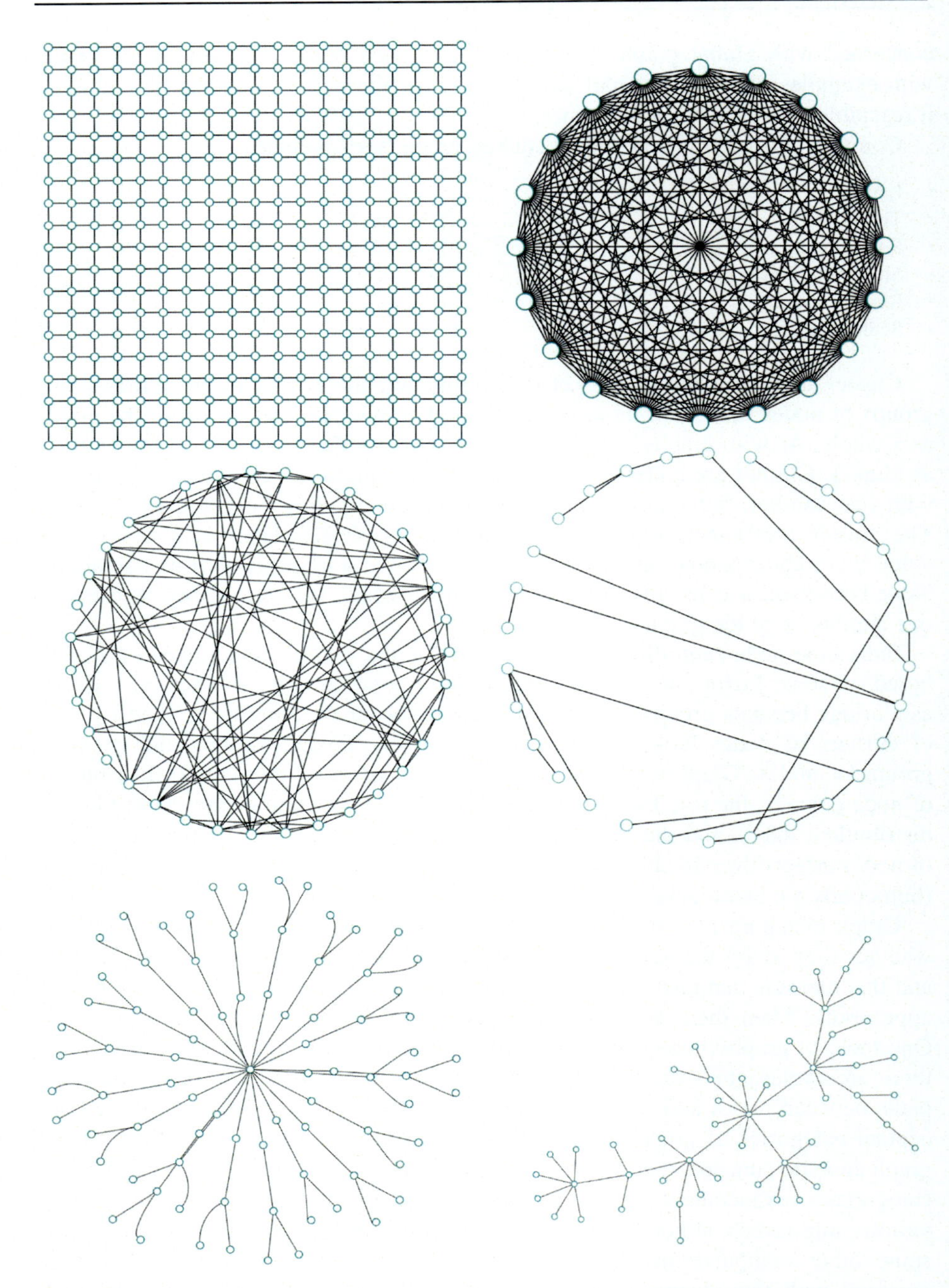

Figure 2.1 Six types of graphs, from top left, lattice, regular, random, small world, scale free, and tree graph.

theorists who study graphs in general tend to focus more on graph-wide metrics, distributions and determining how similar a given graph is to reference graph models such as random, small world, or scale-free network. Researchers in individual disciplines tend to be skeptical of this approach, preferring to focus on groups of nodes, clusters, and the flow of information or patterns of interaction in a localized portion of a graph. Some have even referred to graph-wide metrics and their application to every problem everywhere as a fad.

Both perspectives are valid. If the graph is very large, then certainly localized phenomena may be the only manageable aspect of the graph. If the network models a small and specific aspect of a system or process, then the granularity of the model may be such that graph-wide metrics are useful. Consider the example of a scale-free network. These tend to exhibit fractal-like characteristics, where they are self-similar at different scales. Zoom in and you see a similar pattern of graphs and connections as you do when you zoom out. So a portion of a scale-free network may still contain hubs and lots of nodes with low degree values. Graph-wide metrics are certainly not a fad, but their broad application tends to be. It is not wise to assume they are uniformly reliable predictors of significance for all graphs. That's why it is important to familiarize yourself with as many tools and techniques as possible. This is also why it is useful to understand graph modeling and the domain related to the system that the graph is modeling. This will help you determine how best to analyze your graphs and to interpret the results of that analysis.

There are many ways to represent graphs. In this book, we will explore textual representations such as adjacency matrices, numerous structured formats for documenting nodes and edges in a graph, software models for representing and working with graphs, and various ways of visualizing graph data. All of these things represent graphs, but a graph is a simpler abstraction. All of these techniques boil down to making sense of a system of things and the relationships among them.

The main goal of this book is to provide you with an overview of graph theory, the Semantic Web, and the relation between them. It will help you assemble your own toolkit to explore this exciting field!

Graphs and the Semantic Web

3

"...memory is transitory"

It is time to go to work, which in this particular future, means moving from the kitchen to your home office, where resides a traditional desk, but with a few upgrades.

Now your desk is retrofitted with things like an "improved microfilm, translucent screen, multiple projection displays, a keyboard, a smattering of specialized buttons," and, finally, even "a lever to simulate page turns." In this environment, one would perform a sort of mechanized cataloging by association—in other words, construct an index organically. And while this particular vision suffers many of the tropes of early twentieth century science fiction, it remains acutely prophetic in anticipating the importance of association in information retrieval systems.

In this future envisioned by Vannevar Bush, every person maintained their own personal library. Already a prescient notion, but not extraordinary, until you become aware of the rest of the vision, which is that each person's library would not be organized alphabetically or numerically or by any other conventional method. Instead, in a Vannevarian future, our personal libraries are organized by a machine (Vannevar called it "the memex") that constructs a unique path among all the items in our collections.

This idea was Vannevar Bush's answer to what he considered a towering shortfall of all current library and indexing approaches: that one of the main barriers to getting at information was "the artificiality of the systems of indexing." As a result, he suggested that our future information systems would be modeled after the associative nature of human thought, resulting in *trails through information that resemble human memory, but with greater permanence*. This is only one of the myriad insights that makes Vannevar Bush's 1943 essay "As We May Think" such a transcendent vision of the future. For it was in this essay, that he wistfully noted that "trails that are not frequently followed are prone to fade, items are not fully permanent, *memory is transitory*." Thus permanence emerges as an essential aspect of the value of information and one area where he thought we could—and eventually, would—improve over memory.

The accelerated speed and efficiency of the Vannevarian memex would make vast amounts of content available at the press of a few buttons. But perhaps his vision's most insightful element is his description of the creation and use of paths through information, which he referred to as *trails*: "Before him are the two items to be joined, projected onto adjacent viewing positions. The user taps a single key, and the items are permanently joined. Out of view, but also in the code space, is inserted a set of dots for photocell viewing; and on each item these dots by their positions designate the index number of the other item." The results, he suggested, would make

A Librarian's Guide to Graphs, Data and the Semantic Web.

"wholly new forms of encyclopedias...appear, ready made with a mesh of associative trails running through them." This mechanism for joining two pieces of content and thus forming "a mesh of associative trails" was not just uncanny, it was highly sophisticated and sounds remarkably like today's Semantic Web.

The RDF model

The Semantic Web defines a model for information called RDF. It is the means by which the Semantic Web facilitates "cataloging by association", as envisioned by Bush. At its core is the notion of a statement which describes an association. A statement has several characteristics. It identifies the thing it is about. It expresses a relationship to another thing. It has a truth value, that is to say, every statement is either true or false. Here are some examples of statements:

Birds have feathers.
The Earth orbits the sun.
Absolute 0 is 0 degrees Kelvin.

An RDF statement is intended to be consumed by software. In other words, it is written in such a way that a computer can unambiguously identify each of its components so that it can relate them to other statements. To avoid ambiguity, the components of statements consist primarily of unique identifiers. A URL is an example of a unique identifier. RDF uses Internationalized Resource Identifiers. IRI looks very much like a URI/URL except that Unicode characters are allowed throughout.

An RDF statement can be modeled in two ways, without changing its meaning or its truth value. You can represent an RDF statement as a triple, which looks like a sentence. A triple consists of a subject followed by a predicate followed by an object. You can also represent as a graph segment consisting of two nodes with a directed edge between them. In the graph version, the start node is the subject (also called "resource"), the target node is the object, and the edge is the predicate pointing from the subject to the object. Thus every RDF statement is a statement of truth regarding some relationship a subject has to an object.

In RDF statements, unique identifiers are used to identify the subject, predicates and sometimes for object values for RDF triples. Like URIs and URLs, an IRI uniquely identifies something. But unlike a URL, it is not required that this IRI resolves to anything. So, if you plug this IRI into a Web browser, you may or may not get anything back.

Here are a couple of examples of IRIs from DBPedia, which is a collection of RDF derived from Wikipedia. One identifies an author, and the second identifies a book:

```
http://dbpedia.org/resource/Cormac_McCarthy
http://dbpedia.org/resource/The_Road
```

The RDF model requires that you be able to relate any subject, predicate or object IRI to a vocabulary. A vocabulary, such as a taxonomy or ontology, identifies what the IRI is and provides information about its relationship to other items in that vocabulary. You do this with a statement that indicates the IRI's type. The possible values fall into two categories: classes or properties. Classes and properties are defined in formal vocabulary descriptions such as taxonomies or ontologies (see chapter 5). Classes define things. Things have properties. Some classes are subclasses of other classes. That means they have the characteristics of their parent class, and some additional characteristics that set them apart from their parent. The same is true of properties: they can be subproperties of other properties. Both classes and properties have unique IRIs, which are defined in an external vocabulary. Here are two more IRIs from DBPedia. One identifies a class of thing (WrittenWork) and the second identifies a property (author):

```
http://dbpedia.org/ontology/WrittenWork
http://dbpedia.org/property/author
```

With the various identifiers we have seen so far, combined with the requirements we have identified for RDF statements, and the requirement that each statement has a truth value, we can construct an RDF triple that meets all these requirements:

```
http://dbpedia.org/resource/Cormac_McCarthy   http://dbpedia.org/prop-
erty/author http://dbpedia.org/resource/The_Road.
```

This statement says that Cormac McCarthy is the author of The Road, which is in fact true.

In this example every part of the triple statement is an IRI. But an object does not have to be an IRI. An object can be a raw data value such as a number, a date, a string, or some custom data type. For raw data values, it is important to specify the type of data, again, to reduce ambiguity. The Semantic Web uses the same data types defined in XML. Core types are xsd:string, xsd:boolean, xsd:decimal, and xsd:double, but there are many others for types of numbers, dates, binary data, and data encoded in other formats. So, we could have expressed the triple about Cormac McCarthy like this:

```
http://dbpedia.org/resource/Cormac_McCarthy   http://dbpedia.org/prop-
erty/author "The Road".
```

This is the only exception to RDF's IRI requirement. It is best to use an IRI even in the object portion if possible, because IRIs uniquely and unambiguously identify a thing. Since RDF lives on the World Wide Web, you can achieve this uniqueness in the same way that the Web ensures every page URL is unique, starting with the name of the computer that does (or could) host this RDF data. In fact, it is good practice to make RDF IRIs work. That is, if you type one in a Web browser, the browser would retrieve some information about the thing represented by the identifier. This is a requirement if you want to add your data to the Web of Linked Open Data, a vast collection of RDF data that is accessible on the Web (Figure 3.1).

Figure 3.1 A single RDF statement visualized as a graph.

Modeling triples

Even though triples are not a linguistic construct, there are instances when it is helpful to think of them as simple sentences. For example, if you are prototyping some information as triples with colleagues, you can use the triple structure as a model for that information. This is a good way to explore how to represent information in RDF without initially identifying a source vocabulary for predicates.

It is not uncommon to play fast and loose with RDF when first modeling your data as triples. Let us say you wanted to create a triple about a boy named Paul who is 9 years old. You do not yet know what ontologies or vocabularies might apply, you are just trying to outline things and relationships. So you just write on a whiteboard: aPerson/NewMexico/Paul hasAge 9. Or, maybe you start by drawing a pair circles, labeling one Paul, the other 9, and draw a line between them labeled "hasAge" These are both RDF models. You won't have a problem creating formal valid triples from them, even if you have to define your own vocabulary to get there.

This is a bottom-up approach to modeling semantic data in RDF. Eventually you have to select vocabularies, create IRIs, make links, and create triples. The resulting triples are called instance data. You can think of instance data as rows in a database table. The vocabularies you use in your instance data roughly correspond to the database schema, which defines the tables and relationships in a relational database. In the example above, the predicate "hasAge" could be a data property from a taxonomy or ontology about people. The statement that Paul hasAge 9 is instance data, a statement of fact about something identified as "Paul."

RDF graphs can be analyzed just like any other graphs, although applying graph analytic techniques to RDF can be a little tricky. One reason is because an RDF graph is a multipartite graph. This means there are different types of nodes and edges within the same graph. Summing up the edges that point to an IRI identifying something will tell you how many statements of some form have been made about that thing, but this rarely leads to insights about an RDF graph. Usually it is necessary to extract a portion of an RDF graph, thus creating some kind of subgraph, before something like degree is a useful metric. So graph analysis of RDF graphs tends to require more work and is not always a useful way to explore the information they contain.

RDF and deduction

You can evaluate and analyze the content of RDF graphs in other ways. A triple is an assertion of fact about a resource (the subject). It has a truth value. Most people can, when presented with a set of related facts can reason about the information and draw conclusions. We can deduce new facts from what we know to be true. The

RDF model is rigorous enough that it is possible to construct rules that a computer could use to reason about triples and deduce new facts. These rules are represented as a series of logical statements. You can express things like "if condition a and condition b are true about resource x, then we can conclude that something else is also true." If you have ever performed a boolean search, then you have at least a passing familiarity with formal logic. Consider the following statements about Bob:

"Bob has daughter"
"Bob has wife"
"Wife is mother."

A human would quickly reason through these statements to conclude that a daughter has a mother. We of course have the advantage of knowing what daughter, wife, and mother are, whereas a computer program does not. Because RDF uses unique identifiers for resources, common shared vocabularies, and because each triple is a statement of a fact, RDF is well suited for rules-based reasoning. You can construct rules that a computer could use to determine that there is an implicit relationship between a daughter and a mother:

if (subject has daughter) or (subject has son)
  and if (subject has wife) and (wife is mother)
    then daughter has mother.

These rules make it possible a infer a new fact if certain conditions are met. This fact can be added as a new edge to the graph, between daughter and mother, with an edge labeled "has." This process is called reasoning. Reasoning over RDF statements can result in the discovery of new facts or allow software to "make decisions" based on how a set of logical rules evaluate, given some collection of facts. In a sense, triples represent a sort of "memory" and rules are a very crude strategy for "thinking."

Graphs are usually used to model complex but well-defined systems. These kinds of graphs have a finite set of nodes and edges of one or a few types. In contrast, RDF is graph-based scaffolding for representing all human knowledge. It is a network representation of information, through which many paths are possible. It can grow and evolve over time as resources and relationships are added. In a sense, it is a vast collective memory.

With the Semantic Web, our machines not only gain an associative memory like ours, they can make use of it. Vannevar Bush, and others before him, anticipated that machines might eventually be able to reason over linked knowledge: "Whenever logical processes of thought are employed—that is, whenever thought for a time runs along an accepted groove—there is an opportunity for the machine. It is readily possible to construct a machine which will manipulate premises in accordance with formal logic, simply by the clever use of relay circuits. Put a set of premises into such a device and turn the crank, and it will readily pass out conclusion after conclusion, all in accordance with logical law, and with no more slips than would be expected of a keyboard adding machine."

RDF and its serializations

4

Abstract notions lead to shared concepts

In the 1880s, naturalist Charles Robertson began observing and recording the visits bees made to various flowering plants within a 10 mile vicinity of the town of Carlinville in northwestern Illinois. He finally published these observations in his 1923 book, *Flowers and Insects: Lists of Visitors of Four Hundred and Fifty-Three Flowers.* Robertson's work was so meticulous and thorough that it established a baseline of bee diversity for this small area. It's not hard to understand why this sort of research is valuable, given the precipitous decline in pollinating insects that have been widely reported in recent years.

The existence of exhaustive, reliable baseline observations of the biodiversity for any given area is rare. Such observations are especially useful in evaluating the impact that human activities may have on local biodiversity, as well as revealing deeper truths about universalities of all ecosystems. Researchers have periodically replicated Robertson's observations over time, most recently in 2009–2010 by researchers who subsequently published their findings in *Science* Magazine in a paper entitled "Plant-Pollinator Interactions over 120 Years: Loss of Species, Co-Occurrence, and Function." In this more recent paper, the investigators developed a simple graph model of the current and past observations, with insects and plants serving as nodes, and visitations representing edges between them.

The authors used simple visual cues to differentiate graph elements. Temporal distinctions were indicated using colors, with past edges colored red, and current edges colored blue. Edges appeared thicker when there are multiple visits recorded between a particular species of bee and a particular species of plant. This graph, and simple visualization made it readily apparent that there has been a loss of biodiversity in this area over time. It provided some evidence that other species were replacing lost bees, but it also illustrated that there is limited resilience in the bee–plant network. This research and the resulting graph model are a great example of insights that graph models can yield.

RDF graph

The plant-pollinator graph is very simple. There is only one relationship: visits, and two types of things: a species of bee and a species of plant. This is a situation where either a graph or a Semantic Web model would work equally well. In this case, the authors used a simple graph model. But, in a paper on a similar topic entitled "A Case-Study of Ontology-Driven Semantic Mediation of Flower-Visiting Data from Heterogeneous Data-Stores in Three South African Natural History Collections," the authors proposed to extend an existing ontology to represent similar data in

A Librarian's Guide to Graphs, Data and the Semantic Web.

RDF. They proposed extensions to Darwin-SW, which is "an ontology using Darwin Core terms to make it possible to describe biodiversity resources in the Semantic Web" to describe the various interactions that insects have with plants. Their extension makes RDF statements like this possible:

```
http://dbpedia.org/page/Bumblebee Darwin-SW:participates_in FlowerVisitRole.
```

This is essentially the same relationship as expressed in the plant-pollinator graph, but it uses a semantic model. One of the more interesting problems associated with creating graph representations of a system of things and the relationships among them is the task of developing a comprehensive, yet flexible graph model. Graph modeling is a topic we will revisit many times, but the bottom line is, there is no wrong way to do it.

Sometimes there may be a particular approach to modeling the data that seems more intuitive, for example, if you want to represent a social network, people will be the nodes, and some aspect of their relationships will become edges. This can be modeled as either a simple object-relationship graph or an RDF graph. Perhaps you want to add weights to the graph edges according to how well two people know one another. Labeling graph models is very common. It provides a way to distinguish node types, individual nodes, and edges. Graphs where this practice is formalized are called property graphs. In a property graph, nodes and edges can have label (key) value pairs that document details for that individual graph element. This allows the model to be focused on things and relationships. At the same time, it ensures that you can find out what kind of things and what types of relationships an individual node or edge represents when you need that information. Thus, a property graph is very much an open-ended construct with few constraints. This makes them well suited for modeling various aspects of a great variety of complex systems with relative ease (Figure 4.1).

To make triples work with the World Wide Web, RDF graphs use IRIs, which both represent a discrete thing and provide a pointer to it. In the example above, http://dbpedia.org/page/Bumblebee is a DBPedia IRI for the "thing" bumblebee. This identifier points at other related data about bumblebees in other RDF graphs. It is part of the Web of linked data. Other portions of a triple often link out to other graphs. An RDF triple predicate, which is an edge between two nodes in an RDF graph, is also a node defined in an ontology. An ontology is a graph model for a vocabulary. Subjects and some objects are usually of a type (called a class) defined in an ontology. Ontologies define types of things, their relationships to other things, and the properties that are applicable to those things. The approach for defining ontologies borrows heavily from another branch of mathematics called first-order logic. First-order logic allows you to express statements about what is true (which is what a triple is) and to represent the logical steps that can be used to reason about these facts. The reason for this (pun intended) is that reasoning can lead to the deduction of new facts or to conclusions based on combinations of facts.

Ontologies build on the concept of taxonomies. A taxonomy is a sometimes hierarchical list of terms describing a domain or a type of thing. Consider a taxonomy for animals: at the top is the term "animal." Children of the term animal include "mammal," "reptile," "fish," and "bird." Mammals might then be subdivided into

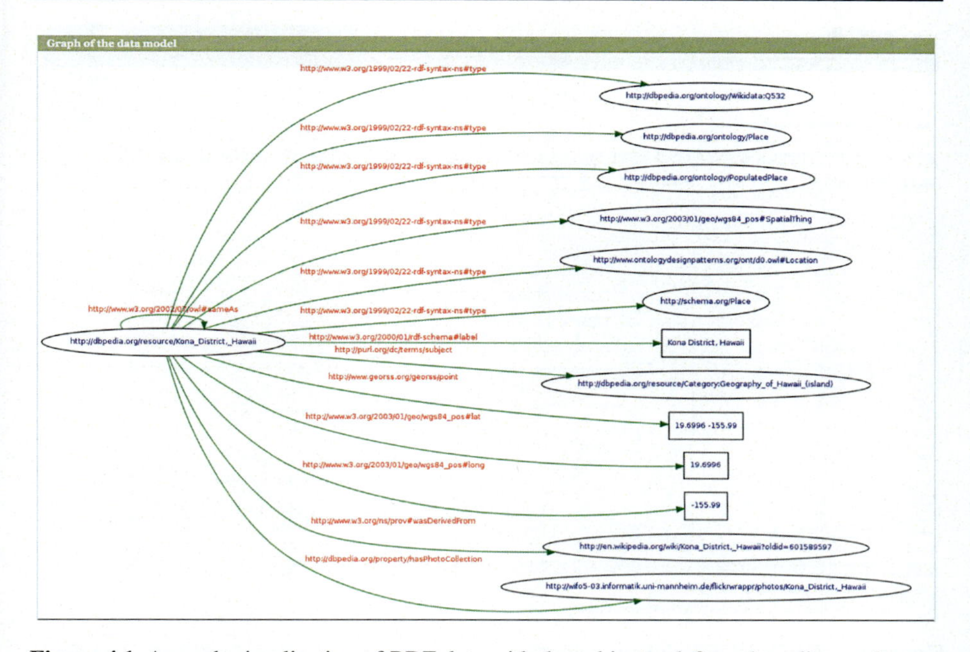

Figure 4.1 A graph visualization of RDF data with the subject at left, and predicate edges connecting it to objects on the right.

"carnivores," "omnivores," and "herbivores." An ontology takes this concept further by allowing for relationships among terms. You can express the fact that an animal cannot be both a reptile and a mammal, and that reptiles, bird, fish, and mammals can all be carnivores, omnivores, or herbivores. Once you define your ontology, you can publish it and others can use and refer back to it. If two different triplestores contain facts about animals, they can both reference the animal ontology and base their predicates on terms from that ontology by using the appropriate IRIs for the terms they wish to use. At that point the concept of animal and the characteristics of an animal are shared across those collections. In effect, they share a basic concept of what an animal is! Chapter 5 covers ontologies in greater detail. Many of the formats described in this chapter can also be used to represent ontologies.

RDF defines an abstract model representing information. The RDF model identifies the parts of a triple, specifies the role of ontologies, when IRIs are required, when literal values like numbers and strings are allowed. However, RDF doesn't tell you exactly how to write a triple. This is the role of serializations. A serialization describes a textual representation for information or data. Serializations like RDF/XML, N3, and Turtle define a particular syntax for RDF statements. As you will see, these various serializations all have their strengths and weakness. Just remember that the RDF model does not change, whether you represent your triples as RDF/XML, N3, or in some other format (Figure 4.2).

Another way to think about serializations is to compare RDF with time. We have numerous ways of representing time (e.g., clocks, calendars, etc.), and the

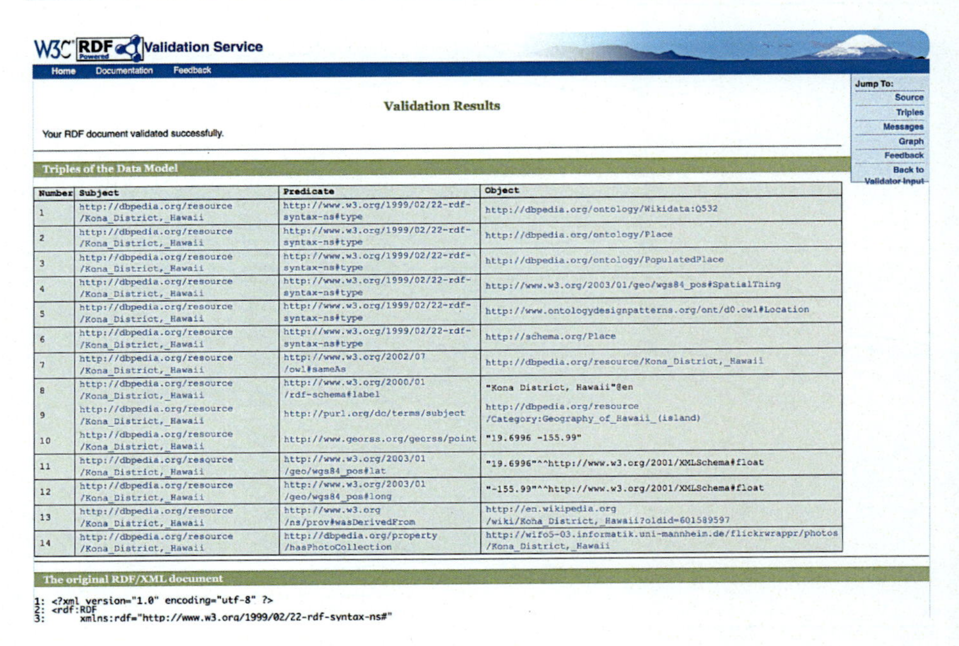

W3C RDF Validation Service

Home Documentation Feedback

Jump To: Source Triples Messages Graph Feedback Back to Validator Input

Validation Results

Your RDF document validated successfully.

Triples of the Data Model

Number	Subject	Predicate	Object
1	http://dbpedia.org/resource/Kona_District,_Hawaii	http://www.w3.org/1999/02/22-rdf-syntax-ns#type	http://dbpedia.org/ontology/Wikidata:Q532
2	http://dbpedia.org/resource/Kona_District,_Hawaii	http://www.w3.org/1999/02/22-rdf-syntax-ns#type	http://dbpedia.org/ontology/Place
3	http://dbpedia.org/resource/Kona_District,_Hawaii	http://www.w3.org/1999/02/22-rdf-syntax-ns#type	http://dbpedia.org/ontology/PopulatedPlace
4	http://dbpedia.org/resource/Kona_District,_Hawaii	http://www.w3.org/1999/02/22-rdf-syntax-ns#type	http://www.w3.org/2003/01/geo/wgs84_pos#SpatialThing
5	http://dbpedia.org/resource/Kona_District,_Hawaii	http://www.w3.org/1999/02/22-rdf-syntax-ns#type	http://www.ontologydesignpatterns.org/ont/d0.owl#Location
6	http://dbpedia.org/resource/Kona_District,_Hawaii	http://www.w3.org/1999/02/22-rdf-syntax-ns#type	http://schema.org/Place
7	http://dbpedia.org/resource/Kona_District,_Hawaii	http://www.w3.org/2002/07/owl#sameAs	http://dbpedia.org/resource/Kona_District,_Hawaii
8	http://dbpedia.org/resource/Kona_District,_Hawaii	http://www.w3.org/2000/01/rdf-schema#label	"Kona District, Hawaii"@en
9	http://dbpedia.org/resource/Kona_District,_Hawaii	http://purl.org/dc/terms/subject	http://dbpedia.org/resource/Category:Geography_of_Hawaii_(island)
10	http://dbpedia.org/resource/Kona_District,_Hawaii	http://www.georss.org/georss/point	"19.6996 -155.99"
11	http://dbpedia.org/resource/Kona_District,_Hawaii	http://www.w3.org/2003/01/geo/wgs84_pos#lat	"19.6996"^^http://www.w3.org/2001/XMLSchema#float
12	http://dbpedia.org/resource/Kona_District,_Hawaii	http://www.w3.org/2003/01/geo/wgs84_pos#long	"-155.99"^^http://www.w3.org/2001/XMLSchema#float
13	http://dbpedia.org/resource/Kona_District,_Hawaii	http://www.w3.org/ns/prov#wasDerivedFrom	http://en.wikipedia.org/wiki/Kona_District,_Hawaii?oldid=601589597
14	http://dbpedia.org/resource/Kona_District,_Hawaii	http://dbpedia.org/property/hasPhotoCollection	http://wifo5-03.informatik.uni-mannheim.de/flickrwrappr/photos/Kona_District,_Hawaii

The original RDF/XML document

```
1: <?xml version="1.0" encoding="utf-8" ?>
2: <rdf:RDF
3:      xmlns:rdf="http://www.w3.org/1999/02/22-rdf-syntax-ns#"
```

Figure 4.2 W3C's RDF Validator output.

same is true for RDF. Representing RDF using different serializations doe not change the original meaning of the statements. All RDF serializations conform to the rules of RDF for the formulation of triples. As a result, it is possible to create converters from one serialization to another. It is also possible to validate a set of statements, to determine if they do in fact conform to the syntactic rules governing that serialization format. Different serializations were developed with different purposes in mind. Some are better at representing RDF in a form that people can understand, others are well suited for embedding RDF in Web pages, and others work best for programs that exchange RDF data.

RDF serializations

RDF/XML co-opts existing tools and standards to express triples using XML. It is the standard interchange format for Semantic Web data and so it is a required format for triples and ontologies. RDF/XML is very difficult to read. Turtle, which stands for Terse RDF Triple Language, is concise, easy to read representation for triples. It is basically a variant of another syntax for representing triples, called Notation 3 or N3. Functional syntax is modeled after logic notation and is especially well suited for defining ontologies and rules. JSON-LD is the JSON (Javascript Object Notation) Linked Data format. Like RDF/XML, it leverages an existing standard (JSON) to facilitate machine exchange of semantic data. Unlike

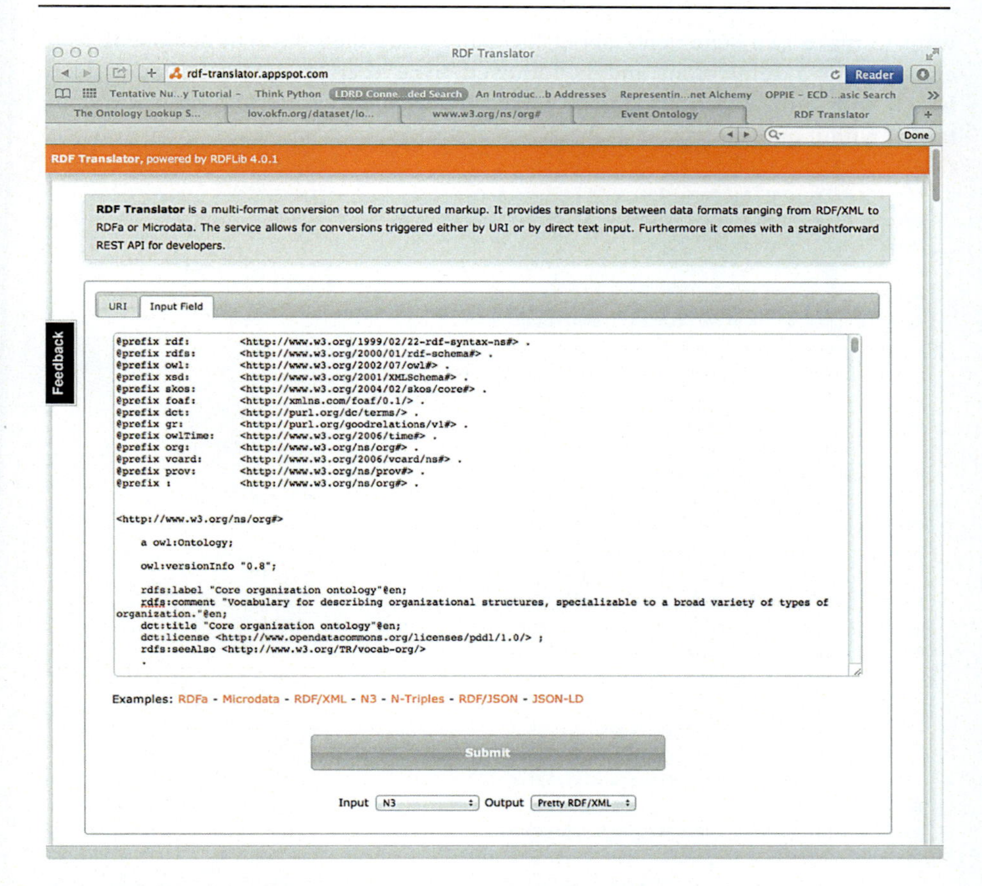

Figure 4.3 RDF Translator displays a portion of a Turtle/N3 document.

RDF/XML, it is actually pretty easy to understand. RDFa is a format for embedding triples into HTML Web pages (Figure 4.3).

Turtle is an RDF serialization that is well suited for human comprehension. It uses some simple syntactic rules also found in English. The resulting expressions of triples, where punctuation such as commas and semicolons are used to combine multiple statements, can almost seem at times like English language sentences. A straightforward representation of a triple in turtle consists of an IRI subject, an IRI predicate, and an IRI or literal object value followed by a period. An IRI is always contained within these characters < >. Turtle allows you to predefine a set of prefixes that correspond to the vocabularies and ontologies that subsequent triples reference. Each prefix definition starts with @prefix. The string that constitutes a prefix for a given namespace follows. This is followed by a colon and then the IRI for the namespace, embedded in < >. When you use a prefix in a triple, you specify the prefix, followed by a colon, followed by a specific element name from the vocabulary (class or property name). If you want to make two statements about the same thing then the first statement concludes with a semicolon, and is followed by a second predicate and object, which ends with a period. Object values represented as literal strings are contained within quotes.

```
@prefix owl:  <http://www.w3.org/2002/07/owl#>.
@prefix ns1:  <http://wikidata.dbpedia.org/resource/>.
@prefix ns2:  <http://id.dbpedia.org/resource/>.
ns2:Distrik_Kona  owl:sameAs  <http://dbpedia.org/resource/Kona_District,_Hawaii>.
@prefix dbpprop:  <http://dbpedia.org/property/>.
@prefix dbpedia:  <http://dbpedia.org/resource/>.
<http://en.wikipedia.org/wiki/Kona_District,_Hawaii>  foaf:primaryTopic
  <http://dbpedia.org/resource/Kona_District,_Hawaii>.
@prefix rdf:  <http://www.w3.org/1999/02/22-rdf-syntax-ns#>.
@prefix geo:  <http://www.w3.org/2003/01/geo/wgs84_pos#>.
<http://dbpedia.org/resource/Kona_District,_Hawaii>  rdf:type  geo:SpatialThing .
@prefix d0:  <http://www.ontologydesignpatterns.org/ont/d0.owl#>.
<http://dbpedia.org/resource/Kona_District,_Hawaii>  rdf:type  d0:Location .
@prefix dcterms:  <http://purl.org/dc/terms/>.
<http://dbpedia.org/resource/Kona_District,_Hawaii>  dcterms:subject
  <http://dbpedia.org/resource/Category:Geography_of_Hawaii_(island)>.
@prefix grs:  <http://www.georss.org/georss/>.
<http://dbpedia.org/resource/Kona_District,_Hawaii>  grs:point  "19.6996 -155.99" .
@prefix xsd:  <http://www.w3.org/2001/XMLSchema#>.
<http://dbpedia.org/resource/Kona_District,_Hawaii>
      geo:lat  "19.6996"^^xsd:float ;
     geo:long  "-155.99"^^xsd:float ;
      foaf:depiction
    <http://commons.wikimedia.org/wiki/Special:FilePath/HawaiiIslandDistrict-
NorthKona.svg>.
@prefix prov:  <http://www.w3.org/ns/prov#>.
<http://dbpedia.org/resource/Kona_District,_Hawaii>    prov:wasDerivedFrom
    <http://en.wikipedia.org/wiki/Kona_District,_Hawaii?oldid=601589597> ;
    foaf:isPrimaryTopicOf  <http://en.wikipedia.org/wiki/Kona_ District,_Hawaii> ;
    dbpprop:hasPhotoCollection  <http://wifo5-03.informatik.uni-mannheim.de/flickrwrappr/
photos/Kona_District,_Hawaii> ;
```

RDF/XML is a way to represent triples using an XML schema. XML is an especially useful format for providing triples in batch to software because processing it leverages existing software that can process XML. An XML document contains data wrapped with special tags enclosed between the < and > characters. When a tag contains some data, it has a start form and an end form <tag> </tag>. Sometimes it is useful to have an empty tag which looks like this <tag />. Sometimes tags include attributes, which express some additional information. They are contained within the start element tag and take the form attribute = "some value". Sometimes tags can be nested inside other tags. Tags are defined in XML schema or XML DTD documents, which are just two ways to define tag names and tag relationships, as well as the overall structure of an XML document that uses the defined tags. Documents containing data tagged based upon a particular tag set are

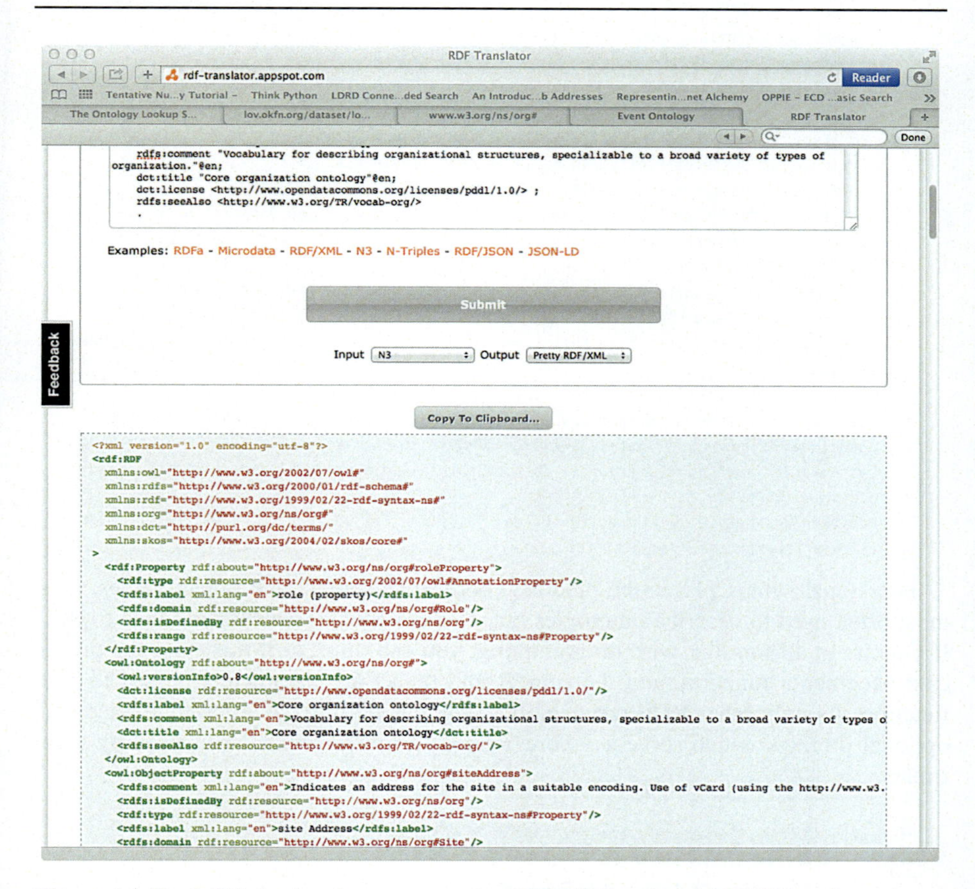

Figure 4.4 Turtle/N3 that has been converted to RDF/XML using the RDF Translator.

called instance documents or instance data. Triples expressed in RDF/XML conform to all of these requirements: there is a schema defining the triple tag and attribute set, and there are instance documents containing sets of triples tagged with RDF/XML (Figure 4.4).

```
<?xml version="1.0" encoding="utf-8" ?>
<rdf:RDF
   xmlns:rdf="http://www.w3.org/1999/02/22-rdf-syntax-ns#"
   xmlns:rdfs="http://www.w3.org/2000/01/rdf-schema#"
   xmlns:owl="http://www.w3.org/2002/07/owl#"
   xmlns:dcterms="http://purl.org/dc/terms/"
   xmlns:grs="http://www.georss.org/georss/"
   xmlns:geo="http://www.w3.org/2003/01/geo/wgs84_pos#"
   xmlns:dbpedia-owl="http://dbpedia.org/ontology/"
```

```
xmlns:dbpprop="http://dbpedia.org/property/"
xmlns:foaf="http://xmlns.com/foaf/0.1/"
xmlns:prov="http://www.w3.org/ns/prov#">
<rdf:Description rdf:about="http://dbpedia.org/resource/Kona_District,_Hawaii">
<rdf:type rdf:resource="http://dbpedia.org/ontology/Wikidata:Q532"/>
<rdf:type rdf:resource="http://dbpedia.org/ontology/Place" />
<rdf:type rdf:resource="http://dbpedia.org/ontology/PopulatedPlace"/>
<rdf:type rdf:resource="http://www.w3.org/2003/01/geo/wgs84_pos#SpatialThing" />
<rdf:type rdf:resource="http://www.ontologydesignpatterns.org/ont/d0.owl#Location" />
<rdf:type rdf:resource="http://schema.org/Place" />
<owl:sameAs rdf:resource="http://dbpedia.org/resource/Kona_District,_Hawaii" />
<rdfs:label xml:lang="en">Kona District, Hawaii</rdfs:label>
<dcterms:subject rdf:resource="http://dbpedia.org/resource/Category:Geography_of_Hawaii_
(island)" />
<grs:point>19.6996 -155.99</grs:point>
<geo:lat rdf:datatype="http://www.w3.org/2001/XMLSchema#float">19.6996</geo:lat>
<geo:long rdf:datatype="http://www.w3.org/2001/XMLSchema#float">-155.99</geo:long>
<prov:wasDerivedFrom rdf:resource="http://en.wikipedia.org/wiki/Kona_District,_Hawaii?
oldid=601589597" />
<dbpprop:hasPhotoCollection rdf:resource="http://wifo5-03.informatik.uni-mannheim.de/
flickrwrappr/photos/Kona_District,_Hawaii" />
```

Functional syntax places the predicate before the subject and object values. It is most often used to describe ontologies but it works equally well for instance triples. If you are at all familiar with programming, you can think of it this way: the predicate becomes a function, and the subject and object are parameters passed to that function. As with other RDF serializations, you can define a default namespace and optional prefixes which serve as abbreviations for other vocabularies used by your triples.

```
Prefix(:=<http://www.example.com/ontology1#>) Ontology(
<http://www.example.com/ontology1>
    Import( <http://www.example.com/ontology2> )
    Annotation( rdfs:label "An example" )
      SubClassOf( :Child owl:Thing )  )
```

Notation 3, or N3, is similar to turtle. It differs primarily in how it handles blank nodes. Like N-triples, you have the option of defining prefixes that stand in for the namespaces for the various vocabularies and ontologies a particular collection of triples use. When a prefix is used subsequently, it is preceded by a colon. Blank nodes are denoted by an underscore character and the internal identifier assigned to the node. Turtle uses square brackets and omits the blank node label altogether. Otherwise the syntax for N3 is the same as Turtle.

JSON-LD uses JSON (Javascript Object Notation) to represent RDF data. Javascript is a programming language for the Web which runs in Web browsers. The LD portion of the name stands for Linked Data. Because of JSON's Web heritage, JSON-LD is well suited for Web applications written in Javascript. But JSON has become a more general purpose data interchange format. Mongo is a big data database that uses JSON natively. Many REST-based Web applications, which are client–server applications that use Web protocols, send and receive JSON formatted data to each other. JSON defines a very flexible key/value pair format for representing various data structures. Additional syntactic rules allow for data to be grouped in various ways. JSON syntax for an object is to enclose the object components within curly brackets. Each key and value is contained within double quotes and the two are separated by a colon. Key/value pairs are separated by a comma. JSON-LD defines a JSON syntax for RDF data. JSON allows objects to be chained together, and this is how JSON-LD specifies things like multiple predicates and objects for a single subject. A JSON-LD document can define a local vocabulary using context, and it can reference external vocabularies as well. These occur at the beginning of a JSON-LD document

```
{ "@graph": [
   { "@id": "http://dbpedia.org/resource/Kona_District,_Hawaii",
     "@type" : [ "http://dbpedia.org/ontology/Place" ,
       "http://schema.org/Place" ,
       "http://dbpedia.org/ontology/PopulatedPlace" ,
       "http://www.ontologydesignpatterns.org/ont/d0.owl#Location" ,
       "http://www.w3.org/2003/01/geo/wgs84_pos#SpatialThing" ,
       "http://dbpedia.org/ontology/Wikidata:Q532" ] ,
       "http://id.dbpedia.org/resource/Distrik_Kona" ,
       { "@value" : "Kona District, Hawaii" , "@language" : "en" } ] ,
       "http://purl.org/dc/terms/subject" : [
"http://dbpedia.org/resource/Category:Geography_of_Hawaii_(island)" ] ,
       "http://www.georss.org/georss/point" : [ { "@value" : "19.6996 -155.99" } ],
"http://www.w3.org/2003/01/geo/wgs84_pos#lat":[{"@value":
       19.69960021972656,"@type":"http://www.w3.org/2001/XMLSchema#float"}],
"http://www.w3.org/2003/01/geo/wgs84_pos#long":[{"@value":-
       155.9900054931641,"@type":"http://www.w3.org/2001/XMLSchema#float"}],
"http://www.w3.org/ns/prov#wasDerivedFrom" : [
       "http://en.wikipedia.org/wiki/Kona_District,_Hawaii?oldid=601589597" ] ,
```

RDFa defines a handful of HTML attributes that can be used with existing HTML markup elements to encode RDF into various contexts such as Web or XML pages. Some aspects of RDFa are implicit. For example, it is understood that an RDFa attribute, when it represents a portion of an RDF statement, is generally referring to the child element or the HREF attribute value, if applicable, of a document. The vocab attribute allows you to define one or more ontology namespaces that will be used in the HTML markup of your Web page. The prefix attribute allows you to define a string prefix for each namespace, just as with other RDF serializations, to designate the ontology for a given property. The property attribute associates the contents of the element it is embedded in with an ontology property. If you want to indicate that something is of a particular class, there is the type of attribute.

Finally, the resource attribute allows you to identify the subject of an RDFa embedded statement explicitly. Full documentation for RDFa core and RDFa lite is available at the W3 website. A similar format called HTML + microdata, which also uses attributes to embed RDF in a Web page. In this case, the itemscope and itemid attributes identify the subject for one or more triples. The item prop and href attributes identify predicate and their associated object values for the specified itemscope subject, until a new itemscope is specified.

```
<dl itemscope itemid="http://dbpedia.org/resource/Kona_District,_Hawaii">
<dt>Subject Item</dt> <dd>n2:_Hawaii</dd>
<dt>rdf:type</dt> <dd>
<a itemprop="http://www.w3.org/1999/02/22-rdf-syntax-ns#type"
    href="http://dbpedia.org/ontology/Place">dbpedia-owl:Place</a>
<a itemprop="http://www.w3.org/1999/02/22-rdf-syntax-ns#type"
    href="http://schema.org/Place">n9:Place</a>
<a itemprop="http://www.w3.org/1999/02/22-rdf-syntax-ns#type"
    href="http://dbpedia.org/ontology/PopulatedPlace">dbpedia-owl:PopulatedPlace</a>
<a itemprop="http://www.w3.org/1999/02/22-rdf-syntax-ns#type"
    href="http://www.ontologydesignpatterns.org/ont/d0.owl#Location">d0:Location</a>
<a itemprop="http://www.w3.org/1999/02/22-rdf-syntax-ns#type"
    href="http://www.w3.org/2003/01/geo/wgs84_pos#SpatialThing">geo:SpatialThing</a>
</dd>
<dt>dcterms:subject</dt> <dd>
<a itemprop="http://purl.org/dc/terms/subject" href="http://dbpedia.org/resource/Category:
Geography_of_Hawaii_(island)">n28:</a>
</dd>
<dt>grs:point</dt> <dd>
<span itemprop="http://www.georss.org/georss/point">
    19.6996 -155.99</span>
</dd>
<dt>geo:lat</dt> <dd>
<span itemprop="http://www.w3.org/2003/01/geo/wgs84_pos#lat">
    19.6996</span>
</dd>
<dt>geo:long</dt> <dd>
<span itemprop="http://www.w3.org/2003/01/geo/wgs84_pos#long">
    -155.99</span>
</dd>
<dt>dbpprop:hasPhotoCollection</dt> <dd>
<a itemprop="http://dbpedia.org/property/hasPhotoCollection"
    href="http://wifo5-03.informatik.uni-mannheim.de/flickrwrappr/photos/Kona_District,
    _Hawaii">n5:_Hawaii</a>
</dd>
<dt>foaf:depiction</dt> <dd>
<a itemprop="http://xmlns.com/foaf/0.1/depiction" href="http://commons.wikimedia.org/wiki/
Special:FilePath/HawaiiIslandDistrict-NorthKona.svg">n24:svg</a>
</dd>
<dt>prov:wasDerivedFrom</dt> <dd>
<a itemprop="http://www.w3.org/ns/prov#wasDerivedFrom" href="http:// en.wikipedia.org/wiki/
Kona_District,_Hawaii?oldid=601589597">n11:601589597</a>
</dd>
```

Ontologies

5

Ontological autometamorphosis

The Semantic Web has its origins in the decades long struggle to enable computers (which until recently lacked means for perceiving or manipulating the world) to understand and interact with information as we do. A similar struggle for understanding occurs in the 1961 scifi novel *Solaris*, by Stanislaw Lem. In *Solaris* humankind had discovered alien life on the planet Solaris. Solaris was inhabited by a single organism that encompassed the entire planet as would an ocean. Despite a hundred years of effort and study (much of which was documented in imaginary books and journals which populated the library of the Solaris outpost), neither human nor alien had managed to communicate with the other. The inhabitant of Solaris was made up of a strange viscous liquid and had a tendency to mimic shapes of things that it perceived or encountered. In the novel, some scientists who studied Solaris suggested that the alien was engaging in a process they called ontological autometamorphosis; that is, in order to perhaps comprehend things, it took their form for a time. Fortunately for us, we can engage in a similar process as purely a mental exercise and document and share the results with others, by using our innate classification skills to create Semantic Web ontologies.

It is perhaps fitting that "ontology" is a vaguely alien sounding word that is a bit hard to define. With ties to both philosophy and linguistics, ontology is the embodiment of something that comes naturally for humans: categorizing and classifying things around us. We categorize to help us recognize things and to predict their behavior. We categorize so we can make guesses about new things that we encounter. Very young children sometimes use a simply classification strategy when learning new words, referred to as a taxonomic assumption. Stanford psychology professor Ellen Markman explains how this works:

> *[we] conducted a series of studies which compared how children would organize objects when an object was referred to with a novel label versus when it was not. When presented with two objects, such as a dog and cat, and a third object that was thematically related such as dog food, children would often select a dog and dog food as being the same kind of thing. If, however, the dog was called by an unfamiliar label such as* dax *and children told to find another dax, they now were more likely to select the cat. This illustrates the basic phenomenon: When children believe they are learning a new word, they focus on taxonomic, not thematic, relations.*

It is often challenging to unambiguously express the structure of a domain of knowledge and facts within it to another person, let alone an alien. Imagine that you had to describe the desk you are perhaps sitting in front of right now. How would you describe this particular desk to someone who has never seen it?

A Librarian's Guide to Graphs, Data and the Semantic Web.

How would you describe a desk in general terms to someone who didn't know what a desk was? How would you describe the category of things we refer to as furniture to a lost tribe of Amazonian Indians who had never been contacted by the outside world? In each case, there are probably different characteristics you would emphasize first, in order to provide a context for the more specific descriptive features. In cases where the target audience's context is less similar to yours, you would build on these descriptions in order to provide all the necessary information. One way to do this is by developing an ontology.

Introduction to ontologies

In this chapter we have four main goals:

1. To convey the thought process for constructing an ontology
2. To give you a sense for what roles ontologies play in the Semantic Web
3. To introduce you to the ontology description languages RDFS and OWL
4. To help you be able to read and understand an ontology when you find one online

An ontology is, in a sense, a skeletal framework for knowledge. An ontology is a description of things, relationships, and their characteristics, usually in a well-bounded domain, for example, ecology or astronomy. It is in part a taxonomy, which is a graph structure that describes the hierarchical relationship of a group of things. Things that occur farther down in the taxonomy inherit characteristics from one or more parents that occur above them. In an ontology, the taxonomy is extended so that you express logical relationships among things, membership in groups, multiple inheritance relationships, the symmetry of relationships, exclusiveness, and various characteristics of a given thing.

Semantic Web ontologies are concerned with logical consistency and expressiveness to allow for machine reasoning. Semantic Web ontology languages employ first-order predicate logic. Logic is a mathematical field concerned with expressing simple statements of fact as axioms, and for expression rules as logical expressions, which, given some initial conditions, can be evaluated against the axioms using inferencing and deduction. Since ontologies are grounded in logic, they can facilitate a process that mimic human reasoning. This is how ontologies can be used in artificial intelligence applications.

In this chapter, we introduce the two languages used to create Semantic Web ontologies, RDFS and OWL. Like RDF, the description of ontology can be serialized in various formats, including N3, functional logic, and RDF/XML. Only RDF/XML is required, and only if you plan to publish and share your ontology with others. The RDF/XML document describing your ontology should be accessible via the IRI that corresponds to its unique namespace. This IRI is used to reference the ontology when its classes and properties are used in RDF triples. In triples, elements of an ontology typically occupy the predicate portion of a triple. In some cases, they can also be subjects (for example, in the ontology definition file itself), or objects, if the statement is expressing that some item is of a type defined in an ontology, for example. In other words, the edges in RDF graphs are usually properties defined in some ontology. In fact, the use of ontologies is one of the defining characteristics of the Semantic Web.

While it is important to be able to read and comprehend an ontology, in practice, you will rarely need to create an entirely new ontology from scratch. There are Web and desktop ontology authoring tools that handle some of the complexity of generating an ontology and make it easier to focus on your model. Protege is one example. You can use Protege to create an ontology from scratch, extend an existing ontology, or simply to load an existing ontology to browse it. It enforces RDFS and OWL language requirements, and can even be used to generate instance triples using your ontology. There's also a Web version of Protege called WebProtege. If you have a basic knowledge of RDFS and OWL, you will be able to more effectively use any ontology authoring tool (Figure 5.1).

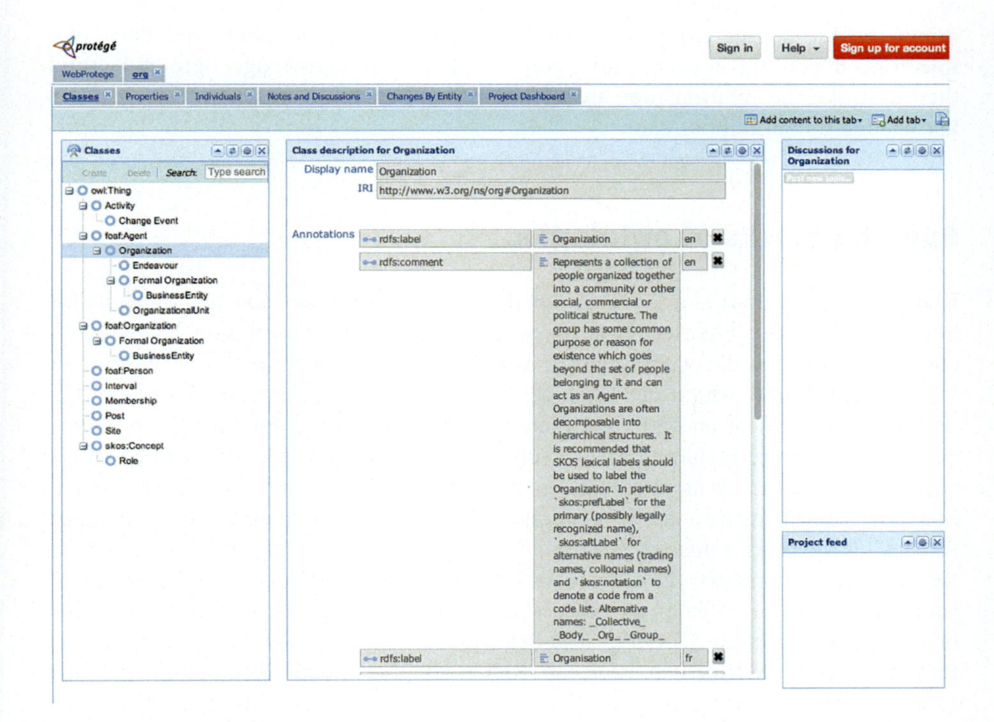

Figure 5.1 WebProtege ontology editor displaying an ontology's class hierarchy and some properties for a selected class.

Ontology development steps

1. Identify your rough taxonomy—what are the things and sub-things?
2. What things have non-relationships with one another?
3. What things inherit from multiple things?
4. What are the uniquely defining characteristics of an individual?
5. What are the measurable characteristics of a thing?
6. What things are described by referencing other things?

Some researchers in this field recommend that you build a separate object and knowledge ontology. They suggest that the object ontology might be reusable in other contexts if it is defined separately. In this approach, the object ontology defines the generic things that can exist, their placement in a hierarchy of classes, and their properties. The object ontology defines a language for the domain. The knowledge ontology in a sense extends the object ontology to express the relationships among its things in the context of a particular domain. This semantic modeling approach is embodied in a formal language called Gellish. Gellish is a representation-independent table of things, their identifiers, their labels in various languages, acronyms that apply to them, etc. If you define an object model for engines, the various possible parts of an engine could be defined in this model. It might include engine components such as a combustion chamber, cylinders, fuel injectors, a cooling system, and a super charger. A knowledge ontology could then describe the relationships among these components in a separate table for a knowledge domain about cars.

Building blocks of ontologies

RDFS (RDF Schema) is a language for describing basic types and relationships for Semantic Web vocabularies. It is essentially a taxonomy description language. A clue to this fact is the word schema, which is a term used for the definitions of XML vocabularies, which are hierarchical taxonomies of elements. To model the taxonomic aspects of an ontology, there are some primitives for specifying hierarchical relationship, including Class, subClassOf, Resource, and subPropertyOf. A class is a type of thing in an ontology—an animal, a vehicle, a name, etc. Mammal, marsupial, and kangaroo are all examples of classes in a domain defining animals. A subClass defines a hierarchical relationship—mammal is a subClass of animal for example. A property is a characteristic of a class, such as a measurement of some type, or a value from a control vocabulary of properties, or a numeric value or string literal such as 3.14159, "100 degrees C," or "blue." As you may recall, the Property class is defined in RDF, so RDFS simply extends this notion with the subPropertyOf property, to enable properties to inherit characteristics from one another in the same fashion that classes can do so.

```
<rdfs:Class rdf:resource="#Novel">
  <rdfs:subClassOf rdf:resource="#Book" />
</rdfs:Class>
```

If a class is defined as a subclass of another class, then it has the properties of that class. There's no need to redefine the properties of the parent class for the child. If a mammal has properties that express the fact that it has fur and its metabolism is "warm-blooded," and if a kangaroo is a subclass of a mammal, then by definition it has fur and is warm-blooded. You can add additional properties to a subclass which help to differentiate it to make it more specific. For a kangaroo, you might define a "means of locomotion" property, to which you assign the value "hopping." Properties can also inherit from one another. This can be used to narrow the range of potential values for the subproperty. Birds could be defined to have a color property that includes green and blue, but for mammals, you might elect to define a mammal color subproperty for which green and blue would be invalid values. These aspects of a property are defined with RDFS domain and range.

OWL, or the Web Ontology Language, was first published as a standard by the W3C in 2004. It is a language for modeling ontologies for the Semantic Web. In practice it is always used in conjunction with RDFS. For the remainder of this chapter, we will introduce the OWL language and use it in conjunction with RDFS to define some aspects of an ontology about libraries. Although this is a simple "toy" ontology, it should give you enough of a sense for what the Semantic Web ontology languages can do and the ability to read an ontology specification and understand most of what you would encounter. Once you complete this chapter, if you want to delve more deeply into ontology development, there are many good tutorials on the Web, including the well-known "Pizza Ontology Tutorial" (http://owl.cs.manchester.ac.uk/tutorials/protegeowltutorial/) which is used as an exercise with an ontology editor called Protege. It can also be very helpful to download an ontology editor such as Protege and use it with an existing ontology that describes a subject area you are well acquainted with and use the software to explore the ontology (Figure 5.2).

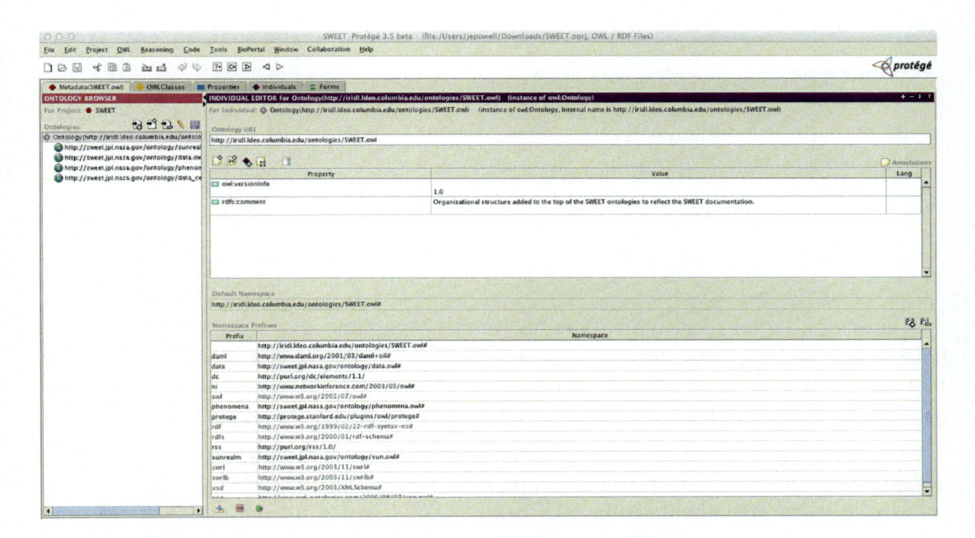

Figure 5.2 Protege displaying metadata about the SWEET ontology.

Ontology building tutorial

For our ontology, we will use RDFS and OWL to express various aspects and relationships among the following list of things:

- library
- librarian
- person
- book
- novel
- journal
- article
- chapter
- page
- director
- figure
- birthdate
- publication date
- genre
- patron
- call number
- publication

These terms represent the knowledge domain we want to model. The resulting ontology could be used to make statements about specific libraries, authors, books, etc. This is an interesting list from which to derive an ontology in part because there really isn't a strong taxonomic arrangement for the elements. Also, some of the items represent characteristics of other items in addition to, or instead of, things that exist. But in preparation for creating an ontology, let's go ahead and explore how these items might be reorganized into a taxonomy.

```
person
 + --librarian
 + --patron
library
publication
 + -- book
 + -- novel
 + -- journal
...
```

There aren't a lot of insights to be had in this taxonomy. For the most part, we still have a list of things that exist at the same top level, thus it is a shallow taxonomy. We do now know that a librarian and a patron are also a person, and that a journal and a book are a publication, and that a novel is a book. That's about it so far.

An ontology will tell us much more as you will soon see. Next we'll construct parts of an ontology to provide more information about these things and the relationships among them using RDFS and OWL. Since an ontology has to have a unique dereferenceable IRI, let's call ours: http://example.org/library#, which we will refer to henceforth with the prefix lib. Here is how this is declared in RDF/XML:

```
<rdf:RDF
xmlns = "http://example.org/library#"
  xmlns:owl = "http://www.w3.org/2002/07/owl#"
  xmlns:rdf = "http://www.w3.org/1999/02/22-rdf-syntax-ns#"
  xmlns:rdfs = "http://www.w3.org/2000/01/rdf-schema#"
  xmlns:dc = "http://purl.org/dc/elements/1.1/">
  xmlns:xsd = "http://www.w3.org/2001/XMLSchema#">
  <owl:Ontology rdf:about="http://example.org/library"/>
  <dc:title>Example Library Ontology</dc:title>
```

The first line defines our ontology namespace prefix for all our ontology elements that will follow. The remaining attributes for the rdf:RDF element reference other languages that our ontology model uses, including OWL, RDF, RDFS, and XSD. The last two lines declare the ontology namespace according to OWL 2 requirements and specify a title for the ontology.

An ontology defines classes for the things that exist in the domain you are modeling. Most of the things in our list and taxonomy above will be classes in our library ontology. OWL language elements for describing classes fall into six categories. The first kind of class description establishes a unique identifier for a thing. Here's an example that establishes librarian as a Thing:

```
  <owl:Class rdf:ID="Librarian" />
```

lib#Librarian can then serve as a predicate to indicate that something (well, someone) is a librarian. This statement is a shorthand way of asserting that a Librarian is an owl:Thing in your ontology. Owl supports two predefined classes, Thing and Nothing. Formally, every class in every ontology is a subclass of Thing. The other predefined class is Nothing, which is an empty set construct for instances where it is necessary to be explicit about the fact that you've logically reached the end of the line, so to speak. Or you may prefer to think of it as the logical equivalent of zero. The need for a Nothing class will become more apparent when we look at reasoning, in Chapter 7.

The next class description defines a class that is a collection of things. Since books and journals are both publications, we'll say there is a collection that can consist of books or journals, or both (Figure 5.3).

```
<owl:Class rdf:ID="Publications">
  <owl:someValuesFrom>
    <owl:Class>
      <owl:oneOf rdf:parseType="Collection">
        <owl:Thing rdf:about="#Book">
        <owl:Thing rdf:about="#Journal">
      </owl:oneOf>
    </owl:Class>
  </owl:someValuesFrom>
</owl:Class>
```

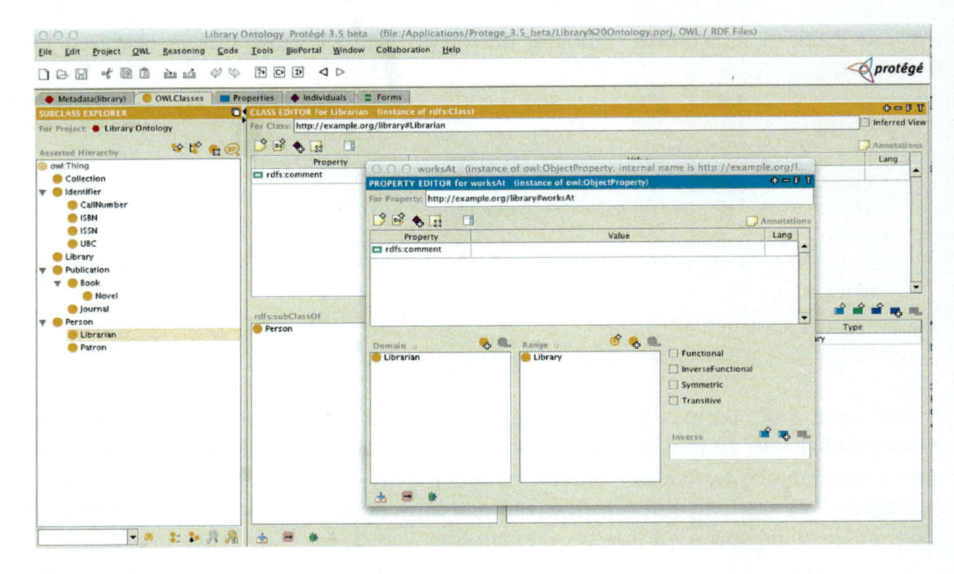

Figure 5.3 Composing a library ontology in Protege.

This states that a particular class Publication can be a Book or a Journal. This is called a class description. A class description is an anonymous class with no identifier. Class descriptions describe property restrictions, intersections, unions, and complement. Since we haven't yet discussed what a property is, we'll revisit the property restriction class description in a moment. Meanwhile, let's look at the "set" class descriptions' intersection, union, and complement. Since it's likely you've been exposed to the Boolean concepts of AND, OR, and NOT, we will use these to illustrate these class descriptions. Here's an example of a union (OR) set:

```
<owl:Class>
  <owl:unionOf rdf:parseType="Collection:>
    <owl:Class>
      <owl:oneOf rdf:parseType="Collection">
        <owl:Thing rdf:about="#CallNumber"/>
        <owl:Thing rdf:about="#ISBN"/>
      </owl:oneOf>
    </owl:Class>
  <owl:Class>
      <owl:oneOf rdf:parseType="Collection">
        <owl:Thing rdf:about="#ISSN"/>
        <owl:Thing rdf:about="#PMID"/>
      </owl:oneOf>
    </owl:Class>
  </owl:unionOf>
</owl:Class>
```

In this example, there are two collections. Whatever occurs in one or the other is added to the union, so the results are merged. The intersection (and) extension takes the same form as the example above except that it uses owl:intersectionOf instead of owl:unionOf. Only items that appear in both collections would be included in the intersection of the two collections. The complement extension looks a bit different:

```
<owl:Class>
  <owl:complimentOf>
    <owl:Class rdf:about="#UBC"/>
  </owl:complimentOf>
</owlClass>
```

where this extension indicates that this class describes things that do not belong to a class called UBC (Figure 5.4).

Once you establish your classes and how they can be grouped, you will likely want to make some additional explicit statements regarding them. There is, as we've seen, some overlap in terms of class extensions and axioms. If you use an IRI in conjunction with class descriptions, then you quickly cross the line between extending a class and making statements about a class. But there are also three language elements for making axiomatic statements about classes in an ontology.

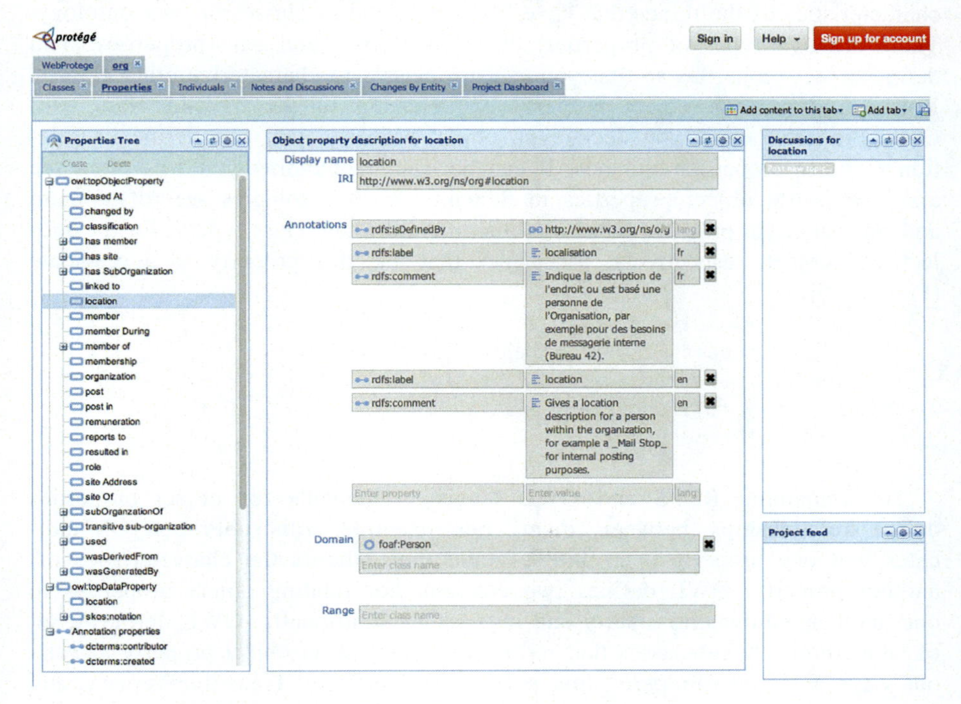

Figure 5.4 WebProtege property view.

They are rdfs:subClassOf which is used to define a hierarchical relationship between two classes:

```
<owl:Class rdf:ID="Novel">
  <rdfs:subClassOf rdf:resource="#Book" />
</owl:Class>
```

owl:equivalentClass which as its name implies says that two classes are equivalent or identical:

```
<owl:Class rdf:about="Journal">
  <owl:equivalentClass rdf:resource="#Magazine" />
</owl:Class>
```

and owl:disjointWith, which is used to indicate that one class is different than another (not equal). Here is an example:

```
<owl:Class rdf:about="CallNumber">
  <owl:disjointWith rdf:resource="ISSN" />
</owl:Class>
```

Most ontologies define both classes and properties. Properties represent characteristics of the things that have been described as classes in your ontology. There are two types of properties: object properties and data properties. You define object properties so that you can use classes to characterize other classes. You can define an object property by referring to the built-in class owl: ObjectProperty. Once you declare an object property, you can define its relation to other properties and how it can be used. Something you will often see associated with object properties in Semantic Web ontologies are rdfs:domain and rdfs:range. In practice, these establish the allowable class type(s) for the subject and object, respectively, for triples that use this property as a predicate (Figure 5.5).

```
<owl:ObjectProperty rdf:ID="hasPatron">
  <rdfs:domain rdf:resource="#Library" />
  <rdfs:range rdf:resource="#Patron" />
</owl:ObjectProperty>
```

The remaining RDFS and OWL language elements for object properties define relationships between them. For example, rdfs:subPropertyOf indicates that one property is a child of (and thus inherits the characteristics of) another property. OWL defines two elements for relating object properties to one another: equivalentProperty and inverseOf. Additionally, OWL defines a set of ObjectProperty subclasses that refine the notion of an object property in various ways: FunctionalProperty, InverseFunctionalProperty, TransitiveProperty, and

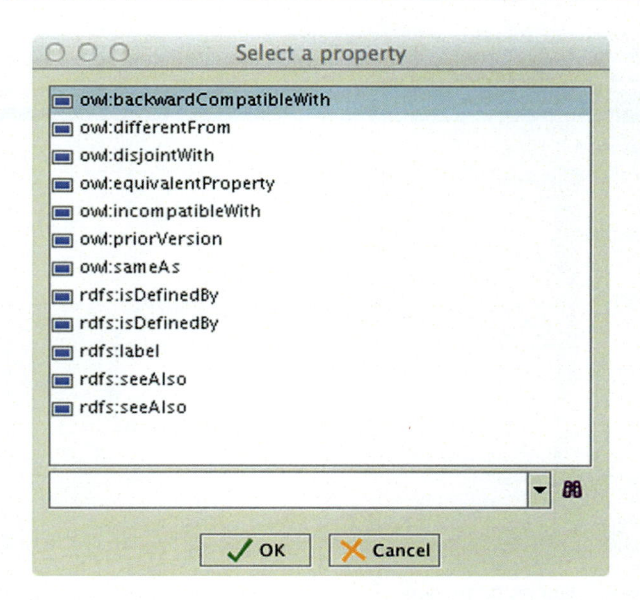

Figure 5.5 Protege data property view.

SymmetricProperty. Let's add a property that allows a patron to indicate that they "like" a certain publication:

```
<owl:ObjectProperty rdf:ID="like">
  <rdfs:domain rdf:resource="#Patron" />
  <rdfs:range rdf:resource="#Book" />
</owl:ObjectProperty>
```

Datatype properties primarily address individuals which are referred to as instances of some class. It is more typical in Semantic Web data sets to define individuals in instance data triples, but there are also various scenarios in which individuals are defined within the ontology itself. A data property is declared using owl:DatatypeProperty and is subsequently referred to as a modifier for some class or used to establish a characteristic of the instance of a class. Here is an example that declares a data property "birthDate" and subsequently uses it to establish that an individual Person named "Mary" has a birthdate of October 2, 1987:

```
<owl:DataProperty rdf:ID="birthDate" />
  <rdfs:domain rdf:resource="#Person" />
  <rdfs:range rdf:resource="&xsd;dateTime"/>
</owl:DataProperty>
<Person rdf:about="Mary">
  <birthDate
</Person>
```

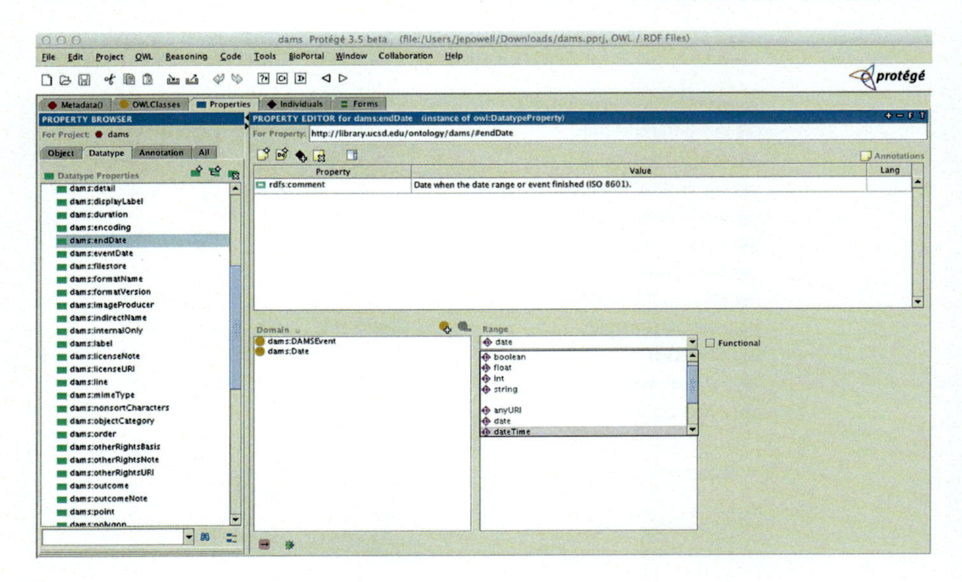

Figure 5.6 Protege data property view.

When we think about things in the world, we categorize things by naming them, grouping them, and identifying characteristics they have without hardly thinking about it. But representing this kind of information formally, and in such a way that software can reason about this data, it is important to be exhaustively explicit (Figure 5.6).

There's one OWL property you will encounter more often in instance data triples than in ontologies. It's intended to eliminate ambiguity across semantic repositories in cases where two repositories have elected to use a different identifier for the same thing. The owl:sameAs property domain and range are both IRIs. Unlike rdfs:seeAlso, which points to an identifier that provides additional information about something, owl:sameAs indicates that the two different identifiers refer to exactly the same thing.

Ontologies and logic

OWL 2 comes in two flavors: OWL 2 DL and OWL 2 Full. OWL 2 DL (where DL stands for descriptive logic) is a more restrictive syntax that better facilitates applications such as reasoning over triples. Descriptive logic is concerned with modeling concepts, roles, and individuals. These terms correspond with class, property, or predicate, and object respectively in Semantic Web. The W3C provides documentation about the differences with respect to modeling and interpretation of these two versions of OWL 2.

Another level of refinement of OWL is realized with profiles. Profiles are intended to facilitate various use cases including particular uses of instance data that contain triples based on the resulting ontology. They do this by defining a subset of OWL 2 language elements that are appropriate for that profile.

OWL 2 defines three profiles: OWL EL, OWL QL, and OWL RL. OWL EL is named for a descriptive logic model that is focused on defining what exists in a domain of knowledge (classes), rather than on the characteristic of a given class. It is easier (and thus faster) for software to process, so think of it as OWL Easy (not an official name!). OWL QL is geared toward supporting queries and reasoning, so you can think of it as OWL Query. The OWL RL profile is bounded so that it is well suited for rules languages, so you can think of OWL RL as OWL Rules. As you can tell, each profile is tuned to support a different type of machine processing. An important aspect of these profiles is to specify which components of OWL and RDFS (e.g., what class description types) can be used when defining an ontology. It sounds complicated, and it can be. In many Semantic Web applications, the predominant use case for the data might be searching or applying rules to determine actions based on the data, and for those uses, it is pretty clear which profile best fits the requirements.

We humans are adept at processing vast amounts of information about the world around us quickly and seemingly without much effort. With incredible speed, we apply a well-defined worldview, consider our assumptions, fill in the fuzzy parts, so we can in a split second conclude that this large clawed, fanged, growling, striped creature we've never seen before probably represents danger. We can start with some facts and draw new conclusions based on them, or figure out what set of circumstances would have to occur in order for something to be true.

In the Semantic Web world of deduction and logic, depending on how the ontologies you use are constructed, it may be essentially impossible for a computer to slog through all the data describing all the things this animal could be, and it could end up as lunch or a plaything for a tiger before (or if) it sorts it all out. If a reasoner can assume that anything that isn't explicitly stated is false, for example, then it bounds what is known to what is explicitly stated to be true. We generally don't think this way, but many judicial systems have a notion of innocent until proven guilty, and this lays a foundation for the machination of their court systems. This is known in logic as a closed world assumption. OWL uses an open world assumption, which means that whatever isn't explicitly stated is left as "undefined"—neither true nor false. This obviously implies further constraints on the ontology model.

Use cases for ontology models and resulting instance data can include searching, application of rules that examine the data to determine actions, and reasoning. Unambiguous modeling of facts and ensuring that data based on an ontology is machine processable were design considerations for OWL. As the global graph grows, and as various collections of triples make reference to the same thing in their instance data, and make use of the same ontologies, it becomes possible for software to connect the dots so to speak. But the vastness of the data set and the degree of expressiveness of the ontology, coupled with the assumptions that can be made in the absence of certainty, determines whether or not it is actually possible for this to occur. We will revisit modeling and reasoning in Chapter 7.

SPARQL

6

Triple patterns for search

Tim Berners Lee once said of the Semantic Web "Trying to use the Semantic Web without SPARQL is like trying to use a relational database without Structured Query Language (SQL)." Search is still the killer app for data. Every major advance in information technology has been driven by search. Card catalogs moved online so that users could sit in front of a terminal, and later a computer, and search by authors, titles, subjects, and even by keywords that could occur in any field. As soon as storage and computational speed allowed for it, solutions were devised for searching collections of full text documents.

Gerard Salton revolutionized document searching with the vector space model, which transformed documents into mathematical constructs called vectors. A term frequency vector maintains a slot corresponding to each word in a document. In this slot resides a number that indicates how many times the word occurred. With Salton's term frequency vectors, searching text documents became a problem that could be solved with basic geometry. Google revolutionized the World Wide Web when they debuted their fast, comprehensive, simple search for Web pages. Google leveraged the explicit graph within the Web by taking into account links among Web pages. Many big data algorithms in machine learning rely on search. A well-known clustering algorithm, k-means clustering, can operate on Salton's vectors to identify groups of related documents automatically. You can use links to meander around the Semantic Web without search, but finding just the right piece of information is like looking for a needle in the proverbial haystack. The Semantic Web needed its own search, so they baked one into the core suite of standards. That search is based on a search language called SPARQL. It seems that search, like quality, will never go out of style.

Search requires some kind of optimized representation of a collection of data. We often use the term database to refer to a system that stores data and makes it searchable. Semantic Web databases are sometimes referred to as an RDF graph database, a semantic repository, or simply a triplestore. A database for Semantic Web data is different because the underlying data is different. For example, there's no predefined schema for RDF. Content producers are free to mix and match various ontologies as they see fit. An RDF description of a person might start off with triples for their name, address, telephone number, and e-mail address. Sometime later, you might need to add some more information such as a twitter ID, a Facebook URL, a second phone number, or a birth date. With a relational database, you'd have to change the structure of the database, perhaps create new tables, new columns, etc. There are no such restrictions on a triplestore. If you need to use a new predicate, reference a new ontology, or load data from another source, you just do it.

A Librarian's Guide to Graphs, Data and the Semantic Web.

Since RDF is different, search is also different. RDF is a graph. We're looking for nodes and edges when we search RDF. If you are searching by edge, then you would want to know the predicate name and the ontology from which it comes. If you are searching by object values, then you'll want to know if the object is a literal value like a number or a person's name, or an URI for a class or instance of some class. So an RDF query is formulated at least in part as node—edge—node patterns and these patterns take the form of a triple. Some parts of the triple are explicitly identified in this pattern, and others are specified with placeholder variables, indicating that any value is acceptable.

Ontologies play a role in how the triplestore responds to certain queries. If the triplestore supports inferencing, then it can look at the data as if it had parents, so to speak. A resource has a type. The type is a class. That class might have a parent class. So the resource is like its parent, its grandparent, etc. This is an effect of the subClassOf or subPropertyOf statements in the source ontology. When you search, these relationships might affect the result you get back. There's no equivalent capability in a relational database!

The Semantic Web allows things described in triples to be linked to other things all over the Web. To facilitate this, search capabilities of a triplestore are often open to the public by default. This open-by-default model is very different than the approach taken by relational databases, which are, by default and design, closed systems not typically searchable by the world.

There are many open source and commercial triplestores. Some are better at scaling up to large amounts of data, some have better transaction support, visualization tools, software APIs, etc. The above description provides a general overview of their capabilities. In a later chapter, we'll take a closer look at triplestores. For the rest of this chapter, we'll focus on SPARQL, the query language for the Semantic Web (Figure 6.1).

SPARQL

SPARQL is a self-referential, recursive acronym for the Semantic Web's most widely used and supported query language. That's a long winded way of saying that the name SPARQL is a bit of a (nerdy) joke. It stands for SPARQL protocol and RDF query language. As the name implies, it defines both a search language and a way of communicating with a triplestore. The SPARQL protocol is built on top of the Web request protocol (HTTP). This means a SPARQL query can be transported over the World Wide Web. The SPARQL protocol requires that search results be returned as an XML document. We will look at details about the protocol later. But for starters, we'll focus on the query language itself. It is important to understand how to construct a SPARQL query since the query structure is the same whether you use the network protocol, a software library, or a triplestore's built-in interactive interface for performing SPARQL queries.

A SPARQL query is a search string that specifies what to search, an RDF pattern that results need to match, and details about constructing the results set. There are

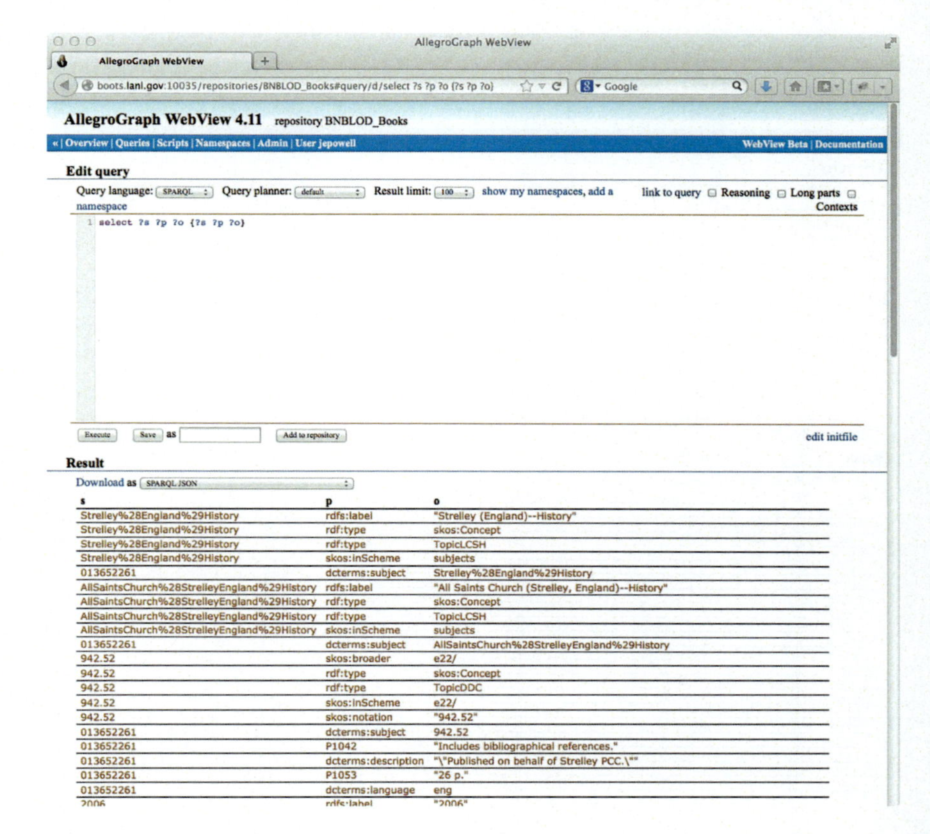

Figure 6.1 A simple SPARQL query in AllegroGraph.

keywords that indicate the aspect of the query that's being defined. The PREFIX keyword defines one or more namespace abbreviations that are subsequently used in the query. The SELECT keyword is one of four possible return clause keywords, indicating what data should be returned in the results set. The WHERE prefix defines the where clause that specifies one or more the graph patterns to be matched. These patterns are specified in RDF. Finally the result modifier clause uses various keywords to indicate how the collection of results is to be presented. Here is an example (Figure 6.2):

```
PREFIX foaf: <http://xmlns.com/foaf/0.1/>
SELECT ?id ?name
WHERE { ?id foaf:name ?name. }
ORDER BY ?name.
```

In many ways, this ought to look familiar. The syntax is concise like Turtle and uses many of the same conventions. A prefix means the same thing here as in Turtle—substitute the IRI inside brackets for the prefix foaf. The content

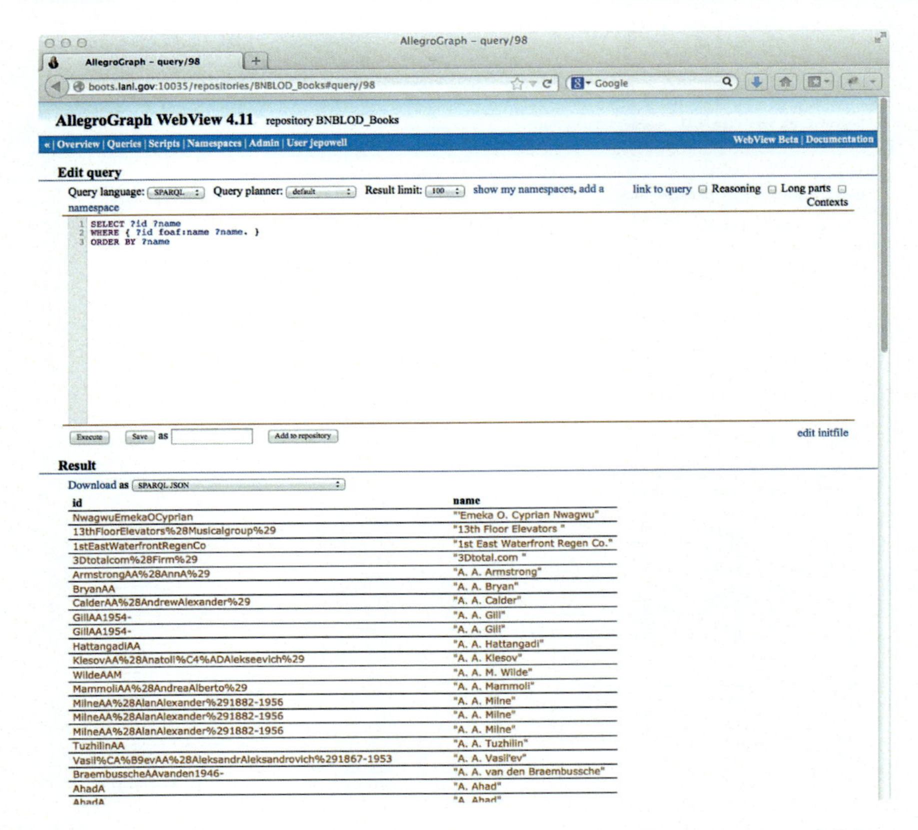

Figure 6.2 SPARQL query that limits results to triples that have foaf:name as a predicate.

between the curly brackets after WHERE constitutes an RDF graph pattern. A graph pattern can be as simple as a pair of nodes and an edge, in other words, a single triple, or include multiple triples, blank nodes, essentially a subgraph that results ought to match. Here is perhaps the simplest SPARQL query you will ever encounter:

```
select *
where { ?s ?p ?o. }
```

You are probably wondering about all these names and letters preceded by question marks. These are variables. They will assume any value from any triple in the repository that matches this pattern. In the first example, the only requirement this pattern specifies for a match is that the triple has foaf:name as the predicate. The subject and object can have any values. For all matching triples, the subject of each triple will be assigned to the ?id variable and the corresponding object to the ?name variable. Once all the results are retrieved, these pairs of values will be sorted by the contents of the name variable and then output as a table. In the second example, any triple matches, regardless of subject, predicate, or object value.

A very useful SPARQL query that can be performed on data sets you may not know much about is this:

```
select distinct ?pred
where { ?x ?pred ?y. }
```

This query will return the names of all of the distinct predicate values used in a given repository. Using this you can identify the ontologies and properties used in the instance data triples.

Here's an example that binds title and name values by using a multi-statement where clause (Figure 6.3):

```
select ?id ?title ?name
where {

  ?s dcterms:title ?title.
  ?s dcterms:creator ?name.

}
```

If you know anything at all about the relational database search language SQL, the role of SPARQL in the context of triplestores is identical. In some ways, SPARQL

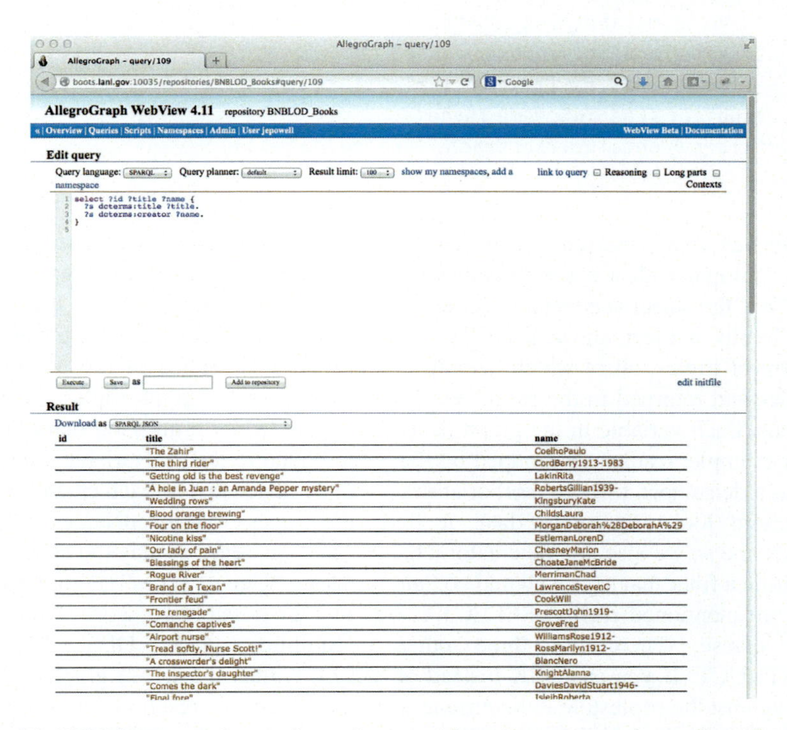

Figure 6.3 SPARQL query that retrieves dcterms title and creator property values for every matching triple.

attempted to emulate SQL. For example, they both have a select clause, which indicates what ought to be displayed in the results list. They diverge because the underlying data model in a relational database and a triplestore is different. SPARQL is designed to search RDF data, while SQL is concerned with columns and rows in tables.

A SPARQL query almost always includes variables, which are placeholders and receptacles for data as the query is executed. Variables are called bindings. This is where the data that matches your search pattern resides as matches are found. The RDF graph pattern in the where clause is a collection of triples that use the Turtle syntax. Where clauses can become very complex, containing many patterns of subjects, predicates, and objects, with dependencies between them.

Here's a more complex example of a SPARQL query:

```
prefix dcterms:  <http://purl.org/dc/terms/>
prefix foaf:     <http://xmlns.com/foaf/0.1/>
prefix skos:     <http://www.w3.org/2004/02/skos/core#>
select  ?id ?title ?given ?family ?subject ?scheme
where {

      ?id dcterms:subject ?subject;
          dcterms:title ?title;
          dcterms:creator ?creator;
          dcterms:abstract ?abstract.
      ?creator foaf:givenName ?given;
               foaf:familyName ?family.
      ?subject skos:inScheme ?scheme.
      filter (contains(?abstract, 'United States'))

}
```

In this example you can see the Turtle style prefix definitions that associate short strings that end with a colon to namespaces that occur in the graph patterns defined later. Next the select statement specifies a set of binding variables. These are id, title, given, family, subject, and scheme. The where clause specifies seven graph patterns in the form of triples, all of which need to be matched in order for data to be bound to variables and returned in the result set. Some portions of the graph triple patterns are variables. Each variable in the graph patterns is preceded by a question mark symbol. In this example, results are grouped by the value bound to the ?id variable. Any triple that has a dc:subject, title, creator, or abstract will be matched. For each creator it finds, the pattern looks for more data. It finds the edges foaf:givenName and foaf: familyName so we also get the creator's name. Note we never display the abstract. We just define a filter that says it should contain the string "United States" (Figure 6.4).

As we mentioned earlier, SELECT is one of four possible keywords used in the return clause. There are three other possibilities: ASK, DESCRIBE, and CONSTRUCT. If you use ASK instead of SELECT, then the where graph pattern is tested against the triplestore to determine whether at least one result matches. If there's at least one match, then it returns true, otherwise it returns false. DESCRIBE is a way of getting some preliminary information about something in a triplestore. Since you

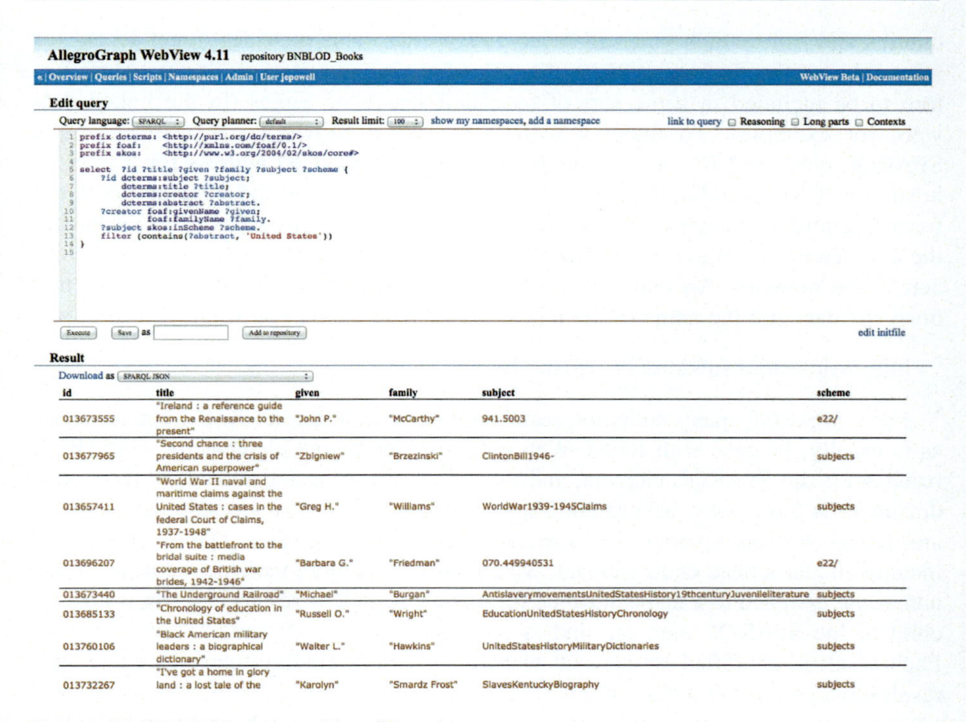

Figure 6.4 SPARQL query with a filter clause.

may be searching a triplestore that contains data you've never seen before, you don't necessarily know what ontologies it uses or what aspects of a thing are described in the instance data. DESCRIBE gives you a way to get at this information. Finally, CONSTRUCT will allow you to specify a new graph pattern into which the results that match the where clause will be mapped. You can use it to transform data in various ways, or to extract subgraphs from a larger data set.

Even though RDF data constitutes a graph, SPARQL 1.0 provided an incomplete solution for exploring that data as a graph. For example, it is very difficult to take paths into account when exploring RDF graph data using SPARQL. SPARQL was modeled after SQL and it very much feels like a database search language at times. If you're just looking for resources in other triplestores to link to, this kind of search works well enough. SPARQL 1.1 addresses the need for path traversal capabilities with property paths, which are covered briefly in the overview of what's new for SPARQL 1.1 at the end of this chapter. Most of this chapter will cover SPARQL 1.0, as 1.1 is backward compatible with it.

SPARQL query endpoint

SPARQL is not just intended for local, interactive use. A SPARQL query endpoint is a Web protocol (HTTP) accessible address to which you can submit SPARQL queries and from which you will receive responses. This provides direct access for users who might not have API level access, for example, if you allow your triplestore to be included in some sort of federated search of triples (in the linked data web, for example). To make a request against a SPARQL query endpoint, a SPARQL query is URL encoded and combined with the URI address for the server hosting it. URL encoding converts characters such as spaces and punctuation into a form that utilizes numeric values and a few special symbols, so as to avoid having the characters in a request inappropriately mapped as they pass between machines across the network. An endpoint address includes the name of the computer that hosts the data and the name of the repository or RDF graph you want to search.

http://triplestore.subdomain.org:10099/repo?query =

For a SPARQL query endpoint, results are converted into an XML representation as is usually the case with REST Web services. The parent element for a SPARQL result set is the SPARQL element, and the default namespace declared for the results document is http://www.w3.org/2005/sparql-results. So all of the results set elements are defined by this schema. The variables declared in the select clause, if any, are included under a head child element, which has one or more variable elements. Their names are assigned to a name attribute for this element. The results element is another child of the SPARQL element, and as its name suggests, it contains query results. Each result is identified by a result element. Multiple binding elements occur in a result block, associating data in this result block with variables defined in the header using the same name attribute. A binding element usually has either a literal child element for literal values or an uri element for identifiers, whether subject, predicate, or objects. Any tool or application that processes data returned by a SPARQL query endpoint can use an XML parser to extract the results, which are attribute values of variable or binding elements, or text nodes of literal or IRI elements.

```
<sparql xmlns = "http://www.w3.org/2005/sparql-results#">

  <head>
    <variable name = "identifier"/>
    <variable name = "author"/>
    <variable name = "title"/>
  </head>
  <results>
    <result>
      <binding name = "identifier">
          <uri>http://</uri>
      </binding>
      <binding name = "identifier">
        <uri>dc</uri>
      </binding>
```

A SPARQL query endpoint can be a huge resource drain if it is heavily used. They tend to be viewed as generally unreliable and even somewhat risky to deploy or enable. A recent standard called Linked Data Fragments attempts to address some of these problems. The general idea is to provide subsets of linked data either through static data dumps or through an intermediate server that constitutes subsets of data that an external entity might have reason to want. These collections are made available through a Linked Data Fragment Server, which might be a SPARQL query endpoint, a page of linked data content, or a compressed data dump for various data sets. An example of a common Linked Data Fragment would be collections of triples associated with a common subject IRI. In other words, a set of triples that would be appropriate in response to a question that could be phrased like this: "tell me everything you know about London."

SPARQL 1.1

Discrete collections of triples are usually organized into repositories, or named graphs. Like any collection of data, sometimes changes need to be made to it. CRUD is an acronym that describes basic transactional capabilities found in data management systems and software. It stands for create update and delete. A triplestore will typically provide some mechanism for creating, updating, or deleting triples. Until SPARQL 1.1, the mechanism for updating a triplestore was not specified by any standard. Most triplestores provide some sort of bulk import option, which can be used to load a file containing serialized triples in various formats, with RDF/XML universally supported. Other capabilities such as update and delete were supported in some interactive fashion. Update explicitly defines the following keywords for managing named graphs: create, drop, copy, move, and add. For transactional functions on triples within a graph, SPARQL 1.1 defines these keywords: insert, delete, and load. SPARQL 1.1 query is significant revision to the core search language that includes support for nested queries, path expressions, and new results formats such as JSON, XML, and comma separated value output. Another notable addition to SPARQL 1.1 is SPARQL 1.1 Graph Store HTTP. Prior to SPARQL 1.1, there was no defined standard for interacting with a triplestore via HTTP, so the REST interface tended to differ from one triplestore to another.

SPARQL 1.1 provides comprehensive support for data administration capabilities that have long existed in other data management systems. And it goes a long way toward making SPARQL a comprehensive graph search language. Alternate approaches to sharing Semantic Web data sets such as Linked Data Fragments are still by and large based on SPARQL, Like SQL for relational databases, SPARQL is likely here to stay.

Inferencing, reasoning, and rules 7

Mechanical thought

The Countess of Lovelace, Ada Lovelace—daughter of scoundrel-poet Lord Byron—was schooled in mathematics but also had some of her father's creative flare. So for her it was no great leap to make many novel observations as she translated into English a paper by Luigi Menabrea about a mechanical computing device called the *Analytical Engine*. The Countess made several crucial connections and they whispered to her....hinted at what steps might be involved, portended the capabilities it might manifest. She could not resist speculating about these possibilities and incorporated her ideas into a series of now-famous notes that accompanied her 1842 English translation of French mathematician Mederier de Frenchelouse's original text.

Charles Babbage a wealthy and restless inventor, and a close friend of the Countess was the inventor of the *Analytical Engine*. It was in part based on a previous invention of his, called the Difference Engine, which was an intricate assembly of numbered cogs that could perform calculations. The Analytical Engine would advance the concept so that it could be controlled by punched cards. It was inspired by a punch card controlled loom invented by Joseph Marie Jacquard in 1801. The *Jacquard Loom* could reproduce images in woven fabric, meaning that it was in a sense "programmable." Mechanization of labor was inspiring some to think about mechanization of thought. The computer revolution was dawning.

The Countess noted with uncanny prescience, but with almost none of her father's poetic aplomb, that the Analytical Engine "might act upon other things besides number, were objects found whose mutual fundamental relations could be expressed by those of the abstract science of operations, and which should be also susceptible of adaptations to the action of the operating notation and mechanism of the engine."

Imagine a mind that could envision such a machine at a time when cutting edge technology consisted of steam engines, rotating gears, and automated looms!

Intelligent computers

Fast forward to the twentieth century, a time when the first Analytical Engines became a reality. At first they were little more than warehouse sized calculators. In mere decades, these humming metal giants grew smaller and faster, and stealthily supplanted calculators and typewriters to become an indispensable tool in every home and office. It was the dawn of the information age. As computing technology continued to grow and advance, a plethora of programming languages were developed to utilize it—including Ada, which was named for the Countess.

A Librarian's Guide to Graphs, Data and the Semantic Web.

Various theories of how computing might evolve, augment, or replicate the human mind were inevitable. Alan Turing, who was first to propose the notion of intelligent computers, imagined a scenario in which a human is communicating with an unseen agent only through typed questions and answers. Nodding to a then-popular parlor activity called the Imitation Game, participants try to determine the gender (and other information) about each other only by exchanging notes. Turing crafted one of the earliest and most persistent thresholds for how we can determine when a computing system has become truly intelligent. He said that there would come a time when a machine could act as one of the participants and fool all the other players. He was trying to illustrate that it was possible to reframe the question "can machines think?" to "can a machine do what we do?"

The Semantic Web technologies we've examined so far (RDF, ontologies) could be said to fulfill the first part of the Countess's vision for the Analytical Engine: "mutual fundamental relations could be expressed by those of the abstract science of operations." In this chapter, we explore technologies that fulfill the remainder of the Countess' vision, which make RDF statements "susceptible of adaptations to the action of the operating notation and mechanism of the engine."

Language to logic

Willard Van Orman Quine in his book *Elementary Logic* describes logic as follows:

"Certain basic locutions, including 'if,' 'then,' 'and,' 'or,' 'not,' 'unless,' 'some,' 'all,' 'every,' 'any,' 'it,' etc. may be called logical." They appear in statements on any and every subject. "Quine" refers to the use of these statements in conjunction with other "special ingredients" as the logical structure of a statement. Quine provides these two examples of statements that have the same logical structure:

1. Every microbobe is an animal or a vegetable.
2. Every Genevan is a Calvinist or a Catholic.

Note that both statements use words the same logical terms "Every" and "or" and their pattern of use in the two statements is identical. "Logic" Quine notes, "studies the bearing of logical structure upon truth and falsehood." The fundamentals of logic include concepts we are all familiar with, such as logical truth, equivalence, and implication. Quine says that a statement is logically true if "all other statements having the same structure are, regardless of their subject matter, likewise true." He offers this example to illustrate the point: "Every microbe is either an animal or not an animal." As to logical equivalence, he asserts "two statements are logically equivalent if they agree in point of truth or falsehood by virtue solely of their logical structure," for example, "If something is neither animal nor vegetable, it is not a microbe" is logically equivalent to statement 1 above. Regarding implication, he explains that "one statement logically implies another if from the truth of the one we can infer the truth of the other by virtue solely of the logical structure of the two statements." He notes that the statement

"Every Genevan is a Calvinist" implies statement 2 above. Quine suggests that logic can be thought of as having three areas of concern:

1. the theory of truth functions—compound statements assembled using words such as and, or, not, unless, if . . . then
2. the theory of quantification—truth functions that incorporate words such as all, any some, none
3. the theory of membership—sets, set operations

RDF statements have a consistent logical structure and truth values. Ontologies can express statement with truth values, quantifications, and memberships. What then can we do with all these logical statements?

Inferencing

Inferencing is a form of logical deduction. Among a collection of triples, there's almost always more information than is explicitly stated. Sometimes this is by design. What could you infer from these two statements?

A dog is a mammal.
A cat is like a dog.

Depending on your interpretation of the word "like," you might infer that a cat is a mammal. In fact, you almost certainly inferred that, even though the word "like" is pretty vague.

Let's look at another example. There are statements that identify a person named Carl, and a person named Susan. A third triple indicates that Carl is married to Susan. Yet another indicates that Carl has a son named Todd. To a human, it is pretty obvious that Susan is Todd's mother (or stepmother). How do we express what we did logically? Let try writing it as a sentence.

If Carl is married to Susan **and** he is the parent of Todd, **then** Susan is parent of Todd.

There's a logical pattern which makes use of the words if . . . and . . . then. So, this sentence is a compound logical statement. Before the word "then," there are two statements joined by the word "and": Carl married to Susan and Carl is parent of Todd. The statement Susan is parent of Todd was not included among the statements that have been made. The logical structure of this statement is such that if the truth value of the joined statements is true, then it implies, that is we can infer that the statement after the word then is also true.

We can create an abstract version of this logical compound statement by replacing the names that identify specific people with variables that could represent any people:

If x is married to y and he is the parent of z, then y is the parent of z.

This looks pretty useful, because now we have a compound logical statement that can be used to evaluate a collection of statements in an attempt to infer additional instances of parent of relationships. This is the general idea behind rules. Another way of representing the compound logical statement above is to replace each statement with a variable that represents it. The convention for this is to use a capital letter for each statement. You can also include parentheses to further clarify this statement:

if (A and B) then C.

Rules are statements that conform to a specified logical structure, with some variables so that they can be evaluated using existing statements of fact. A rule is made up of an antecedent, which is one or more simple logical statements that are tested, and a consequent, which is one or more logical statements that are inferred if the antecedent is true. In the statement "if (A and B) then C," (A and B) is the antecedent and (C) is the consequent. You can use various conjunctions such as and, or, not to combine statements in the antecedent and the consequent. You can even use the statements that are inferred in subsequent statements, for example,

If (A and B) then C.
If (C or D) then E.

Chaining refers to the process of evaluating a set of compound logical statements. When you start with what you know and infer new information from it, you are evaluating the antecedent to arrive at a consequent. This is forward chaining. There's another way to perform deduction, by examining the consequent first, to determine what rules and conditions would be required in order for it to be true. This is called backward chaining. Some triplestores that support inferencing use backward chaining, some implement forward chaining, and some even do a little of both. Of the two, forward chaining is used more often in Semantic Web applications (inferencing and reasoners).

Logic notation

We've introduced a few conventions for representing logical statements. Different forms of logic have their own notation which is used in place of the various "basic locutions." RDF, OWL, and rules are based on predicate logic and first order logic. First order logic is relatively easy to understand. It is a simplified version of the deductive reasoning we apply to everyday situations. It also happens to be a branch of mathematics and there is a corresponding mathematical notation for representing logical statements. The notation specifies the form of logic statements and some symbols. Semantic Web rules languages (SWRL) often borrow aspects of this notation. There are some core logic symbols used in first order logic statements that are worth remembering, because they reinforce the fundamental tenants of first order logic (and will impress your friends) (Figure 7.1).

Figure 7.1 Logic operator bar in Protege.

Logic statements use the universal quantifier ∀ or the existential qualifier ∃ to indicate the following conditions: for every, for all, for some, or there exists. A statement starts with one of these two symbols, followed by a variable that is a stand-in for the thing you are reasoning about. This is followed by a colon, and then a pair of functional statement, where the predicate precedes the subject. The subject is usually the same variable that appears in the left half of the statement, which is surrounded by parentheses. The first functional statement may be read as "if" (predicate applied to variable is true). The functional statements are separated by a symbol ⇒ that can be read as "it follows that," "implies" or "then." Every predicate and subject in a first order logic statement is represented by a variable. It is usual to capitalize the predicate variable and use a lower case character for the subject. Logical statements can incorporate Boolean operators (and, or, not) and characters that define sets, such as union of and intersection of, to define more complex statements. Let's look at a few examples, and their "English" translations. We reproduce and expand on these examples later using Semantic Web rules.

$B \Rightarrow C$	B implies C
$\forall x: B(x) \Rightarrow C(x)$	For all x, B of x implies C of x
$\exists x: D(x) \Rightarrow E(x)$	For some x, D of x implies E of x

When using first order logic, you typically start with axioms. In the Semantic Web, you can express axioms in ontologies, triples, and rules. Semantic Web ontology statements are generally equivalent to first order logic statements. What first order logic refers to as a predicate is closer to a predicate + an object in RDF.

Challenges and pitfalls of rules

It would seem that you could use rules to effectively emulate one of the things we can do, deduction. Wouldn't Alan Turing be impressed? Probably. But this mechanized approach to deduction has some not so obvious limitations. Eventually you will encounter the word "undecidable" in reference to an ontology or Semantic Web rule. It turns out that it isn't difficult to create statements in the course of expressing axioms and rules that can neither be proven true or false. What's an artificial intelligence (AI) system to do in that case? Well, fail, most likely, possibly inelegantly, and probably at the worst possible place or time.

Sometimes what seems logical and obviously true to a human is actually quite difficult for a rules engine to arrive at given a particular set of triples, ontologies, and rules. With logic, you have to be extremely specific. The closed world assumption states that if something isn't known (i.e., been expressed) to be true, then it is false. The opposite is assumed in the open world assumption. In reality, neither is always true, but a rules engines cannot process rules effectively without starting with a closed or open world assumption. Even then they can quickly bog down with essentially undecidable rules, that is, the aggregate statements and rules cannot be determined to be true or false. In that case, the rules either never finish being evaluated, or the outcome is indeterminant. This is why there are different versions of OWL that constrain the kinds of relationships that can be expressed among classes and properties. Abilities we take for granted are still largely beyond the ability of computers and software, unless the "world" in which they are expressed is bounded.

This is the essence of what's known as the "frame problem." It is easy to produce a set of rules that evaluate to true based on severely restrictive assumptions about the world. To a computer, there's no certainty that one statement doesn't have an effect on another which follows it, even if the two seem to you to have no relation to one another. Consider these two statements: W(x) where x is a person named Tom and W is a predicate indicating "wrecked his car", followed by a statement that expresses Y(z) where z is a robotic rover and Y is "landed on Mars". What do we know about the state of the car after Y(z)? Well presumably it is still wrecked. To a person, the fact that a robotic rover just landed on Mars has no relation to the condition of the car. But if you don't explicitly indicate that the two have no relation, the only statement that logically can still be assumed to be true is the presence of the rover on the surface of Mars. For all the computer knows, this event may have "unwrecked" Tom's car. To us, it is intuitively obvious that these two events have no effect on one another. Logic is at times unforgiving. If you have no facts, then you can draw no conclusions. But if you have only a few facts, you may very well reach the wrong conclusions.

Reasoners and rules

SWRL specify how you represent rules. This is similar to the relationship between RDF and RDF serializations. You can model rules using first order logic notation, but for the Semantic Web, you create a textual representation of your rules that is supported by the reasoner that will evaluate them. Some Semantic Web rule serializations use description logic, some use XML, and others are based on N3. Rules are interpreted by specialized software called a reasoner. Some reasoners can process more than one type of rules language. A reasoner uses triple statements along with rules, so a reasoner is usually connect to or integrated with a triplestore.

The remainder of this chapter will focus briefly on two rules languages: SWRL and N3 Logic. SWRL is supported by Protege, with an add-on called SWRLTab. N3 is supported by a reasoner called EYE, which stands for Euler Yet another proof Engine. A version of EYE is available online at http://eulersharp.sourceforge.net.

SWRL

The SWRL is an RDF model for representing rules based on first order logic. SWRL provides some ways of comparing and evaluating certain types of data and conditions. These primitive evaluation capabilities are built into SWRL and allow it to compare various kinds of literals, reason about time intervals, etc. SWRL rules use functional syntax. Conditions are expressed so that classes and properties from applicable ontologies act as "functions" and variables representing the value to be evaluated are the parameters to that function.

An SWRL rule consists of an antecedent, one or more conditions, and a consequent, which specifies a pattern for a new triple that will be inferred if the antecedent evaluates to true. The conditions are evaluated using data from statements extracted via a graph pattern from a triplestore. Rules bind elements from triples to variables in the same way that SPARQL does.

Each SWRL rule is evaluated for truth separately, one after another, until all evaluation is complete, or until some condition evaluates to false. This allows for the consequent of one rule to become part of the antecedent of another. Boolean operators can be employed to express more complex, nested conditions. SWRL built-ins support temporal reasoning such as durations and overlaps, evaluations of strings and mathematical conditions, general comparison of class and property types, Boolean evaluations, list enumeration, and conditions having to do with the URIs of things. Here's a rule that uses a SWRL built-in to deduce that a Person who is older than 18 is of the class Adult. In this example, Person, Adult, and hasAge come from an ontology. Person and Adult are classes, and hasAge is a property. This syntax is based on the RDF serialization called description logic.

```
Person(?p), hasAge(?p, ?age), swrlb:greaterThan(?age, 18) -> Adult(?p)
```

The variable ?p assumes the value of an identifier for an instance of class Person, and we can surmise that ?age is a literal object value from a statement of the form <ex:John> <ex:hasAge> 19. So when this rule is evaluated for John, a new statement of the form <ex:John> rdf:type <ex:Adult> will be inferred, because the antecedent evaluates to true for this instance data.

N3 rules

There are other SWRL. One is called N3 rules. As the name implies, N3 rules take a similar form as N3 triple statements. Like N3, N3 rules have the advantage of being easier to read and encode. The antecedent and consequent are separated by a logical operator, such as =>, and rules are grouped together as needed using curly brackets. Like SPARQL, variables are strings preceded by a question mark. Here is an N3 rules example (Figure 7.2):

What we know in the form of two triples:

```
PREFIX lib: <http://example.org/library#>
<http://people.lanl.gov/jepowell> lib:like
<http://dbpedia.org/page/Roadside_Picnic>.
<http://dbpedia.org/page/Solaris_(novel)> lib:similarTo
<http://dbpedia.org/page/Roadside_Picnic>.
```

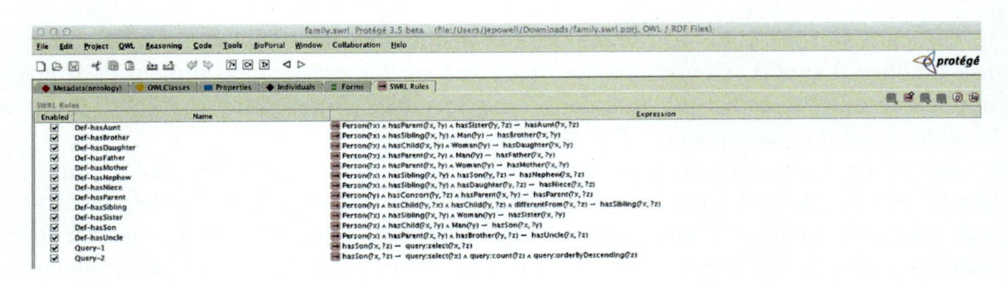

Figure 7.2 Editing rules in Protege.

Rules that can deduce whether someone will like a book based on its similarity to a book we know they liked:

```
@prefix lib: <http://example.org/library#>.
{

      ?personA lib:like ?bookA.
      ?bookB lib:similarTo ?bookA.

}
=>
{

      ?personA lib:like ?bookB.

}.
```

The Eye Reasoner deduces that this person will like Solaris because they liked Roadside Picnic and the two books are similar, so the Eye Reasoner results include a third statement (Figure 7.3).

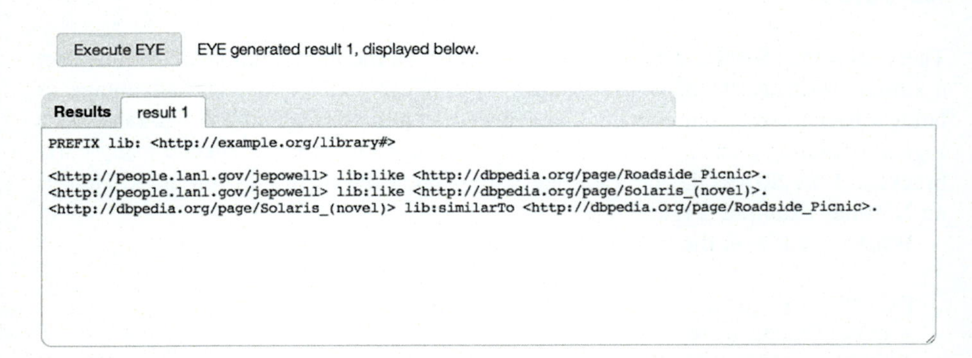

Figure 7.3 The Eye Reasoner executes N3 rules.

In this example we're using the mini ontology from Chapter 5. We've introduced another object property called similarTo. Our rule deduces that if personA liked bookA and bookB is similar to bookA, the personA will like bookB. So, we could recommend that personA might want to read bookB. Logically SWRL and N3 allow you to express most of the same conditions. Like SWRL, N3 rules can incorporate built-ins. These built-ins are specified by the reasoner and can vary from reasoner to reasoner. They can include math, comparison, and temporal built-ins.

Final considerations

There are several things to keep in mind with regard to rules engines and rules. First, you will need to select a rules engine that can parse rules expressed in the rules language you used. Second, you need to make sure that the logical statements you make in the rules language you selected are supported by the rules engine you intend to use. Third, the built-ins supported by a rules engine may only be available in a particular implementation. Although it is generally true that many built-ins are supported across different rules engines, how they are referenced may vary from one rules language or reasoner to another.

Reasoning is a specialized area within the Semantic Web. It touches on mathematics, logic, computer science, AI, and even philosophy. It is well suited to tasks ranging from data mapping to semantic search to generating recommendations or any task where machine deduction might reliably augment or replace human assessment of a large amount of data that might not be practical for a person to realistically digest. This chapter was intended to introduce you to some of the core concepts. If you decide to incorporate rules-based reasoning into a project, here are some areas to explore further:

- OWL Description Logics
- Rules languages and rules parsing
- Practical applications of rules
- Rules engines
- Open and closed world assumptions
- Meaning and implications of entailment
- Forward/backward chaining
- First order predicate logic and Semantic Web rules
- Decidability of rules and inferencing
- Semantic Web rules languages
- Inferencing and triplestores

Sometimes thinking logically is hard enough. Telling a computer how to do it is even more of a challenge. The "logical world" in which your RDF statements exist has major implications for inferencing and rules. So if you plan to use logic-based technologies such as reasoners or inferencing in your Semantic Web applications, select your ontologies with great care. Use statements that are true without regard to place or time. Be careful of your assumptions. Limit your use of these technologies to a very specific problem space.

Final considerations

Understanding Linked Data

Demons and genies

Artificial intelligence (AI) refers to software that is capable of processing information in a fashion equal to or beyond human cognition. AI is like many human inventions with its risks and benefits two sides of a Janus head. Noted physicist Stephen Hawking has become the most noteworthy critic of AI as a potential existential threat, but also a defender of the vision of an AI that can serve and better mankind. Tesla Motors CEO and entrepreneur Elon Musk put his reservations about thinking machines more bluntly: "With artificial intelligence we're summoning the demon."

But why would such a promising technological advance also threaten humankind? Because if an AI gains the ability to continually improve itself and harness vast resources, it may rapidly gain a level of intelligence and ability far beyond our own. Ultimately, it may replace or dispose of us, rather than deigning to continue its existence in the servitude for which we originally designed it. Fear of AI as an existential threat comes at a time when AI is advancing rapidly on many fronts. Corporations such as Google, Facebook, IBM, and Amazon are using a variety of AI techniques to solve problems and provide new services. In some of these projects, data from the Semantic Web has played a role—an important role.

There are two (at least) schools of thought regarding AI, some believe AI starts out as blank slate, merely endowed with ability to learn (like a neural network), while others believe AI must start as a fully informed "mind" that can use logic to deduce things (an encyclopedia that can reason). Both camps seem to agree that linkages and associations among data, whether preprogrammed or the result of experience, are essential if AI is to ever reach its full potential.

The original name for the Linked Data Web was the Global Giant Graph (GGG). This was the name Tim Berners Lee coined for the Semantic Web when he developed the idea in 2001, because he envisioned that all these RDF graphs would ultimately form a huge global graph of structured knowledge. RDF and related technologies were intended to do more than just provide a new way for representing information. They were envisioned as the foundation for an information sharing environment potentially equaling or surpassing the impact of the World Wide Web. The GGG, Semantic Web, LOD, or Web of Linked Data were intended to do for information what the World Wide Web did for content: provide a comprehensive, open infrastructure for publishing information and building connections between your data and other data on the Internet. Linked Data, also referred to as Linked

Open Data (LOD) constitutes a loosely coordinated crowd-sourced project that intends to formally encode relationships between bits of knowledge so computers can make sense of it. Some envision Linked Data as a sort of classroom for AI. We don't know if there will be an AI apocalypse, but perhaps contributing LOD may be something we can do to help avert it. In any case, knitting together data into something more akin to knowledge is definitely a worthwhile undertaking.

Characteristics of Linked Data

LOD augments data with context, meaning, and relationships. These are characteristics that most data lack today. Silo is a popular term used to describe an organization or a collection of information that has become isolated in some fashion. A lot of data resides in silos. Sometimes there are good reasons for limiting access to information. None of us want our bank accounts or personal data searchable through a public database.

There are other kinds of data silos. Unstructured data may be readily accessible, easy to find, but not easy to use or get at. Articles, book chapters, blog posts, tweets, and other content have limited or no metadata. They have little to no internal structure. What facts are contained in this content? Today, it would take a person reading the content to figure that out. That level of granularity of information is simply not available. If you want to explore the relationships among this data, then you have to function as the integration point. Linked Data attempts to tear down some of these silos by encouraging content creators and metadata owners to convert their data to RDF graphs, create links to other data, and share it openly. It is a navigable Web of knowledge crafted for computers.

So what do you have to do to make your Semantic Web content part of the Linked Open Data effort? Nothing changes within the RDF itself, but every distinct thing you make statements about has to have a universally unique IRI. If someone clicks on or enter an IRI in a Web browser, they'll be taken to some actual content about that thing. The format of this content must be some serialization of RDF, such as RDF/XML or N3. Your data should be available for discovery and linking, and it should be linked to other data whenever appropriate.

Linked Data requirements summary

- An IRI for everything (resources)
- IRIs for predicates (context from ontologies)
- RDF data model (graph)
- Links to other data (relationships)

As we mentioned, you should always be able to access Linked Data using a Web browser. This is useful if you are looking for other content to link to. Many times, sites that publish Linked Data will employ stylesheets or Javascript to render a user-friendly HTML version of the RDF. The raw RDF in formats such as RDF/XML is really intended for machine consumption and processing. Semantic Web

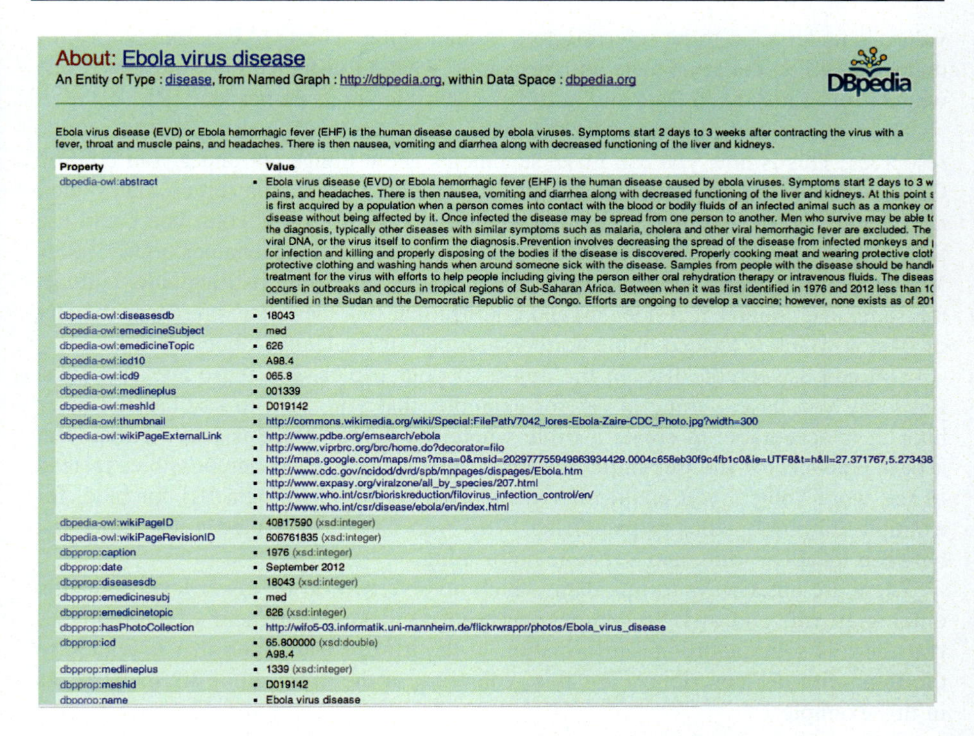

About: Ebola virus disease

An Entity of Type : disease, from Named Graph : http://dbpedia.org, within Data Space : dbpedia.org

DBpedia

Ebola virus disease (EVD) or Ebola hemorrhagic fever (EHF) is the human disease caused by ebola viruses. Symptoms start 2 days to 3 weeks after contracting the virus with a fever, throat and muscle pains, and headaches. There is then nausea, vomiting and diarrhea along with decreased functioning of the liver and kidneys.

Property	Value
dbpedia-owl:abstract	• Ebola virus disease (EVD) or Ebola hemorrhagic fever (EHF) is the human disease caused by ebola viruses. Symptoms start 2 days to 3 w pains, and headaches. There is then nausea, vomiting and diarrhea along with decreased functioning of the liver and kidneys. At this point is first acquired by a population when a person comes into contact with the blood or bodily fluids of an infected animal such as a monkey or disease without being affected by it. Once infected the disease may be spread from one person to another. Men who survive may be able t the diagnosis, typically other diseases with similar symptoms such as malaria, cholera and other viral hemorrhagic fever are excluded. The viral DNA, or the virus itself to confirm the diagnosis.Prevention involves decreasing the spread of the disease from infected monkeys and for infection and killing and properly disposing of the bodies if the disease is discovered. Properly cooking meat and wearing protective clot protective clothing and washing hands when around someone sick with the disease. Samples from people with the disease should be handl treatment for the virus with efforts to help people including giving the person either oral rehydration therapy or intravenous fluids. The diseas occurs in outbreaks and occurs in tropical regions of Sub-Saharan Africa. Between when it was first identified in 1976 and 2012 less than 1 identified in the Sudan and the Democratic Republic of the Congo. Efforts are ongoing to develop a vaccine; however, none exists as of 201
dbpedia-owl:diseasesdb	• 18043
dbpedia-owl:emedicineSubject	• med
dbpedia-owl:emedicineTopic	• 626
dbpedia-owl:icd10	• A98.4
dbpedia-owl:icd9	• 065.8
dbpedia-owl:medlineplus	• 001339
dbpedia-owl:meshId	• D019142
dbpedia-owl:thumbnail	• http://commons.wikimedia.org/wiki/Special:FilePath/7042_lores-Ebola-Zaire-CDC_Photo.jpg?width=300
dbpedia-owl:wikiPageExternalLink	• http://www.pdbe.org/emsearch/ebola • http://www.viprbrc.org/brc/home.do?decorator=filo • http://maps.google.com/maps/ms?msa=0&msid=202977559498639344229.0004c658eb30f9c4fb1c0&ie=UTF8&t=h&ll=27.371767,5.273438 • http://www.cdc.gov/ncidod/dvrd/spb/mnpages/dispages/Ebola.htm • http://www.expasy.org/viralzone/all_by_species/207.html • http://www.who.int/csr/bioriskreduction/filovirus_infection_control/en/ • http://www.who.int/csr/disease/ebola/en/index.html
dbpedia-owl:wikiPageID	• 40817590 (xsd:integer)
dbpedia-owl:wikiPageRevisionID	• 606761835 (xsd:integer)
dbpprop:caption	• 1976 (xsd:integer)
dbpprop:date	• September 2012
dbpprop:diseasesdb	• 18043 (xsd:integer)
dbpprop:emedicinesubj	• med
dbpprop:emedicinetopic	• 626 (xsd:integer)
dbpprop:hasPhotoCollection	• http://wifo5-03.informatik.uni-mannheim.de/flickrwrappr/photos/Ebola_virus_disease
dbpprop:icd	• 65.800000 (xsd:double) • A98.4
dbpprop:medlineplus	• 1339 (xsd:integer)
dbpprop:meshid	• D019142
dbpprop:name	• Ebola virus disease

Figure 8.1 The DBPedia page at http://dbpedia.org/page/Ebola_virus_disease that aggregates a collection of triples about Ebola.

crawlers, for example, follow links within and between collections of triples. Semantic Web browsers and reasoners are designed to consume RDF directly. Ontologies form yet another network of connections among Linked Data Web through reuse of formalized vocabularies across triplestores (Figure 8.1).

A triple about Ebola

Subject: http://dbpedia.org/page/Ebola_virus_disease
Predicate: http://www.w3.org/TR/2013/REC-prov-o-20130430/#wasDerivedFrom
Object: http://en.wikipedia.org/wiki/Ebola_virus_disease?oldid = 606761835

Relationships are obviously an important aspect of Linked Data. Predicates are IRIs and in Linked Data predicates function as links. They establish the relationship between a triple and the vocabulary it uses. All Linked Data predicates should reference published ontologies. Published ontologies, or Linked Open Vocabularies (LOV), are an important component of Linked Data. Ontologies are valuable to humans and essential to Semantic Web applications, because they provide context, that is, they establish the sameness of certain kinds of relationships across Linked Data collections. For example, a foaf:Person is understood to always refer to and be a type of Friend of a Friend Person object from the FOAF ontology. If a triple indicates that some resource is a foaf:Person, then it, and any other triple which uses this value, is understood to be referring to a human being. The FOAF ontology ensures that we're all on the same page with respect to what a foaf:Person is. An LOV is one which is used in Linked Data and must be accessible via its namespace IRI.

The subjects and objects in RDF Linked Data can be IRIs that point to remote resources. This is how you can make statements about things not under your control. Geonames is a Linked Data collection of geographic information (cities, states, etc.) as a feature. If you wanted to create a triple that says Boston is cold, you could use their IRI for Boston as the subject of your triple: http://sws.geonames.org/4930956. You can look at their statements about this resource, including its longitude, latitude, the state, and country it resides in, and confirm that this identifier references the city of Boston which is located in the northeastern part of the United States.

You can use remote IRIs in the object of your triples, and these are also links. Let's say you have a thing, a car for example, that you want to say has the color blue. It is acceptable to create a triple where the value "blue" is just a string. But a best practice for the Semantic Web is to use an IRI whenever possible. Instead of the word "blue," you could reference a DBPedia Linked Data IRI for blue, for example, http://dbpedia.org/page/Blue. Now you have established a semantic link between local car thing and a remote color thing.

There are other ways to link data, which involve two of the lower level semantic ontologies, rdfs and owl. Sometimes you want to make a statement which indicates that there is some additional information in the Linked Data Web that is related to the thing you are describing. For this, you can use the predicate "rdfs:seeAlso" as in this example:

```
<ex:Boston> <rdfs:seeAlso> <http://dbpedia.org/resource/Boston>.
```

Other instances you may wish to explicitly indicate that your local thing is the same as a remotely defined thing. In this case, you can use the "owl:sameAs" predicate:

```
<ex:Boston> <owl:sameAs> <http://dbpedia.org/resource/Boston>.
```

There is nothing inherently different about using rdfs or owl classes to express a link as opposed to other values from other ontologies, but these are well understood and well supported by Semantic Web tools.

Discovering Linked Open Data

The Web of Linked Open Data has grown significantly in the last decade (Figure 8.2, Figure 8.3). But how do you go about discovering LOD resources to link to? Well, as with anything on the Web searching and browsing are the two best strategies. If you know the SPARQL query endpoint address for a collection of Linked Data you can directly search that collection. But many times you won't be

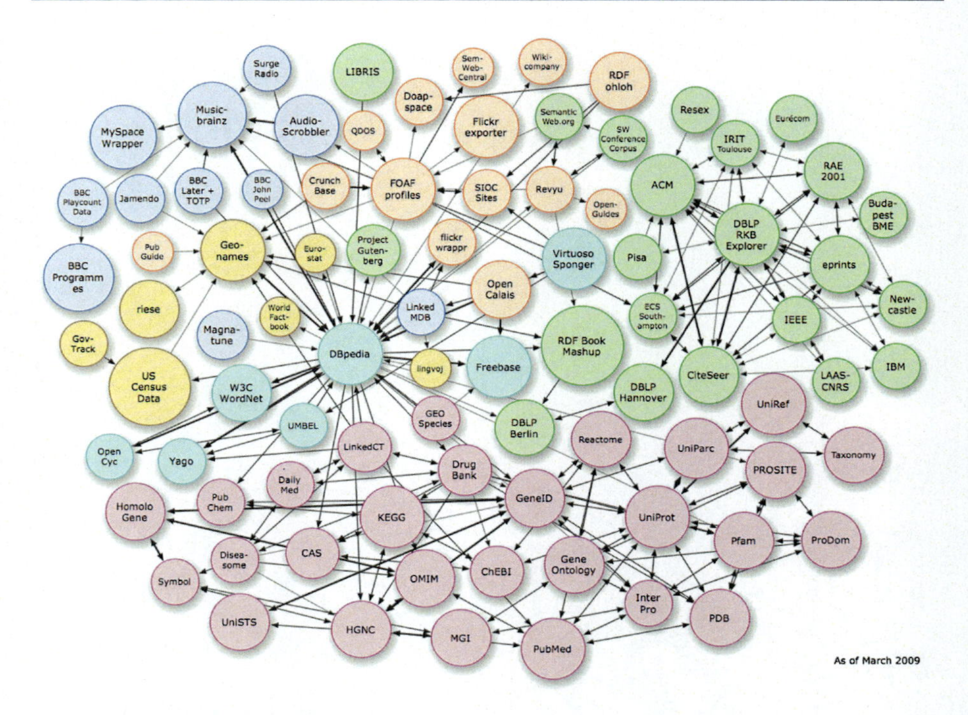

Figure 8.2 Linked Data collections as of March 2009.
Source: Bizer, C. <http://en.wikipedia.org/wiki/File:Lod-datasets_2009-07-14_colored.png>.

able to do this, either because you don't know the address or there is no public endpoint available. You can instead consult a semantic search engine. There are several which crawl and index Linked Data and ontologies. These typically offer a keyword search initially. Keywords searches target object literals, identifiers, ontology class, or property values. Semantic search engines leverage the RDF model. Advanced search options can narrow the location where a keyword must occur in order for a triple to match your query, or target values associated with particular classes or properties in an ontology. Two of the more comprehensive Web search engines for Linked Data are Watson (not to be confused with the IBM Watson project) and Sindice. Watson (http://watson.kmi.open.ac.uk/WatsonWUI/index.html) provides a fast default keyword search that returns identifiers for triples where your keyword occurred in any part of the statement. You can follow links to the RDF or human-readable page about a given item. At that point navigation is no different than navigating Web content. Sindice (http://www.sindice.com) is another semantic search engine with comparable coverage and speed as Watson. Sindice provides many more search options, including limiting results by date or RDF format, and searches based on n-triples and filters.

You can also browse the Web of Linked Data. DBPedia is a good starting point. It covers many topics and its content is based on Wikipedia content. You can often

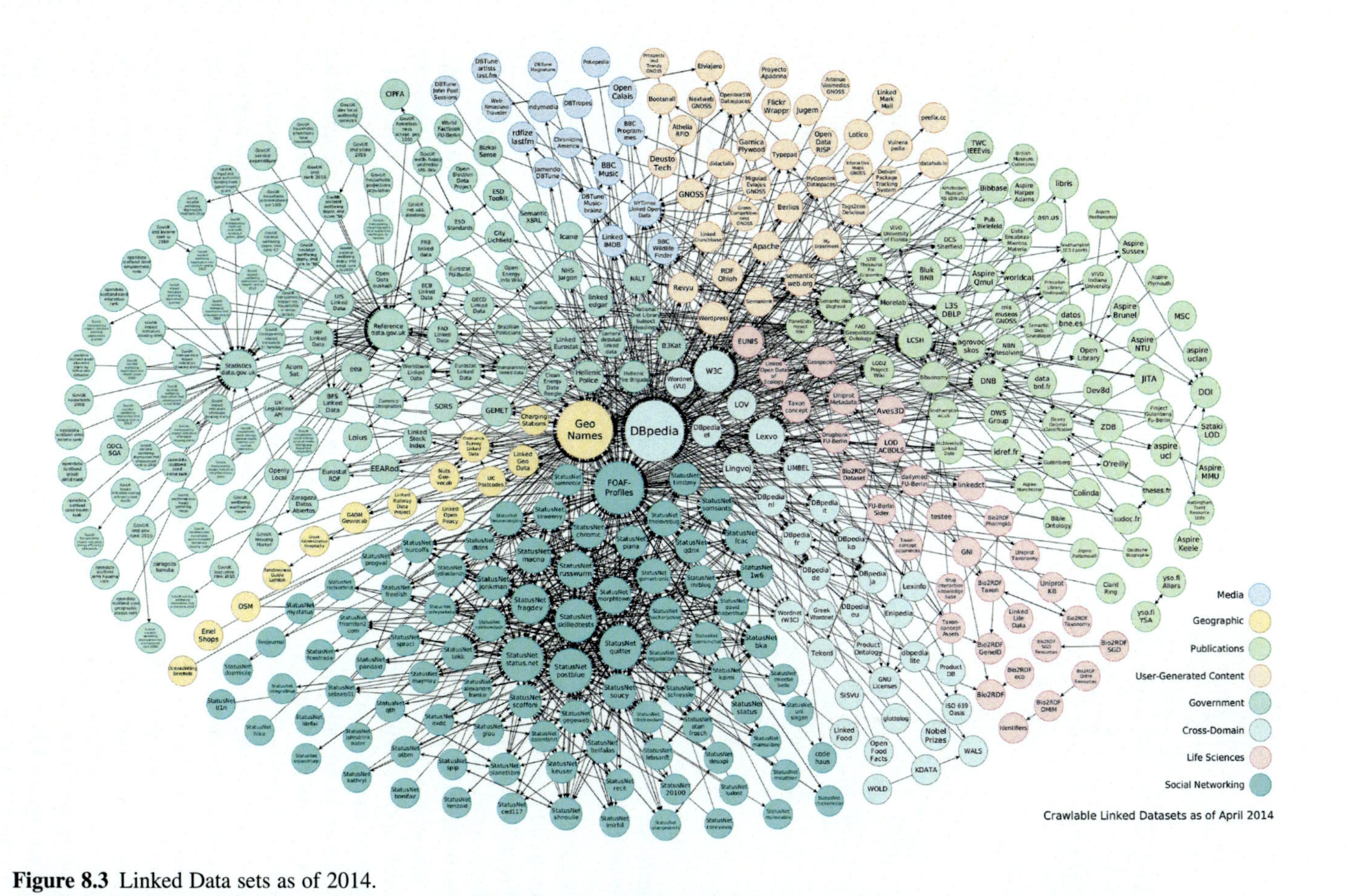

Figure 8.3 Linked Data sets as of 2014.
Source: Linking Open Data cloud diagram 2014, by Max Schmachtenberg, Christian Bizer, Anja Jentzsch, and Richard Cyganiak. <http://lod-cloud.net/>.

guess DBPedia IRIs. The best way to go about this is to use this partial URL as a starting point: http://dbpedia.org/page/. If you are interested in finding DBPedia triples about astronomy, try http://dbpedia.org/page/Astronomy. For triples about the Columbia River, combine the two words by replacing the space with an underscore like this http://dbpedia.org/page/Columbia_River. When you access a page in DBPedia, it returns a HTML with embedded RDFa content. This page will contain all of the triples about this topic.

You can navigate to other properties associated with a given topic by simply clicking links on this page. You can also retrieve various serializations of the collections of triples that are the basis for a given page using links provided in the footer of a DBPedia page. RDF serializations include N-triples, Turtle, RDF/XML, and JSON-LD.

Geonames is another source of Linked Data which is focused on geographic information. It contains over 10 million place names, of which 8 million represent unique features including cities, countries, states, rivers, and mountains. Because the tool is location-centric, it provides a graphical interface for locating and visualizing results on a map. A keyword search for Columbia River returns a list of potential matches and when you select an item in the result set, the map location is adjusted to correspond to that results' location. You can view additional details through a set of icons in a pop-up window, or download RDF triples about the place. Geonames also provides a REST Web service interface that can be used to discover and create links to geonames entities from other applications. Since most of the data Geonames is based on is in the public domain, you have the option of downloading any or all of the various data sets which it uses.

OpenCyc (http://sw.opencyc.org) is a general knowledge base organized into an ontology. It defines upward of 250,000 terms about places, organizations, businesses, and people. OpenCyc has many links into other Linked Data resources. You can search the collection online, or even download a copy of it if you want to use it internally or mirror it locally for your particular applications (be forewarned, it is quite large). Astronomy is represented in OpenCyc with this triple: http://sw.opencyc.org/2012/05/10/concept/en/Astronomy a ScientificFieldOfStudy.

It links out to another set of Linked Data about astronomy with this IRI: http://umbel.org/umbel/sc/Astronomy. OpenCyc uses CSS and XSLT to transform RDF into Web friendly content when one of their Thing IRIs is retrieved through a Web browser. Some browsers support a "view source" option which should allow you to see the original RDF for an OpenCyc concept as RDF/XML. You can navigate among classes, properties, and instance data via this Web interface, to find things that might be appropriate for your to link to.

Europeana (http://www.europeana.eu) is a European Union funded effort to build a Semantic Web repository and portal for dissemination and exploration of data about European scientific and cultural heritage. It includes metadata describing over 30 million books, paintings, films, and music from more than 2000 museums, libraries, and universities across Europe. The Europeana project aggregates and ingests data from many different sources from every member country in the European Union. The project maintains the full metadata as provided by the contributing institution, utilizing a Semantic Web data model called the Europeana Data Model (EDM) which attempts "to transcend the respective information perspectives of the various communities constituting Europeana." EDM's requirements include maintaining the distinction between physical objects and their digital representations, maintaining the distinction between metadata and the objects they describe, supporting multiple records for the same object even if they contradict each other in some way, supporting objects that are composed of other objects, accommodating concepts from controlled vocabularies, and more. The Europeana project makes RDF data for over 20 million objects available as a data dump and also provides a SPARQL query endpoint for search (http://labs.europeana.eu/api/linked-open-data/data-downloads/).

Europeana, Geonames, OpenCyc, and DBPedia are just a sample of the hundreds of LOD collections available. The Web of Linked Data doesn't tend to grow fact by fact, as the Web grew page by page. Instead LOD grows in bursts, as new collections of data are added. Individual researchers may have some motivation to convert small data sets to RDF graphs and publish their data online. Libraries, universities, and businesses convert data sets, identify relationships to other data, and publish their semantic data online in RDF/XML, embedded as RDFa into Web content, or via a triplestore and SPARQL query endpoint. Other projects are developed much like open source software—open data is converted by an ad hoc group of contributors, and eventually makes its way online as with Geonames and DBPedia. Governments are getting involved too with open data initiatives funded to convert and make available data that is the result of other publicly funded projects.

Linked Open Vocabularies

Linked Open Vocabularies (LOV) are an important aspect of Linked Data. Ontologies, taxonomies, and vocabularies constitute shared meaning. LOV constitute a crowd-sourced consensus of knowledge in a given domain of knowledge, whether they were collectively created, or just widely used. Linked Data sets often use properties and classes from multiple published vocabularies. It's common for vocabularies, especially upper ontologies to overlap, reference, and extend classes and properties in other vocabularies. So it's important that these vocabularies be published and made discoverable.

There are many places to search for ontologies—Sindice and Watson index ontologies as well as instance data, so ontology links will be included in their results sets. Swoogle (http://swoogle.umbc.edu) is another search tool for locating ontologies. It works much like Google and claims to index over 10,000 ontologies. The LOV site (http://lov.okfn.org) is one of the best ontology discovery sites available. Hundreds of ontologies are cataloged here, with detailed descriptions, pointers to their RDF/OWL descriptions, and handy visualizations

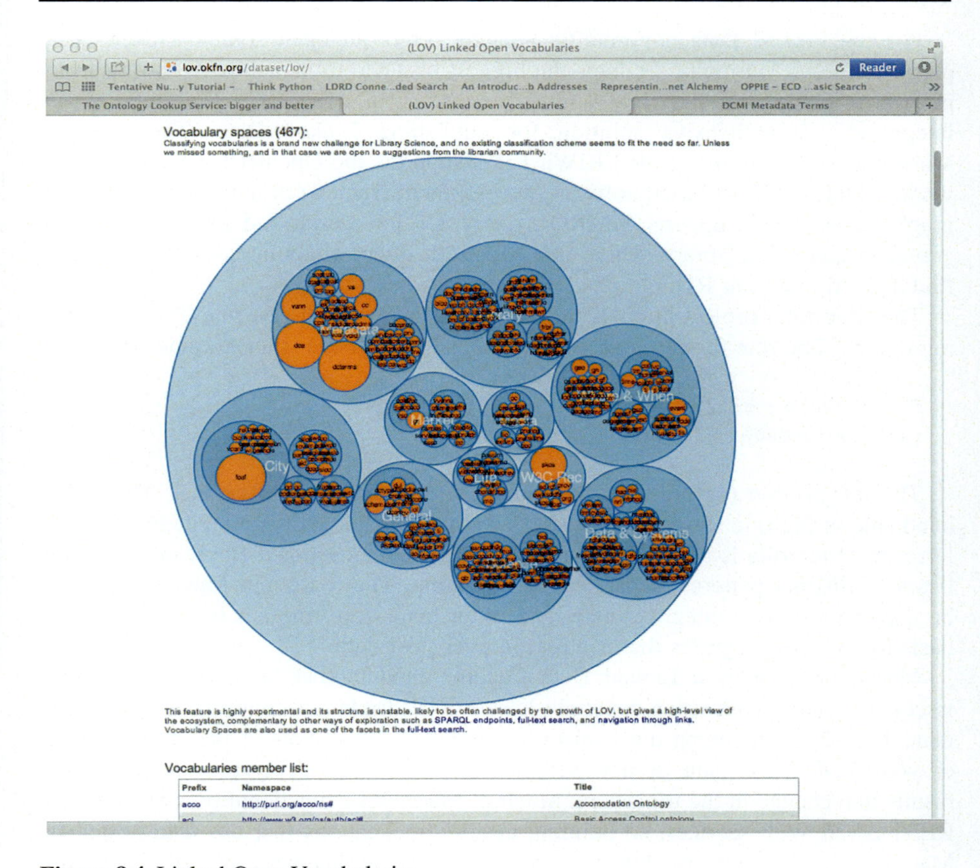

Figure 8.4 Linked Open Vocabularies.

that provide an overview of their relationship to other ontologies. The site is searchable, so you can just enter a few terms that describe or might occur in the type of vocabulary you are interested in, and the LOV Web site will return links to related ontologies. Using public ontologies reduces ambiguity in the Web of linked data. Ontologies can also give you an idea of what kinds of data may reside in this GGG (Figure 8.4).

Linked Data platform

Apache is home to numerous open source software projects including the Apache Web server, Tomcat java application server, the Giraph platform for scalable graph computing, Hadoop, and many other tools and libraries. Two projects that are widely used in libraries are Apache SOLR and Apache Lucene. These applications can be used in combination to index and make searchable structured and unstructured text.

For the Linked Data community, Apache offers an open source Linked Data platform called Marmotta. Perhaps the biggest obstacle to launching a Linked Data project is getting all the right software together in one place. Marmotta is an integrated, comprehensive solution for publishing Linked Data. The core of Marmotta is a triplestore called KiWi. KiWi supports the OpenRDF Sesame framework, which is a Java-based software development framework and toolkit for RDF graph stores. Kiwi supports SPARQL query 1.1 for search and includes an integrated visualization library. There is a SPARQL query endpoint so that others can find and explore your RDF graphs.

The Marmotta project bundles the KiWi reasoner, which is a rule-based reasoning engine. The rule format is based on triple patterns. Here is an example:

```
@prefix skos: <http://www.w3.org/2004/02/skos/core#>
($1 skos:broader $2) -> ($2 skos:narrower $1)
```

The left portion (before the -> symbol) is the condition to be met. The right-hand side of the rule specifies the pattern for a new triple that can be deduced if the left side of the rule is true. Multiple conditions (with an implied Boolean AND) are listed as distinct patterns, separated by a comma. The reasoning functionality can be used to test data integrity, map data, infer, and store implicit triples, or as the basis for custom programs that can reason over your data.

Marmotta includes a Linked Data Caching module that helps address latency issues associated with using remotely hosted RDF triples in conjunction with local data. There's a versioning mechanism that maintains snapshots of previous versions of your RDF graph data. A new version entry is created every time a transaction results in a change in the triplestore. Much of Marmotta's functionality is available as REST-based Web services, so building custom applications that use data hosted in Marmotta is relatively straightforward and programming language agnostic. This API is fully compliant with the SPARQL 1.1 Graph Store API protocol. The Marmotta project is available at http://marmotta.apache.org/index.html.

Library networks—coauthorship, citation, and usage graphs

9

"Uncritical citation...is a serious matter"

Few of us enjoy social networks so extensive and varied that we personally know experts in every single field. If we did, then when our research interests or curiosity sent us after the most authoritative papers on say, the diseases of early hominid tribes, we could just consult that particular expert. This person would have read all the relevant papers—had perhaps written many of them—and could recommend those of highest quality that shaped the field. More likely, we will not know an expert for every such question, and we will instead consult a general source of information.

Citations are an important part of an academic paper. The word citation has several meanings, some of which involve granting an award or receiving recognition for some achievement. When an author includes citations in a research paper, they are often, although not always, recognizing some positive contribution the cited work made to their own work. But some minority of citations are negative citations. There is no suggestion of this in a paper's reference section, so one would have to read the paper to realize this. "The uncritical citation of disputed data by a writer, whether it be deliberate or not, is a serious matter." Researchers and librarians alike feared that even if an author took care to note the character of the citation, that this fact would be "overlooked with the passage of time."

As references gained in importance, a librarian and information scientist named Eugene Garfield observed the utility of citations in information discovery and qualitative evaluations of sources. He also recognized that this was a self-organizing activity that librarians, historians, and information seekers could take advantage of. "By using authors' references in compiling the citation index, we are in reality utilizing an army of indexers, for every time an author makes a reference he is in effect indexing that work from his point of view." It was his opinion that this resulted in a more natural organizational strategy. "By virtue of its different construction, it tends to bring together material that would never be collated by the usual subject indexing. It is best described as an association-of-ideas index." From this idea the citation index was born. Garfield went on to develop and refine a number of strategies for evaluating and organizing citation indexes. He obviously recognized the value of this implicit network.

History and evolution of science

One area of keen interest to Garfield was the history of science. One of his collaborators a geneticist named Gordon Allen diagrammed the relationship of citations

A Librarian's Guide to Graphs, Data and the Semantic Web.

related to staining nucleic acid. The diagram was a graph model which represented publications as nodes and citation relationships as edges. Furthermore, it was organized vertically, with older works appearing above newer ones. Garfield recognized that this could be applied more generally to any field of science, and he named it the historiograph. He felt that this network diagram would in many cases "constitute a fairly reliable outline for the history of a field of science." Garfield also developed the Science Citation Index, pioneered the notion of an impact factor for authors, and developed other research tools, which are widely available in libraries throughout the world.

It should then come as no surprise that a historian of science, Derek J. de Solla Price, went on to refine some of Garfield's ideas. In a 1965 paper entitled "Networks of Scientific Papers," he fully recognized the value of studying citations as a network. He observed that "each group of new papers is knitted to a small, select part of the existing scientific literature but connected rather weakly and randomly to a much greater part." He thought of the sum total of citations as a vast, comprehensive network, but in his day he was only able to analyze portions of this network and extrapolate characteristics of the larger network based on that analysis. Incidentally, de Solla Price is now recognized as the first person to have discovered and described what we now call a scale-free network.

Only many years later was it possible to evaluate and provide a new context for de Solla Price's theories. In 2006, Johan Bollen and his colleagues at Los Alamos National Laboratory's Research Library analyzed vast amounts of usage data and modeled it as "the click-stream map of science"—a graph visualization based on a data set de Solla Price could have only dreamed of having access to in 1965. The map of science provided a stunning visual verification of the theory that there was significant interconnectedness among scientific disciplines, from the perspective of content users. The map of science and subsequent work it inspired has led to the development of new tools and theories about measures of quality and author impact. These efforts continue to leverage "an army of indexers" in this sharply accelerated digital publishing age, but they also leverage "armies of clickers" making it possible for content usage patterns to play a role in aiding information discovery. And so it is that another generation of graph analysis techniques are finding their way into libraries (Figure 9.1).

Librarians as network navigators

A patron of a library may conduct an information search on their own, or they may do so through a proxy, like a librarian. A library is not just a warehouse of information, but a guide to that information. A librarian's job includes answering questions about topics he knows nothing about and might never have even thought about before. His approach cannot be the same as the expert. He cannot read every paper in a field nor learn the information well enough to be able to judge the body of papers with the same assurance. To make the point more distinct, imagine an English-speaking librarian tasked with finding the most important or relevant articles from a body of literature written entirely in Indonesian.

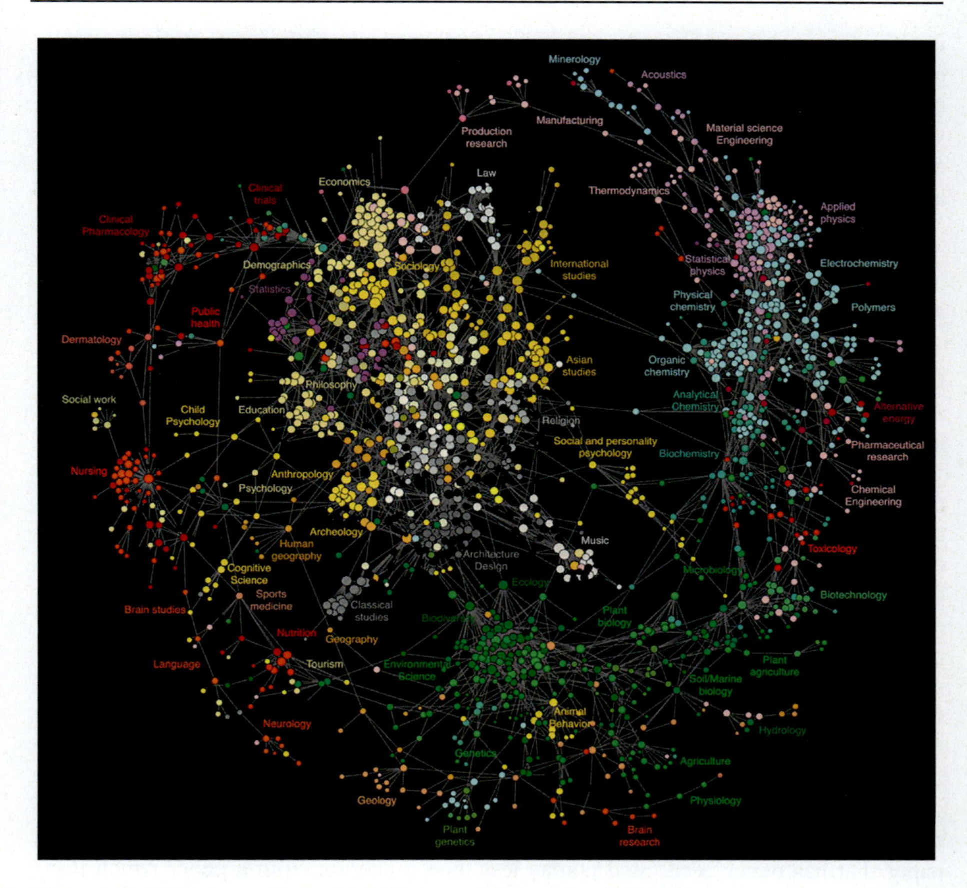

Figure 9.1 Clickstream Data yields high-resolution map of science.
Source: Bollen, J., Van de Sompel, H., Hagberg, A., Bettencourt, L., Chute, R., et al. (2009) Clickstream Data yields high-resolution maps of science. *PLoS ONE*, *4*(3), e4803. <http:\\dx.doi.org\10.1371/journal.pone.0004803 >.

The librarian requires a method of search and assessment that does not rely on the content itself—which she cannot understand—but instead relies on metrics independent of the content. She might look to connections between the content, such as citations. She may know that, in general, the most important papers in a field tend to be the most highly cited. The librarian may consult a citation index to cull a list of recommended papers, and in so doing, she is using graph theory.

An academic paper contains additional information beyond the ideas explicated within its text. First, it has an author, or perhaps multiple authors. Those authors are connected to each other through this shared paper. They may have published other papers, with other coauthors, who have themselves published with other coauthors, and sometimes the same coauthors, building a network of coauthorship. Second, each of those authors hails from a certain institution. Papers connect various institutions, and if we want to generalize further, each of those institutions can be reduced to a geographic location, allowing us to graph output among or within countries, cities, and states. Third, each paper has a subject or topic. And finally, within the paper itself, there are direct references to other, earlier papers. Note that each of these areas exist independent of the content of the paper itself, and can be analyzed even if one ignores or does not understand the content of the paper.

Author metrics and networks

Citation analysis is one of the more familiar types of bibliographic analysis. A researcher may look at cite counts without realizing that he is seeing a metric of a citation network or graph. But when we view bibliographic citations as a network, we realize that there are many graph theory metrics to consider. In a citation network, where papers are nodes and citations are edges, those nodes with the most citations will have the most edges and the highest degree centrality. The degree centrality of a node in a graph is simply a count of the number of edges that connect to it. A paper cited five times within a network would therefore have a degree centrality of five. The paper with the highest degree centrality would be the paper most often cited, and it might be the paper that the librarian recommends.

Citation counts by themselves, however, may not reflect what we are looking for. One paper may be cited 10 times, all by low-quality papers, while another is cited by three papers of the highest quality. Is there some way to measure the quality of a citation? Can we weigh certain citations higher than others? We can do this with another graph metric called eigenvector centrality. With this metric, citations to a paper are weighted based on how many times they themselves are cited. A citation from a paper that has never been cited counts less than a citation from a paper which itself has dozens of citations. Google ranks pages in this way, using a search algorithm called PageRank, only it is links that are considered instead of citations. Web sites that are linked to by sites which themselves are often linked to will be returned closer to the top of your search results. So if you decide to eschew these methods and just google your topic, you are still relying on the fruits of graph theory!

Citations are not only used to judge papers. They are also used to judge the researchers who authored those papers, and the journals that published them. A researcher's citations may be considered when he is up for tenure. A common shorthand metric is the h-index—a person who has authored 12 papers with at least 12 citations each would have an h-index of 12. For journals, one common metric is the impact factor, and it might be looked at by researchers who are trying to publish papers that will be cited highly. There is great incentive to publish highly cited papers. One way to do so, often, is just to get there first. The first papers to stake a claim in a new field of research tend to be cited much more often than those which come later, an effect which has been called the first-mover advantage. (Citation graphs are often examples of scale-free networks, in which a few nodes have most of the connections. They often form by preferential attachment: nodes with many connections are more likely to form new connections.) Researchers would like to be the first to discover these untapped fields. Can graph theory show not just what is, but what isn't yet? For this question we will look at another type of bibliometric graph, the coauthorship network.

Analyzing coauthorship networks

In coauthorship networks, authors are the nodes, and they are linked by collaboration over papers. Centrality measures will tell you who collaborates with the most people, and perhaps these authors also have the most influence in their field. But what if you are the author represented by one of those nodes, and you are looking for someone new to collaborate with? What can the graph tell you? For this need, path length is the more useful metric. Take any two nodes in a graph. If they are connected to each other, then they have a path length of one. If they are not directly connected, then they may be connected through other nodes. Suppose A is connected to B which is connected to C which is connected to D, so that A and D have a path length of no more than 3. No more than, because they may be connected in other, shorter paths via a different series of nodes. The shortest of these paths constitutes the path length (Figure 9.2).

Following paths in a graph to discovery new information is called searching the graph. Two common ways to search a graph are breadth-first and guided search. A breadth-first search starts at some node, then finds all the nodes to which it is connected. From that list of nodes, the process is repeated, until all connected nodes are found. This is a time-consuming and often inefficient process, but it is also thorough. Guided search uses some criteria to select certain paths over others. This criteria might be some path or node characteristics (a property in a property graph, for example), some node metric, or some aspect of the structure of the graph. To locate potential collaborators, you may want to ignore those who have published

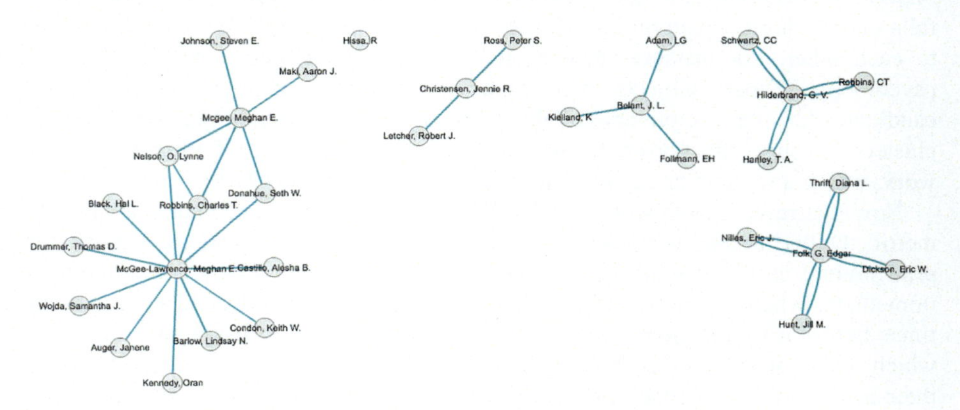

Figure 9.2 A small co-authorship network.

only infrequently or who have few co-authors, for example. A guided search could help you do that.

A random walk is another way to explore a graph via paths. Martin Chester maintains a Web site that illustrates the concept of a random walk at http://www.physics.ucla.edu/~chester/TECH/RandomWalk/. He offers a colorful explanation for the random walk: "[a] proverbial drunk is clinging to the lamppost. He decides to start walking. The road runs east and west. In his inebriated state he is as likely to take a step east (forward) as west (backward). (Probability 50% in either of the two directions.) From each new position he is again as likely to go forward as backward. Each of his steps are of the same length but of random direction-east or west." A random walk starts at some initial node and selects one of the nodes that share a path with that node at random. When it arrives at the node along this step, it repeats the process. The path that results from this process is a random walk. Random walks effectively model the observed behavior of various systems that can be modeled as graphs in ecology, biology, chemistry, physics, and even economics. They are also used in recommender systems where a probability distribution can be used at each step to influence the subsequent step.

A path length of 1 does not tell our researcher anything new—after all, this indicates a researcher he has already collaborated with, and chances are he already knows that. But a node with a path length of 2 represents an author he has never collaborated with, yet who has collaborated with at least one of his coauthors. If this person has collaborated with many of his coauthors, then he may be someone the author himself would like to collaborate with. On the other hand, a high path length represents an author whose research interests are perhaps "distant" from your own. But what if they are not? What if someone has a high path length, but you know that their research is tangential to yours. This might indicate an unexplored area of research in which you can achieve first-mover advantage. Finding these areas might be easier if we add subjects to our coauthorship network.

In a subject–author graph, nodes with high-degree centrality might represent researchers who publish in many different fields. Another centrality measure is betweenness centrality. A node with high betweenness centrality is one which often falls on the shortest path length between two nodes in a graph. It connects clusters to each other. For instance, papers on brain research might connect biology to psychology. Those subjects with high betweenness centrality indicate good candidates for interdisciplinary collaboration. If the path length between two subject clusters is longer than average, it may indicate the absence of interdisciplinary work, which a researcher can exploit to his advantage (Figure 9.3).

Now that researchers predominantly find articles online, usage data is a valuable metric. Online access is tracked, a task that proved difficult and incomplete for print journal usage. One advantage of usage data over citation data is that usage is immediate, where citation data lags. An article may be downloaded thousands of times before it is first cited. There is also a greater volume of usage than citations, which makes sense—researchers read many more articles than they actually cite in their own works. And finally, usage data encompasses a wider base of people, not just publishing researchers. Usage data has been used to generate Maps of Science.

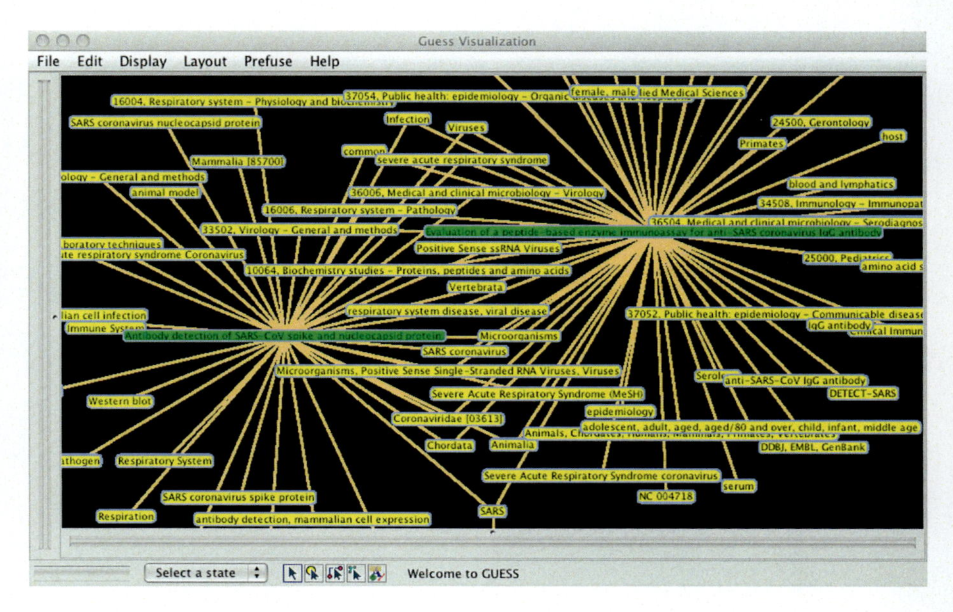

Figure 9.3 A topic graph.

Because usage is immediate, these maps can be updated almost in real time, which makes trends easier to spot. This is another way for researchers to spot emerging fields early.

But what about our original example of a researcher who only wants to find the best articles? Usage data can generate recommendations by spotting patterns of co-use. If you access a particular article, you might like to know that many people who read that article also read this article. Or if you access many articles by a certain author, you might like to know about this other author who often publishes with the same set of collaborators. Of if you read a handful of articles, you might like to know about this other article that cites all of them. As Garfield noted in later years "citations symbolize the conceptual association of scientific ideas as recognized by publishing research authors." The quest for quality that leads to the development of citation networks makes these discoveries possible.

Networks in life sciences

10

In 1854, arguably the world's most advanced city, London, had been brought to its knees by rampant cholera. Government officials, medical doctors, and clergy alike were unable to slow the onslaught. It was through the innovative approach of one man, John Snow, that London was able to trace back to the source of the epidemic and then, finally, help put an end to it.

Today, Snow is often considered the father of modern epidemiology. He investigated an outbreak of cholera in London; he talked to individuals who had fallen ill and eventually found that the cases clustered around a particular well, which was contaminated by an old cess-pit (which is just what it sounds like) located a few feet from the well. His sleuthing, which included exploring the local social connections among infected individuals, led to a resolution of the outbreak, and a broader theory of how a disease such as cholera could spread in a community.

Another way infectious diseases spread is through social contacts. This is why the technique known as contact tracing is so widely used to track the spread of communicable diseases. We can overlay contacts onto a social network and track how the disease has spread through a population over time or predict how it will spread.

The path of an infection

An infectious disease is an illness caused in a host organism by another organism, referred to generically as a pathogen. A pathogen can be a virus, fungus, or bacteria that has the ability to take over cells in the host. In the case of viruses, hijacked cells become factories for churning out new copies of the organism, and through accident or design, they impair functions in the host and, at some point in their life cycle, they use the host as a means to spread to others. It is at this point that a host, for example a human with the flu, is considered infectious. During the host's infectious phase, the host might spread the pathogen to others through the air, by contact with surfaces touched by others, or through intimate contact. Other more complex life cycles are possible, but for the purpose of exploring networks in the context of infectious diseases, we will restrict ourselves to scenarios where host-to-host transmission occurs.

Host-to-host transmission is also referred to as linked cases. In linked cases, there is clear evidence that a disease was somehow passed from host to host, regardless of the mode of transmission. Note the use of the word "linked" in the definition. The links between hosts that allow a disease to spread is what makes disease contagious. Disease transmission lends itself particularly well to network models because they can represent the people involved, the relationship between them (transmission of disease), and the direction of transmission.

Sometimes a disease outbreak expands to become an epidemic. An epidemic is defined as the unchecked spread of a disease through a geographically localized population. In graph terms, it is a highly connected graph, containing many connected clusters. When an outbreak spreads beyond localized geographical boundaries, it is referred to as a pandemic. The swine flu outbreak in 2009–2010, which many researchers believe started on large-scale pig farms in Mexico became a pandemic, reaching many parts of the world, infecting millions of people.

Historically, understanding how diseases are transmitted has led to new methods for short-circuiting epidemics, ranging from simple hygienic practices to vaccines, quarantine, and social isolation. When an outbreak threatens to become a pandemic, more extreme measures such as limiting travel and monitoring borders may be needed in order to protect communities. Any practice that can thwart the spread of disease can potentially be applied during an outbreak, if the way in which the disease is spread (the link) and the persons carrying the disease (the nodes) can be identified. And of course the earlier this information can be determined, the better. This is one reason that graph models of transmissible diseases are so valuable. Individuals with high betweenness and high degree centrality facilitate the chain of transmission for infectious diseases by directly or indirectly linking large numbers of people. An individual who connects clusters of other individuals, such as a teacher or CEO has a higher than average probability of transmitting the illness between those clusters. An individual with high degree centrality, for example an office manager, can directly infect more individuals because they come into direct contact with more individuals. Thus examining the centrality measures of a social network prior to the outbreak of a disease could, in theory, help limit the spread of a contagious illness.

The index case for a disease outbreak is the first person identified as having had the disease. A graph model of the spread of a disease often assumes a directed tree-like form. In many cases, an individual who survives a bout with a disease develops antibodies that provide some degree of immunity to that disease. This immunity reduces or prevents the occurrence of cycles. A cycle is a path through several nodes that ultimately leads back to the starting node. This is also known as a closed path. A directed graph with no cycles is referred to as an acyclic graph, or tree. Immunity conferred by prior infection prevents the formation of links back to previously infected individuals. A notable exception is the seasonal flu that typically spreads through populations during the coldest season of the year. The flu virus makes its way through human, and sometimes animal populations, mutates, and then starts the process all over again. Unfortunately for some of us, that path can return the flu virus to us again and again. A cycle which allows for edges to repeatedly connect to nodes is called a closed walk.

While we're on the topic of cycles, there are two other important types of cycles worth noting briefly. A Hamiltonian cycle is one in which the cycle's path connects

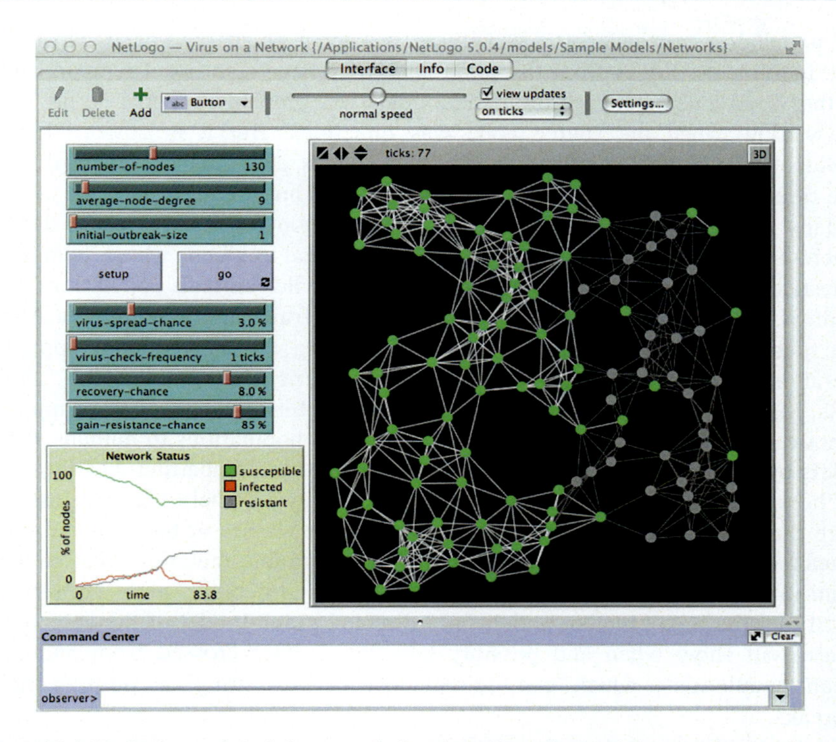

Figure 10.1 NetLogo model of the spread of a virus through a social network over time. *Source*: Stonedahl, F. and Wilensky, U. (2008). NetLogo virus on a network model. <http://ccl.northwestern.edu/netlogo/models/VirusonaNetwork>. Evanston, IL: Center for Connected Learning and Computer-Based Modeling, Northwestern Institute on Complex Systems, Northwestern University.

every node in the graph. In the case of an infectious disease, this would mean that a disease spreads from exactly one person to exactly one other person until everyone in the population had been infected. An Eulerian cycle starts and ends with the same node, and the path from start to end uses each edge exactly once. That means there'd be some unlucky person who would end up getting infected twice before the disease burned out.

In the case of infectious diseases, including the flu, their graph models have a starting point (an index case), even if it cannot be identified. Sometimes researchers can use time to walk backward through the graph to find the index case. Degree measures for directed graphs include in-degree and out-degree values. In epidemiology these measures can be used to identify the reproduction rate (*R*-value) for a disease. Reproduction rate indicates how many other people on average an infected person will infect. Degree measures can also be used to identify the so-called superspreaders, who for some reason manage to infect more people than would be predicted by the *R*-value (Figure 10.1).

The path length between individuals who were infected early in the outbreak and those infected later can help researchers estimate how widely a disease has spread in a population, particularly if something is known about the social network of those individuals. Edges from the same node may have significant temporal overlap, that is, anyone connected to that individual was probably infected during a narrow window when the source node was infectious. But it is obvious that an individual whose path length is two from the index case was not infected at the same time as individuals whose path length from the index case is one.

Many diseases spread from animal to human populations. In recent decades numerous deadly diseases have emerged in tropical regions, where humans or domesticated animals came into contact with wild animal populations. The Hendra virus is endemic (occurs naturally) in wild fruit bat populations in Africa, Asia, and Australia. It was first identified among horses and later spread to several humans before being identified in northern Australia in 1994. AIDS, Ebola, Marburg, and H5N1, often referred to as the bird flu, are other examples of zoonotic diseases, diseases that spread from animal populations to humans. Graph models of zoonotic viruses can not only play a role in combatting an illness, but also help scientists trace the origin of a virus. They can help identify instances where the disease may have co-occurred with other viruses or bacteria and possibly exchanged genetic material, or experienced favorable mutations that gave the organism an evolutionary advantage as far as infecting new populations. Identifying the index human patient in a directed graph model of the spread of a disease will show when and possibly how the disease crossed from animal to human populations, which can be valuable in preventing or limiting future outbreaks.

To review the concepts we've covered so far, let's look at an outbreak scenario. We'll construct a graph of how the infection spreads, and look at how various characteristics and measures of that graph might be used by health care professionals to assist the ill and curtail the spread of the illness.

The CEO of a medium sized corporation returns from a conference in another city and starts to feel ill after returning to her office. After a brief conversation with her secretary, Mary Anne decides to go home. She spends the next 4 days in bed with the flu. The secretary, Barbara, starts to feel ill 2 days later. She works the entire times she's ill, so a stream of middle managers and other employees are exposed to her while she is infectious. Barbara's in-degree measure is one, but since 11 employees caught the flu from her (Barbara was a super-spreader!), her out-degree measure was 11. A further 49 employees were infected, and the longest path length from Mary Ann was 5. Fortunately, some employees had been vaccinated prior to the arrival of flu season, so it soon ran its course. In retrospect, if the company had encouraged at least selective vaccination of employees who are highly connected within the corporate social network, or had been more insistent that sick employees stay home while they were sick, far fewer employees might have been infected. A graph model of the outbreak illustrates these points clearly. Fortunately for everyone, since the vaccinated and previously infected employees were now immune to this strain of flu, no cycles were possible and thus there was no chance the flu would reinfect anyone this season.

Food webs and motifs

Ecology uses networks to model and analyze food webs. The most fearsome predator at the top of a food chain is connected to the humblest microbe often in a multitude of predictable and not so predictable ways. Studying food webs is a powerful tool for understanding the environment. For those of us who aren't ecologists, it can help us understand the importance of a species in conservation efforts.

Ecologists look at ecosystems from many perspectives. One perspective in particular that reveals a lot about a biosphere is the food web. A food web, or food chain, is a representation of how energy makes its way through a community of organisms, as one organism consumes another. Food webs readily lend themselves to graph modeling. We will use food webs to further explore directed graphs and to introduce the concept of motifs.

Motifs are recurring subgraphs, patterns of connections among nodes that exist in statistically significant numbers and are indicative of a relationship among a group of nodes. In some networks, motifs can be the building blocks of the larger network, while in others, they are atypical of the overall network. Regardless, when the network is compared with a similar size random network, the motifs are one of the things that sets a network apart.

In many networks where motifs occur, the motifs themselves tend to be small. Terminology used to describe these small motifs includes sequential size terms such as triad or tetrad (three or four nodes), or simply the word size followed by a dash and numbers indicating the graph size (size-3, size-4, for example). Something important to note about motifs is that three nodes are typically the minimum number required to represent a meaningful motif. A biad is really just an edge between two nodes, the recurrence of which would be extremely common in most networks, and not particularly significant in most circumstances.

Motifs can include cycles and bidirectional links among nodes. It is in directed networks where motifs are meaningful. They provide a technique for looking past the global network characteristics to explore local aspects of graphs. Researchers use terms such as 3-chain graphs (where the edges among three nodes flow through the first, to the second, and then to the third node), contrasted with a three node feed-forward loop (where the connections among the three nodes form a cycle). In some biological networks, this demonstrates a symbiotic relationship or a predator–prey relationship. Food webs are a prime example of a biological network that usually contains motifs. The concept of a food web dates back to at least AD 800, when it was described by an Arab scholar named Al-Jahiz in a quasi-scientific zoological text entitled "Kitab al-Hayawan" or Book of Animals. In this text he noted the relationship between a mosquito and animals such as hippos and elephants which the mosquito fed upon, observing that they became food for other insects and birds. Charles Darwin is also credited with expanding and popularizing the food web. It provides one explanation for natural selection in living organisms, since predation over time favors mutations to resist or deter being consumed, whether through the spines of a thistle or the camouflage wings of a moth.

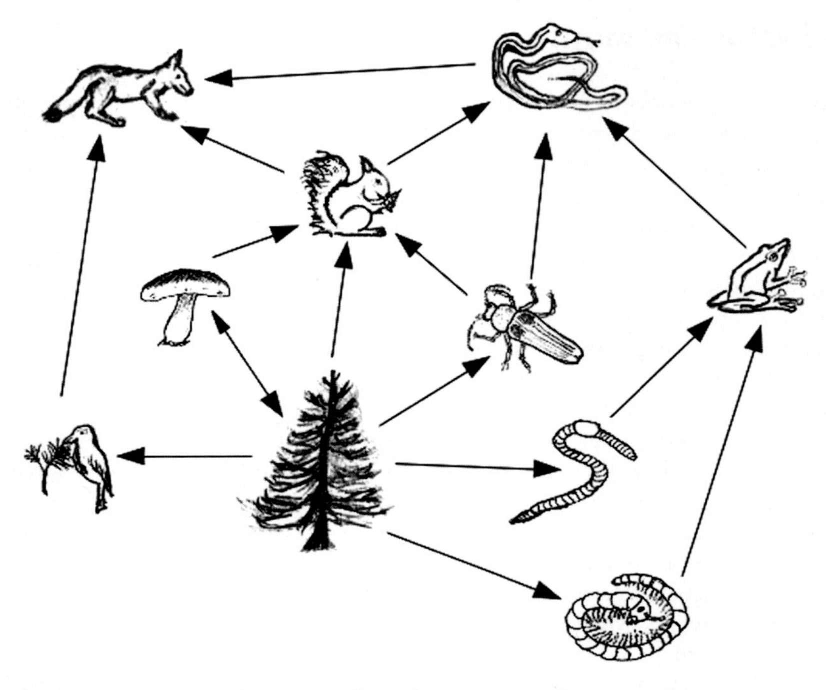

Figure 10.2 A food web where energy flows from one organism to another.

Today biologists are often more concerned with the immediate implications of a food web in an environment, such as the relative health and ongoing viability of a particular ecosystem. Food webs are complex, but at a more fundamental level, there are recurring instances of relationships among groups of organisms. And, there is a readymade relationship that serves to link organisms in a food web: trophic links.

Food webs are concerned with trophic levels and trophic links. Trophic levels refer to the broad category that an organism occupies in a food web. There are three basic levels: producers, consumers, and decomposers. Within these three categories are the trophic links, the relationship between types of organisms that results in the transfer of energy (food). A trophic link is what connects a lion to a zebra, a mushroom to a rotting tree trunk, or a mosquito to a starling. In essence, trophic links trace the path of energy through an ecosystem (Figure 10.2).

As you might imagine, this web of connections quickly becomes quite complex, as predators and omnivores have numerous connections to consumers and producers, with decomposers taking over once the others are done. Various other network measures can reveal many aspects of the productivity and health of an ecosystem, the impact of a given consumer, etc., but these metrics will not reveal patterns of relationships that recur among different organisms.

The best way to understand motifs and what they convey in this context is by way of an example. Consider two organisms that fall into the consumer level, a black bear and a coyote. The bear is an omnivore, with many trophic links to both producers and other consumers. The coyote on the other hand is predominantly a carnivore. The bear and the coyote may both prey upon field mice, but there may be two different species of field mouse and bears prefer one, while coyotes prefer the other. The diet of these field mice includes beetle larva, again of different species. Thus we have a pair of triads, motifs reflecting the same relationship but among different actors in the network. This illustrates two important aspects of motifs: they are distinct subgraphs, and the relationships among the actors are consistent within these subgraphs even though the actors are not the same. When we say the relationships are consistent, we are saying that the edges connect the nodes in the same way, and the direction of the edges is the same among nodes in both subgraphs. In a graph visualization, motifs would look identical, like recurring folds of origami.

So motifs tell us something important about the makeup of a network, something that other graph metrics cannot tell us. In a food web, motifs can help scientists comprehend the complex relationships in an ecosystem, by revealing recurring patterns of relationships among different actors. Motifs are an explicit manifestation of the fact that some complex networks represent systems that have evolved over time, and they are evidence of that evolution.

Discovering motifs is actually quite difficult. As mentioned above, some motifs may be immediately apparent when you look at a visualization of the network. But what's obvious to the human eye and intellect is not necessarily obvious to a computer. Statistical techniques are employed to compare the structures within an instance graph to a random graph with the same nodes. As you may recall, a random graph is one that has been generated by software and each node has an equal probability of have a connection to any other node. In such a graph, there are no meaningful patterns of connections. Motif detection is concerned with finding motifs of varying sizes that are statistically significant when the graph is compared to a random graph of equal size. This is a hard problem however, with the resource requirements to discover motifs increasing exponentially as the size of the motifs of interest grows. In other words, an algorithm searching for triads and tetrads in a graph may be able to complete the task in minutes or hours, but extend the search to size-5 and size-6 nodes, and it may take tens of hours depending on the graph size and computational power at hand. As you might imagine, developing more efficient motif detection techniques is an active area of research.

Biological networks

11

DNA is software

The functions that biologists model as networks are as distinctive as the processes and entities they model. These networks are not something we created, like power grids, or something that arises spontaneously from the fabric of society, like social networks. They evolved in response to environmental challenges to fulfill specific purposes; as we evolve our own networks in the world around us, what can we learn from the structure of networks inherent in ourselves?

Biological systems have had billions of years to evolve. Evolution at the genetic level involves mutations, that is, changes over time in the DNA sequence, that determine how an organism develops and functions. Changes and/or increasing complexity is affected by the environment, competitors, availability of food or sources of energy, impact of viruses, fungi, and bacteria, whether symbiotic or infectious.

Genes also tend to play a more active role throughout the life of an organism than was once understood. DNA is not merely for determining physiological traits of an organism, it also plays an important role in biological processes, including responses to the environment over the course of an organism's lifetime. DNA is software and a catalog. It is information that perpetuates itself and adjusts its contents as the environment changes.

Networks of gene-based biological processes have come into their own as researchers realized that merely sequencing an organism's genome was not sufficient to understand how the organism functioned, or what might make it vulnerable to a particular disease. Various network-based explorations of biological functions have emerged, including biome, genome (role and relationship of gene sequences within and between organisms), connectome (connections and structures in the brain), and proteome (how genes map to biological functions in an organism) analysis (Figure 11.1).

Comparing networks

Regardless of the functions represented, network models of biological systems tend to become very complex very quickly. Unfiltered visualizations of many biological topologies are often useless, because there are simply too many nodes and too many edges for a human to comprehend. Much work has gone into improved visualizations of networks both before and since they were adapted to model biological systems and processes. One approach to rendering a complex network visually involves identifying a way to group nodes into a hierarchy, which tends to work well for processes that have parallel processes between a distinct start and endpoint.

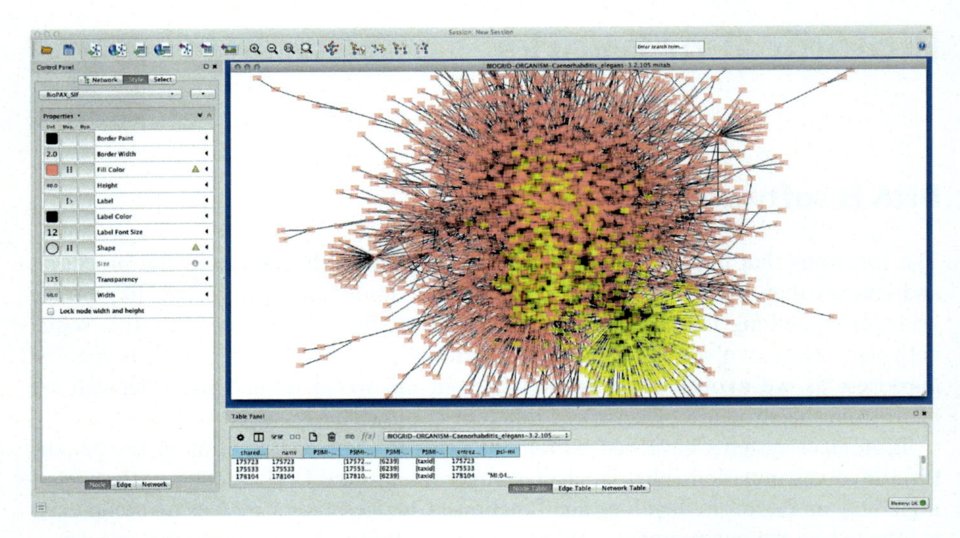

Figure 11.1 Protein interaction network of the well-studied nematode *Caenorhabditis elegans*.

This technique has been used to compare biological and nonbiological networks. In a paper entitled "Comparing genomes to computer operating systems in terms of the topology and evolution of their regulatory control networks," published in Proceedings of the National Academy of Sciences, researchers developed models for a gene regulatory network and a computer operating system. A gene regulatory network describes the steps that lead from a gene to enzyme that supported biological functions. They selected a common bacteria, *Escherichia coli*. They compared this network to a network representing all the function calls performed by the Linux operating system. This study revealed two things: (1) Gene regulatory networks developed over time. We know this because the gene network shows evidence of redundancy and, in contrast to Linux, no evidence that various pathways were ever "re-engineered" to improve their efficiency. (2) Linux shows evidence of intelligent design and the visualization is shaped like a pyramid, which is due to the fact that higher level functions were derived from and entirely dependent upon lower level functions. Furthermore, it illustrates why biological systems are generally less brittle, in other words, less prone to failure, than software systems: redundant pathways may be hard to manage in a software codebase but they are a natural side effect of how biological systems develop, and this redundancy makes it less likely that the "system will crash."

In two 2004 articles, Dr Johannes Berg and colleagues examine how one might reverse engineer the evolution of some biological networks. In one they look at a protein interaction network and try to determine which features were chance fluctuations and which were biologically (evolutionarily) useful. In this network, the protein molecules themselves are nodes; links are formed by their interactions with each other. On that fine scale, it's not easy to see whether this protein interacted with that one, so they apply a technique called high-throughput screening, in which they simulate millions of such interactions, using statistical outcomes to put together a large-scale model of the network, even if each individual link can't be discerned. By letting these networks grow over evolutionary timescales, they can see what processes work to build the existing networks we know. They find that link dynamics—mutations that break existing links between proteins and allow for new ones—shape the structure of the network, while gene duplication mostly grows the network in size. The other article examines the evolution of gene regulation networks—the factors that control the expression of a gene, such as other genes, chemical signals, and primarily, transcription factors (regulatory proteins that bind to part of the gene's DNA). These questions are important, because just as the same four building blocks make up every organism's strands of DNA, those DNA strands make up the same genes, and those genes make up the same proteins for all the diverse organisms—it is how an organism uses those genes that matter. The same proteins may be used in different organisms, but called upon, or expressed, in different ways. Answering how these complex networks evolved may help answer in a sense, how did these complex beings evolve? Again, they produce a model of the evolution of transcription binding sites, including the effects of point mutations, genetic drift, and selection—finding the most efficient motifs for forming new binding sites.

But there's much more to be learned from network representations of biological systems than things we intuitively know about evolution and life. Networks can model very complex, highly interconnected processes as well as intricate interpersonal relationships or processes such as the spread of a disease. Still, it isn't always easy to represent a complex process or system using a network, and it is often necessary to reduce the system to one or a few types of interactions in order to represent it as a network. One of the advantages of network analysis is that something that seems so impossibly complex—not a few interlocking parts with clear functions, but thousands and thousands of connections—actually has consistent high-level properties. In those thousands of separate connections, in the way they interact, they become one thing again, a certain type of graph with certain known characteristics. What types of graphs make up the biology of living organisms? What types of networks does evolution build?

In their paper "The small world inside large metabolic networks," Allon Wagner and David Fell looked at the *E. coli* energy metabolism network, where substrates are nodes and they form links if they participate in the same chemical reaction. These complex networks exhibit both small-world and scale-free characteristics. Albert-László Barabási, a researcher in the field of Graph Theory, found that scale-free networks tend to emerge when you grow a tiny network into a large one by adding nodes and edges in a certain manner—where new nodes are preferentially connected to those existing nodes which already have many links. The authors test this on *E. coli* and find that the most connected nodes are also some of the oldest. The evolutionary advantage to this type of graph, they posit, is that any perturbation is transmitted through the network as fast as possible (it is, after all, a small world), letting the network react quickly to environmental changes.

We've seen how these biological networks might form, but let's consider further their properties. Will different types of networks within a body share similar properties? That is, will metabolism networks look like neural networks and so on? Before considering that, what about different forms of life? Do the biological process networks of mammals resemble those of plants, and do either resemble those of bacteria? Hawoong Jeong at the Korean Advanced Institute of Science and Technology looked across 43 varied organisms and found striking commonalities. Using a genome analysis database called WIT (What Is There?), he and his collaborators extrapolated and compared networks from the genomes of various archaea, bacteria, and eukaryotes. They found a small "diameter" for each network—a feature of small-world graphs. The diameter is the average connection length between any two nodes in the network. But more than that, they found the diameter to be constant across organisms, whether the networks were large or small. This means that as there are more substrates in a network, they must have on average more reactions. (In graph terms, they must form more connections, to keep the diameter down.) It is also a slight difference from nonbiological small-world networks, like the Internet. In those cases, the diameter tends to be relatively low, but it does grow with larger networks. An evolutionary advantage to this, perhaps, is to be able to adapt easier if a certain substrate suddenly becomes lacking in the environment, by making it easier to utilize new paths. A biological network like this is fairly robust, that is, impervious to random errors, as there are only a relatively few crucial nodes—the hubs that form many connections. Finally, another curious commonality was that for all 43 organisms, it was the same specific substrates that acted in the hub roles, even though only 51 substrates were common to all 43.

A fresh perspective

We've seen how the science of networks can act as fresh eyes on problems that have been worked on for centuries. By looking at the question in a different way, from a new angle, scientists can gain new insights. Networks seem to pop up everywhere—connections, it seems, are integral to the underlying nature of things, like numbers—and most questions in some way feature a network component which can be exploited. Take something as simple and as understood as a rock. There are many ways to analyze or study a rock, though networks wouldn't fall high on the list. But the rock may have formed by the cooling of a liquid—a phase transition that can be explained by a dynamic network. If the rock is porous, we can understand just how porous with percolation theory, again drawing on network principles. We'll explore both of these ideas further in Chapter 13. Yet, for most things we want to know about rock—what it is made of, how strong is it—networks are not the primary scientific frameworks.

But in many biological problems, network analysis is the most obvious tool at our disposal. And to find examples, we need to look no further than ourselves. The metabolic networks inside our cells, the pattern of synapses inside our brains: these things *are* networks, first and foremost. If we are ever to fully understand how proteins interact within our cells or how our brains think, we are surely going to need to understand the broader networks they comprise. There's also a granularity question to consider. Can something useful be learned about a system without modeling interactions at physical, biological, molecular, and even atomic scales simultaneously? It tends to be the case that multiple scales introduce too much complexity without adding useful information, making the networks incomprehensible and computationally challenging to explore. Thus choosing what to model in a network representation of a biological system takes a bit of creative thinking.

Scientists have yet to create a comprehensive dynamic graph model of the entire brain, every individual connection, and observe how it evolves and processes information. Olaf Sporns at the University of Indiana has developed some graph models which he uses to investigate the structure, function, and development of the human brain. He and his collaborators developed a dynamic artificial graph model in which they could select for certain known cortical qualities, like complexity. In this way a success is twofold—not only do they have a model to play with, but their selection process may give some hint as to how the brain developed as it did. The brain's complexity they define as the relationship between functional segregation (different hubs in the network control different bodily functions) and functional integration (how those hubs are then connected). Put another way, small clusters behave independently, but they form large clusters that behave in step.

Other qualities allowed for in their model include entropy and integration. But when the model was set to generate graphs of high complexity, they found large clusters with a few reciprocal links to other large clusters, as well as many short cycles (paths that start and end at the same node—similar to the cerebral cortex data matrices of macaques and cats). When they instead modeled that actual animal cortical data into graphs, they measured high complexity. And when they selected not for complexity, but for the cortical patterns observed, they ended up observing an increase in complexity. Finally, they found that any rewiring of the animal model tended to reduce the measure of complexity. Thus, evolution seems to have selected for high complexity, perhaps under volume constraints, and the need for particular functions to maintain separation yet link to those close. (The idea of different functional modules is not limited to the brain. Sergei Maslov at Brookhaven National Laboratory looked at networks within yeast and found that links between hubs were suppressed which kept them isolated and implied different functional modules.)

Some biological systems are real-world networks. Others are more readily comprehensible when modeled as networks. We can even use graphs to represent classification schemes for living organisms. Biological taxonomic classification involves categorizing organisms into a hierarchical graph of categories. Categories and category membership are inferred based on heritable characteristics. The result is typically a tree-like graph. This tree of life starts with kingdom and is subdivided by phylum, class, order, family, genus, and finally species. Sometimes hybrids will cross species boundaries. Further complicating matters, we're still discovering organisms, like Dendrogamma enigmatical, a deep-sea dwelling animal discovered in 1986 but only described in 2014, that superficially resembles a mushroom. Organisms like this challenge our

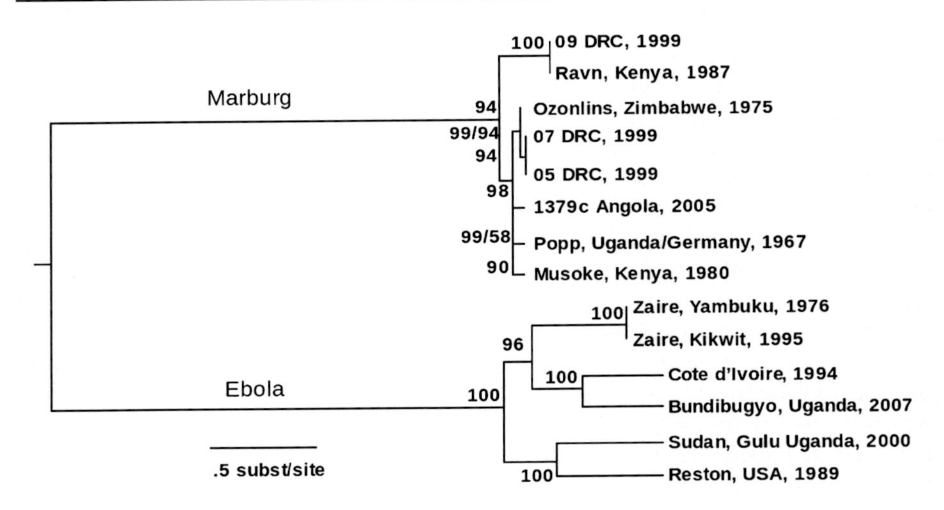

Figure 11.2 Phylogenetic tree of Marburg and Ebola viruses.
Source: <http://commons.wikimedia.org/wiki/File:Filovirus_phylogenetic_tree.svg>.

clean, simple classification models. Increasingly gene-based classification is also used, particularly in cases where the organisms are virus or bacteria or where lineage cannot be clearly discerned based on exhibited characteristics. These are called phylogenetic trees and they are playing an important role in devising new treatments and vaccines for infectious diseases. Phylogenetic trees can reveal what distinguishes one infectious organism from another, when they diverged from one another, and what traits (and vulnerabilities) they may share (Figure 11.2).

Biology has an enviable problem—too much data, too much information, whole sequences, the specification of each protein, its concentration, and so on. This is where networks bring an advantage, offering a way to organize the information. But even so, networks themselves can be too vast, as in a full mapping of the brain—the shortcuts need their own shortcuts. When the data is long sequences of genetic code, biologists use a process called sequence alignment, which looks for the similarities across sequences, the idea being that these reflect useful bits, because there must be some natural pressure that preserves the sequence, keeps it intact against the steady erosion of crossing, mutation, deletion, and other forms of drift. Berg develops the same idea for the vast networks, calling it graph alignment. It looks for similar patterns in the network, which we know as motifs. And this is more profitable, because biologists have long found, to their initial dismay, that it is not always the code itself, but how it interacts with other bits of code within the body that cause functions—that is, regulatory networks, signal transduction, and protein interactions. The "sequence explosion" has given us tools that we can use in the analysis of networks, and in the future, when computational power has caught up to the vastness of the networks within the human body, and the modeling and analysis of such networks has become "easy," then perhaps the work-arounds developed here can be applied to another problem that is before its time.

Networks in economics and business

12

Look at the systems, not the individuals

By the end of 2008, there was a pervading sense that the world as we knew it might very well end. A global financial crash was well under way. Lehman Brothers seemed to be the first of many dominoes about to fall. All because of the failure of several complex financial instruments that almost any person would be hard-pressed to explain. The stock market, global finance, and a web of other esoteric concepts were poised to do damage to our way of life. The graph theory of these arcane mechanisms suddenly became very real and unarguably crucial.

At their core, businesses want customers. In the language of network theory, business nodes want to amass the most customer links. But having the best product is not always enough. W. Brian Arthur of the Santa Fe Institute showed how society can get locked into an inferior technology as networks develop around it. He models the effect as two competing nodes (rival technologies) competing for edges (early adopters). This is a dynamic network, with the Matthew principle at work. The more edges a technology has, the more likely it is to get new nodes—through word-of-mouth, or just increased awareness. A slight, random advantage in the beginning can grow over time into dominance of a technology.

Abhijit V. Banerjee examined the Matthew effect further. He offers herding as an explanation for why nodes grow in certain networks. The idea is that since people tend to have incomplete information, they try to borrow as much information from others as they can to complete their own picture. While they cannot always know the information of others, they can deduce hints of it by observing "signals," that is, what other people do. Thus, as more and more people choose one thing, they herd others to the same conclusion, which herds others, and so on. Banerjee postulates certain scenarios where destroying information can actually be beneficial, because it forces new nodes to use their own independent signals instead of following the herd, which brings more information into play, offering a fuller signal to the undecided and making their resulting choices more reliable.

Information flow

Businesses themselves, though independent of their customers, are complex systems that can be understood and analyzed as networks. One commonly studied feature is communication and information transfer within a business. Patrick Bolton and Mathias Dewatripoint, for instance, found the pyramidal network to be optimal,

A Librarian's Guide to Graphs, Data and the Semantic Web.

where each person in the flow of information reports up to one single agent. They also considered the trade-offs between two different types of pyramidal network structures—more layers and a flatter hierarchy. Roy Radner looked at the same hierarchical models, but actually calculated the time for various information packets to travel from bottom to top (like a tree). Initially a flatter structure seemed best, as there were more processors to divide the information and work on it simultaneously, as well as less hierarchical levels to pass through. But the optimum was actually found when each manager also takes on a processing role himself, in addition to receiving information processed and passed up from subordinates. In this new reduced hierarchy, then, the head node (the boss, or the hub) has a direct connection to each level of the tree. That is, at each level of the organization, there is someone who reports directly to the top (Figure 12.1).

At a meta level, investors play a prominent role in the strategies and ultimately the success or failure of businesses. They supply guidance and capital. They withdraw support for thoughtful reasons—for example, insufficient profits, loss of market share, and reactive reasons—stock selloffs in reaction to some event or some general trend in stock trading volume or share prices. Investment strategies propagate among investors much like fads or highly infectious diseases spread through society. The decision to buy or sell stocks is based in part on whether others are buying or selling that same stock. Between automation and the profit-taking or wealth-preserving desires that motivate investors, there is a tendency toward a herd

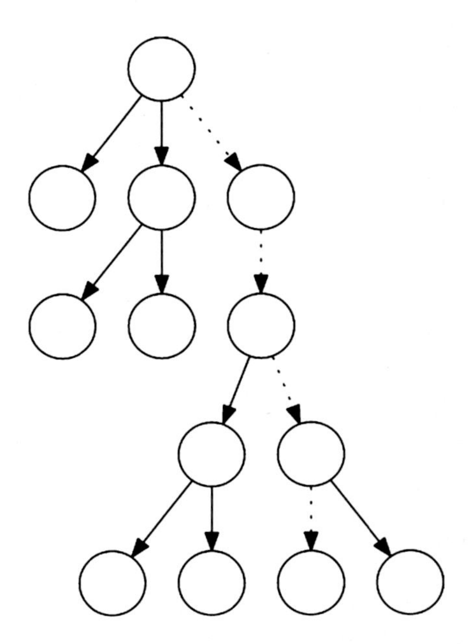

Figure 12.1 The management structure of organizations often resemble a tree.

mentality. This behavior can be represented in a directed or undirected network, depending on whether there is any way to determine the path of information that lead to an investment decision.

Businesses also collaborate and partner with other businesses, as in a supply network. The most famous real-world example of how important these networks can be is the 1997 fire which shut down Toyota's Aisin plant. The loss of this plant removed Toyota's P-valve production capability, which would have brought their output to a halt. However, other factories in the supply chain, not directly under the Toyota corporation and with little hard guidance from Toyota's upper management, learned how to make P-valves and brought production back online. They had a stake, too, in keeping Toyota going. Later supply chain work would take full advantage of network principles. Stephen P. Borgatti and Xun Li looked at supply chains as social networks. They focused on ego networks, which are simply a central actor (the production company) and all its ties (the supply network). A structural hole is an unconnected tie, and Borgatti and Li argued that these can be advantageous, since your supply firms couldn't coordinate with each other. Also, if all your supply companies also supply each other, then when one goes out, you not only lose those supplies, but perhaps others in the network which they supplied. They postulated the idea of structurally equivalent firms. Firms have regular equivalence if they share equivalent suppliers—and they may face similar risks to shock (Figure 12.2).

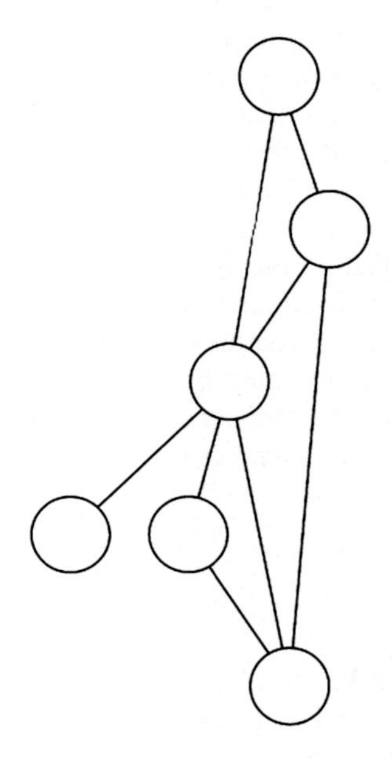

Figure 12.2 A graph with a structural hole.

Figure 12.3 A real-world graph of north American railway lines with apparent structural holes.
Source: <http://commons.wikimedia.org/wiki/File:BNSF_Railway_system_map.svg>.

As we will see in a later chapter, social networks abound in all sorts of contexts, even the corporate boards of major American companies. Gerald F. Davis, Mina Yoo, and Wayne E. Baker examined such boards over a period of two decades and found a small world, an interlocking network of overlapping board memberships. This helps quickly spread corporate practices and structures and ideas. You can look at the company network, with shared board directors as edges, or a director network, with shared boards as edges. Banks are the linchpins, connecting the two clusters. And banks bring us to the encompassing network of the economy as a whole.

Networks have long played a role in the thinking of economic systems, from competing technologies that consumers buy, to the supply chains that support those products (Figure 12.3), from the communication of information within a firm, to the intra-firm communication promoted by the social networks of corporate board memberships. But what about the entire economy? Bringing over the lessons from contagions, let's consider how financial crises can spread in a financial network.

Is it contagious?

In their chapter "Networks in Finance," Franklin Allen and Ana Babus consider the literature. Institutions can be linked in both assets (portfolios of investments) and liability (depositors, or debts). Can looking at these relationships as networks help us answer the important questions? How does the network overall respond to and propagate a shock? Which institutions or nodes in the network are the most vulnerable (and which vulnerabilities are the most dangerous)?

They first consider contagion in the banking system, where literature shows that increasing the number of links might reduce propagation of shocks. The network is more resilient, for there are more connections to absorb the losses of a single bank (or node). The problem, though, is that the well-intentioned impetus to preserve links makes it less likely to close weak banks, and so more of them proliferate throughout the network. Sometimes though, it is not outside events that create propagating shocks, but it is stressed banks reallocating (i.e., breaking their links), which causes others to break their links, or else causes others to preemptively break their own, all of which might propagate through the network.

But the striking cause of the August 2007 banking failure, or at the least a contributing factor, was that bank assets that were rated high actually should have been rated low. Network perspective offers one explanation, if not a solution: credit analysis becomes more difficult in a complicated network where assets can comprise chains through many links. Once the failure happened, the markets froze, and network studies can offer explanations for this too—empty networks can be a type of equilibrium, and part of the collateral necessary for the forming of links might include the relationships between the firms, another nod to the importance of social networks.

Robert M. May, Simon A. Levin, and George Sugihara make the same points from an ecological perspective. Drawing a parallel to fisheries, they argue that too much effort is spent on specific cases of fish species (or risk management within a single bank) rather than the whole ecosystem (or the systemic risk of the financial markets). Ecologies have to survive shocks too—they have done so for millions of years—and so we can look to them for examples of robustness. One, seen in pollinators, is that they are disassortative. What this means is that large nodes preferentially connect to small ones, and vice versa. This would be large banks connecting to lots of smaller ones, rather than each other, and small banks connecting to larger ones, not other small ones. Other examples are modularity, or compartmentalization, and multiple pathways. In a later article, May and Andrew G. Haldane develop a model of financial failure spillovers and come up with the following recommendations. Capital and liquidity ratios should be debated and set to reduce spillovers (cascades)—that is, looking at the system, not the individual bank. But we should look at the individual banks when setting requirements—those bringing more risk ("too big to fail") should have higher regulations. There should be more diversity across the system. Each bank doing the same thing might minimize their individual risk, hidden in the pack like an African savannah grazing animal, but it maximizes the risk for the entire system. And finally, back to the idea of modularity, for example, keeping hedge fund trading separate (closed off) from traditional banking.

Networks can also be used proactively by businesses to increase sales of products to consumers. Marketing is essential to drive adoption of new products, services, or influencing opinions to further some goal, such as the outcome of an election. Networks can be used to model this adoption process. In some instances, a network model of potential customers can help determine how and to whom a product ought to be initially marketed in order to leverage network effects. A product or service can be said to have gone viral when a significant percentage of people in a target network have adopted the product based on their connections. As this effect cascades through the network, adoption rates increase via a self-replicating process not unlike the spread of a disease through a population via social contacts.

In social networks, the method by which information spreads through a social network is referred to as the cascade model. The cascade method relies on social influence to determine the probability that a person in a social network will receive a piece of information, based on how many of their connections already have it. The same can be said of the adoption of new products and services in a social network. The rate of adoption is often determined by the number of immediate connections who have already adopted. The predictive power of the cascade method in marketing is limited because there are other factors that often influence adoption, which are referred to as confounding factors. Confounding factors are people and conditions that are not accounted for in the network model.

Online networks are the product of social media and social networking sites like Facebook. It is often possible to characterize online social networks using graph analysis techniques. Once a social network is better understood, this information can be used to guide targeted marketing efforts. For example, highly connected individuals and individuals who bridge between clusters might make sense as initial targets, provided they also fit the profile of someone who may potentially adopt the product or service. By targeting these well-connected nodes, marketing efforts have a better chance of initiating social influence driven adoption and thus increasing their success. This is the goal of viral marketing.

The city effect

Businesses also influence our world in more fundamental ways. Major corporations tend to lay down their headquarters in major cities. Cities are vast networks of people, ideas, transportation, goods, and so on. They are the "center" of things, where "center" can be measured in different ways. But they are immensely complex. Or are they?

Luis M. A. Bettencourt, with Jose Lobo, Dirk Helbing, Christian Kuhnert, and Geoffrey B. West, has found that when cities are seen as networks, their features at least are much simpler. Many of these features—things related to people, their interactions, or their economy, such as wages or the amount of road surfaces—scale based on a single indicator, city size (measured in population). That is, if you increase the population, these other factors will tend to increase (or decrease) by some percentage. This holds across cities around the world. Said another way, looking at an unknown city's population, you can estimate all these factors (and you can judge then whether specific cities are ahead or behind the curve). But let's look at examples. Many basic human needs are simply linear, as we would expect. That is, more people means more jobs, more houses, more water consumption, without any multiplier effect. But we also see economies of scale at work for the infrastructure of cities. For a given increase in people, the observed increase in the following is around 20% less: gasoline sales (21%), electrical cable length (13%), and road surfaces (17%). And there is an increasing return on social features. The corresponding increase in patents is 27%, inventors 25%, wages 12%, and crime 16%.

Why is this so? Economies of scale may explain the infrastructure savings, while greater social mixing could explain things like the increase in ideas. People are people and their social networks take certain forms (small-world graphs with high-clustering but short path lengths, which obey a power law). As these networks grow, with more people and more connections, they scale with a power law. Is there some connection then to all the infrastructure that supports people, and the social benefits that come out of their interactions—the features of business like patents and innovation and wages?

Bettencourt later developed an explanation for the evolution of cities. He started with four basic principles: (1) population mixing, (2) incremental infrastructure growth, (3) human effort is bounded (increases in social measurements come from greater mixing, which can be either more people or a reduced area of interaction), and (4) social interactions are what matter. The third is measured in a factor G (social output times area per person) which has an optimum. A city's transportation network might be so efficient that social output can be increased by simply adding more people to it. Or, it might be clogged, so that more people won't lead to more social interactions (which leads to the good stuff). This has implications for urban planning. If G is less than optimal, then you want to promote people's mobility or increase their density in the city. If G is greater than optimal, then you need to improve the efficiency of transportation.

For many areas of life, we seek analogy or explanation in biology. Cities, for instance, are often compared to living organisms. But organisms evolved to minimize energy loss. Cities are different in that our transport losses scale with size. Bettencourt instead offers an analogy to physics—stars. With more and more mass, stars increase output and burn brighter.

Networks in chemistry and physics

13

The best T-shirts graph theory has to offer

Anyone who took chemistry in high school (or anyone who has seen a T-shirt emblazoned with the chemical formula for caffeine) can see that there's something about chemistry that lends itself particularly well to graph modeling. Chemistry doesn't have to be viewed through a graph lens because atoms and the bonds between them have obvious mappings to nodes and edges in a graph. Over time it has become difficult to sort out which influenced which.

Certainly the language of graph matching, which is of broad interest to graph theoreticians, borrows from the language of theoretical chemistry. Graph edit distance, that is, the comparison of graphs to determine what changes would need to be made to one to make it identical to the other, uses terminology such as edits, insertions, and deletions. By rewiring graph models of molecules, chemists can perform experiments in silica. Theoretical chemistry uses the same language to talk about how one might change the structure of a molecule. And although chemists are less concerned with comparing two molecules than what molecular structures are possible and what characteristics they might have, they would immediately recognize the similarity (Figure 13.1).

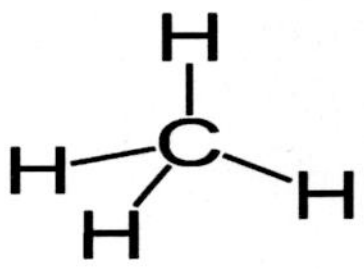

Figure 13.1 A methane molecule in graph form.

Chemical molecules obviously lend themselves to graph theory, but what about the chemical reactions between them? Gil Benko, Christoph Flamm, and Peter F. Stadler created a model for chemical reactions—one that could stand for the swirling mass inside each of our cells or inside planetary atmospheres. There is a selection bias in studying the few reactions which are modeled in great detail, but modeling based on simple rules lets you consider many. One limitation to this kind of study, these networks, is that molecules can react to form new things, not just more of existing things which are already factored into the model.

But this lets you ignore 3D angles and simply look at the connections. Benko et al. must first translate potential reactions into graph language, describing how the graph is reshaped and rewritten as links dissolve and reform in the reaction, bounding it by common chemical rules like conservation of vertex labels (since atoms

A Librarian's Guide to Graphs, Data and the Semantic Web.

must remain). Then they can send together two graphs randomly. These will simply be sent back if no rewiring is possible—that is, an elastic collision. Or, pick random rules for each and see what new graph comes back. Or, specify all the different rules, evaluate each, and pick the one requiring the lowest energy.

In chemistry and genetics research, much effort is devoted to identifying and associating published literature with chemical entities or gene sequences. In some disciplines, such as protein crystallography, authors are required to submit the protein structure to a database at the time that their corresponding paper is published. This explicitly establishes a connection between a protein structure and a research paper. But many disciplines do not have such a requirement. Scientific papers, although conforming to some predictable naming conventions, reference models, and overall structure of narrative are still unstructured documents. Lacking structure, these artifacts of scientific research are data rich, but from an information retrieval perspective, information poor.

There are techniques for establishing these relationships after the fact. For example, various text mining techniques can be used to discover references to entities within papers. These include using natural language processing (NLP) to identify features of interest within individual documents. NLP software uses grammar and syntactic rules to analyze the textual content of a document, identifying parts of speech for example, which can ultimately lead to the identification of things like dates, actions, actors, and named entities. In this case, the ultimate target would be chemical entities. At the level of a corpus of papers, machine learning techniques can be used to group papers into clusters, using unsupervised machine learning techniques such as k-means clustering. These clusters can then be analyzed using more computational intense methods, like NLP. The product of such an effort can be a multipartite graph that identifies for example chemical entities and the papers and authors associated with them, date of publication, co-occurrences of chemical entities within papers. The resulting graph can be used as a resource for planning future research.

Percolation

Many network problems first appeared in physics. We will see how graph theorists have borrowed some of the tools and conclusions developed by physicists. We will also see how physicists and chemists borrowed back the tools of graph theory, an oscillation in the clustered network of scientific research. An early example, from 1960, carries over from the last chapter. In "The Pareto-Levy Law and the Distribution of Income," Benoit Mandelbrot compared the exchange of money in economic markets to the energy exchange of molecular interactions, and postulated that statistical thermodynamics models from physics could be appropriated. Two physical concepts more connected to graphs are percolation and phase transitions.

Percolation asks the basic question: Will a liquid be able to penetrate a porous material, and how far? This becomes a network problem if you look at holes as edges, and it can be related to the robustness of networks to random or targeted attacks, as we'll see in the next chapter. But first let's look at the problem in the context of physics. One early paper which looked at the problem in the language of networks was Michael E. Fisher and John W. Essam's "Some Cluster Size and Percolation Problems" (1961). Their model envisioned a lattice of bonds, which could be chemical bonds, or could be anything—that is the power of graphs. They supposed particles occupy sites on the lattice with probability p, and the bonds they form link up into clusters. This is the "site" version of the problem. An alternative is to look at the bonds of the lattice as being occupied or unoccupied, which puts it more intuitively as a percolation problem. Whatever fluid you are considering then flows through the lattice, via occupied bonds, with unoccupied bonds representing dams. The whole distribution becomes a "randomly dammed maze." There is a critical probability p_c above which a cluster becomes unbounded, extending throughout the lattice. For percolation, this means that flows are indefinite. For the spread of a disease, it might be the point at which an epidemic becomes unstoppable. For a magnet, it might represent the moment of order, when all poles align.

But what does the rigid lattice percolation model have to do with modern networks? How can we understand percolation in the small-world graph, more common to social networks? We don't think of social networks as lattice grids, but that is the way Duncan Watts and Steven Strogatz formulated their small-world model—starting with a lattice, where people know their neighbors and no one else, they systematically broke random links and rewired them, possibly stretching across the lattice. The lattice framework explains one feature of social networks—that if one person knows two people, those two people are more likely to know each other than another pair of random nodes. And the random rewiring of links, acting as bridges between clusters explain the reduced path length that gives "small-world" graphs their name. So the physical basis of percolation carries over nicely. M. E. J. Newman, with Watts, builds on their model and finds a similar critical percolation probability, the point of phase transition where clusters become unbounded, or in modern parlance, form a "giant component." In a later paper with Duncan Callaway, the four extend the model to graphs with power-law degree distributions, a more realistic feature, but also more mathematically complicated. They found that such networks are both robust *and* fragile, a paradoxical arrangement that's found in many other real-world networks.

Phase transitions

Like networks, phase transitions are all around us. For one thing, water is all around us. Sweat evaporates in heat. Ice melts in a drink but reforms in a freezer. But what could it possibly mean in graphs? What "phases" does a graph have? The answer is related to percolation, and we have seen it already with the idea of the giant component. If you grow a graph from the bottom-up, letting links form naturally with probability p, then you have a bunch of unconnected clusters (you don't really have one graph, but many). But if you vary p, making links more common, then you reach a critical point where the graph becomes connected. Those are the phases of a graph—connected and unconnected.

One benefit of Watts and Strogatz developing the small-world model on a lattice is that so many physical models also exist on a lattice. One physical example is the Ising model—a mathematical model that describes phase transitions. At its core, these represent the emergence of order, as when a fluid freezes into a solid lattice structure, or when all the individual dipoles of a metal suddenly point in the same direction, creating a magnet. But how does this simple model look on a complex network? J. Viana Lopes, Yu. G. Pogorelov, J. M. B. Lopes dos Santos, and R. Toral, for instance, successfully update the 1D model to incorporate the long-range bonds of the small-world graph, enabling its conclusions to illuminate the many natural phase transitions that might occur in real-world graphs.

Synchronization

Many physical insights have helped the development of graph theory, as many of its models have given network scientists fields to play on. At the same time, the pendulum swings back, and graph theory can be applied to those and other problems in physics and chemistry. Mathematicians and physicists have long been intrigued by coupled oscillators and their seemingly magical displays of synchronicity—ever since 1665 when Christiaan Huygens, inventor of the pendulum clock, uncovered an area of mathematics when he observed that two clocks, side-by-side, eventually swung in step. This synchronization has since been found in other mechanical ways, and even biologically, like in the lighting of fireflies or animal gaits.

Takashi Nishikawa and Adilson E. Motter asked how one could maximize this synchronization, in light of network theory. Which types of networks synchronize best? They considered "best" in two ways. First, they looked at the range over which networks were able to couple. Second, they defined a cost of synchronization, which they proceeded to minimize. This cost is the minimum node strength at which point the networks first become coupled, or stable. Surprisingly, those networks with maximum synchronization also have minimum synchronization cost—and there are no intermediary solutions to the equation. This gives us a way to look at evolved networks. If they do not contain these signatures of synchronization, then synchronization was likely not a major factor in their evolution, giving way to other potential factors like robustness or scarcity.

Quantum interactions and crystals

The Feynman Diagram (named for their inventor, Richard Feynman) employs a graph notation to describe the interactions of subatomic particles that are responsible for electromagnetic effects. These diagrams omit explicit representations for start and end nodes. Each edge represents a particle. Each node, which is represented by the intersection of various lines in the diagram, represents an interaction. Since nodes within the graph represent interactions, and an interaction must involve

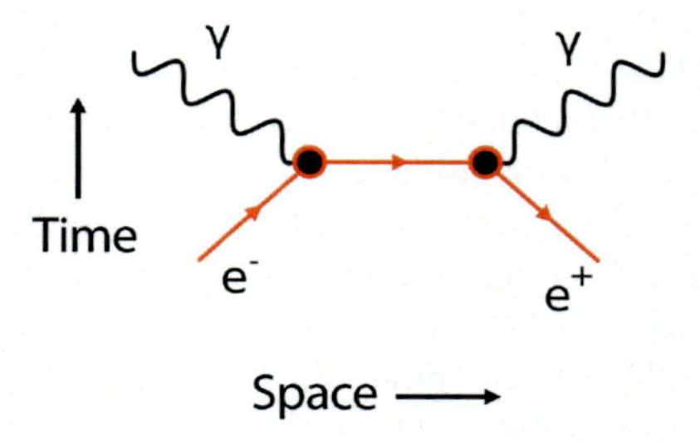

Figure 13.2 A Feynman Diagram.
Source: <http://commons.wikimedia.org/wiki/File:Feynman_EP_Annihilation.svg>.

at least two particles, there are no unconnected edges between the start and end-points of a Feynman Diagram. To convey additional information about the constituent particles involved in the interactions, Feynman introduced wavy edges for force particles and directed edges for matter particles. Feynman Diagrams are intended to be read from left to right, and each tells a particular story about how particles interact over time, and what the results of those interactions are. Thus a Feynman Diagram is a dynamic graph. This shorthand notation revolutionized the way physicists represent and think about problems in quantum electrodynamics (Figure 13.2).

The Hubbard model is a graph model that models the transition between conductive and insulating systems. Most materials ultimately have the ability to become conductive, that is allow the exchange of electrons among atoms, if enough energy is introduced. For some insulating systems, the material is permanently changed once subjected to these high-energy states, and they lose their insulating properties. In the Hubbard model, particle interactions are modeled as a lattice. This model can be used to predict the conductive potential of a material and to model the phase transition that occurs when a material becomes more conductive.

Crystals are often modeled using graphs. A crystal is a solid material whose atoms are arranged in a highly organized fashion. A snowflake is an example of a crystal most of us have encountered in the real world. Salt is another crystal in which sodium and chloride atoms occur with equal frequency. The constituent atoms are arranged in an alternating 3D lattice pattern. This is typical of crystals. The distinct arrangement of atoms found within a crystal is repeating, that is, the characteristic pattern recurs periodically throughout the solid. This recurring pattern is also referred to as translational symmetry. Some solids are not classified as crystals, but are made up of grains that are themselves crystals. These are referred to as being polycrystalline. In polycrystals, the crystals do not recur in a predictable periodic fashion, but may be fused together in various ways as grains within the solid. It is the recurring patterns of atoms in crystals that are most often modeled as graphs. In these graphs, atoms represent nodes and the bonds between atoms represent edges. Understanding and characterizing crystals yields important information about solids since crystals can have special conductive, optical, or mechanical properties. Crystal graph models are used in crystallography which is the science of measuring and modeling crystal structures.

Graph theory has also been applied to physical applications, areas of engineering like electronic circuits. One way to consider such systems as a network is to picture the nodes as the various components—capacitors, logic gates, etc.—and edges as the wires connecting them. There are other independent variables at work. Smaller, digital components allow for larger and larger networks. Ramon Ferrer i Cancho, Christiaan Janssen, and Richard V. Sole look at the resulting topology. Specifically, does it display small-world behavior? (That is, does the network have low path lengths, like random graphs, yet nonrandom high clustering. Additionally, do the distribution of node degrees—how many connections each node has, compared to the others—follow a power-law?) These studies are important, because there is a cost to each connection, in both time and money, just as in the Internet or the power grid. Cancho et al. look at two examples: the analog TV circuit and a set of benchmark digital circuits. They found that small-worldness increases with increases in circuit size. One explanation might be that larger circuits simply connect existing circuits or circuit patterns, which then become clusters in the larger circuit. In electronic devices, however, unlike biological systems, small world does not necessarily equate with resiliency, as there is less redundancy (every connection matters) and an edge failure might lead to system failure. There is a need for in situ rewiring capability, on space missions for instance. One idea for further study is to specify objectives of your system and let an evolutionary algorithm search for the best circuits and connections.

Social networks

14

Six degrees of separation

As far as many people are concerned, network science originated with the study of social networks. Although that's not really the case, the use of networks to study the relationships among people is common, intuitive, and revealing. We are all keenly aware of the connections we have with other people, whether it is our family, friends, or coworkers. We've all experienced situations in our lives where someone moves on and we end up losing contact with the people we knew through that person.

Until that moment, we may not have recognized that person served as a bridge between our close associates, and another group of people to whom we were not really directly connected to. And betweenness centrality works in reverse in social circles as well: we may start dating a new person and soon find ourselves welcomed into a new circle of people to whom our new partner is already connected.

Beyond the intuitive experience that we're all familiar with, there are numerous scenarios in which more rigorous documentation and analysis of social networks has value. Social network analysis (SNA) is the broad general term used for representing connections among people and using graph analytic techniques to explore characteristics of that network. One of the most famous experiments in SNA was conducted by Stanley Milgram in 1967. Milgram's experiment suggested that it may be the case that all people are more closely interconnected than we would otherwise imagine. He found that there were on average only six degrees of separation between any two people (Figure 14.1).

Milgram's experiment involved enlisting the help of 160 people selected at random, in Omaha, Nebraska. Geographically, Omaha is of course centrally located within the continental United States, and it is also fairly far removed from many population centers in the country, and even more so at that time. These individuals were sent a package that was to be delivered to a stockbroker in Massachusetts, whom they did not know personally. These individuals were instructed to try and get the package to the stockbroker by sending it to someone they knew personally. That person was then to follow the same guidance: mail the package on to someone they knew personally with the intention of getting it closer to someone who might know this stockbroker personally, or know someone who knew him. The results were surprising. In some cases there were only two individuals that connected a randomly selected person in Omaha with the stockbroker in Massachusetts. The average number of connections from these 160 individuals and the stockbroker was five, thus the study gave birth to a phrase that often turns up in modern popular culture and is often applied to many different social networks, whether it is in fact accurate or not: "six degrees of separation."

A Librarian's Guide to Graphs, Data and the Semantic Web.

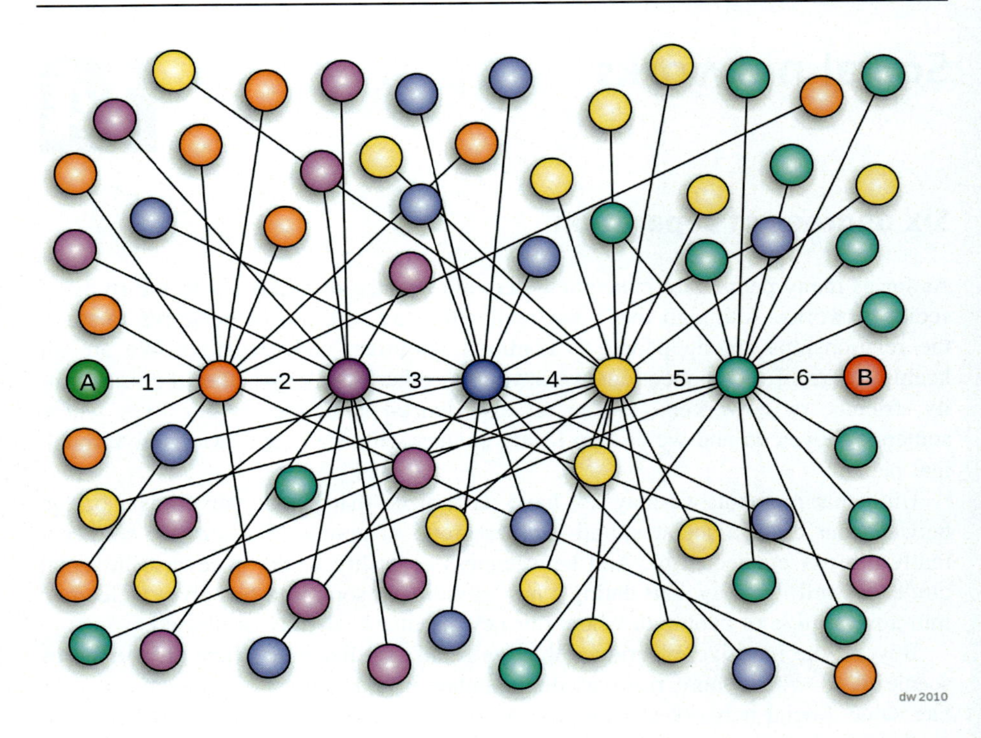

Figure 14.1 Six edges separate person A from person B.
Source: Wikimedia.

It's a small world

Milgram documented the existence of what we now refer to as a small-world network. While most of the individuals in the study did not know one another directly, he found that the network that included those 160 people and the stockbroker included a sufficient number of short paths between people that the average shortest path was far lower than what would be found in a random network. Random networks have long average path lengths between any two nodes, whereas small-world networks include enough short paths beyond what would be expected to occur by chance, thus establishing shorter paths between selected clusters of individuals in the graph. Depending on the size of the network, there may only need to be a few such connections to vastly reduce the average path length. As a result, the number of connections between people in a small-world network may not be much, if at all different than the number of connections in a random network. All it takes is a few select rewired connections that perhaps span large distances geographically or bridge two otherwise unconnected social, business, or community networks and suddenly we we're an average of six degrees from a world leader, a pop icon, or a random stranger in a city literally on the other side of the Earth.

Milgram's experiment used a network to model the relationships, or perceived lack of relationships in this case among a group of randomly selected people. By conducting an experiment on that network, Milgram discovered something unexpected about that network and suggested that it might be generalizable to the whole of human population. It doesn't mean that all of humanity is organized as a small-world network, but it does suggest that, as social organisms, our connection patterns manifest characteristics of a small-world network. Studies of small-world networks that represent other phenomena, such as biological processes within a cell or food webs in an ecosystem, suggest that small-world networks are resilient in ways that random networks are not. That resiliency means that if something happens to one node or even a small portion of the network, there are other paths that can ensure the process or group survives this change.

This in turn suggests a practical reason for human networks to exhibit small-world characteristics: communities are more resilient and thus more durable if they organize in this way. Moreover, if communities in turn develop the same organizational strategy in the context of a geopolitical body such as a country, and this conveys benefit to the country, then it is not hard to imagine that this organizational strategy is so valuable that it might cross geopolitical borders or oceans.

Humans have probably been aware on some level of the benefits of organizing themselves into small-world social networks for thousands of years. Organizing into a loosely connected community lead to developments such as agriculture, technology, and the arts. Division of labor became possible but with it the need to trade, share, and contribute to the common good. It makes more obvious one of the purposes for so many of the traditions and ceremonies that have endured for so long—that is to reinforce connections and provide opportunities for new connections to form , whether at community festivals, team building exercises at work, religious ceremonies, attending college, engaging in hobbies, or participating in political parties. We don't usually make a conscious decision to act so as to establish or perpetuate a small-world network, but it happens.

Social network analysis

SNA is the practice of representing networks of people as graphs and then exploring these graphs. A typical social network representation has nodes for people, and edges connecting two nodes to represent one or more relationships between them (Figure 14.2). The resulting graph can reveal patterns of connection among people. Small networks can be represented visually, and these visualizations are intuitive and may make apparent patterns of connections, and reveal nodes that are highly connected or which play a critical role in connecting groups together. As the network representation of a community grows, it becomes necessary to apply graph analytic techniques to compute the characteristics of nodes and the graph as a whole.

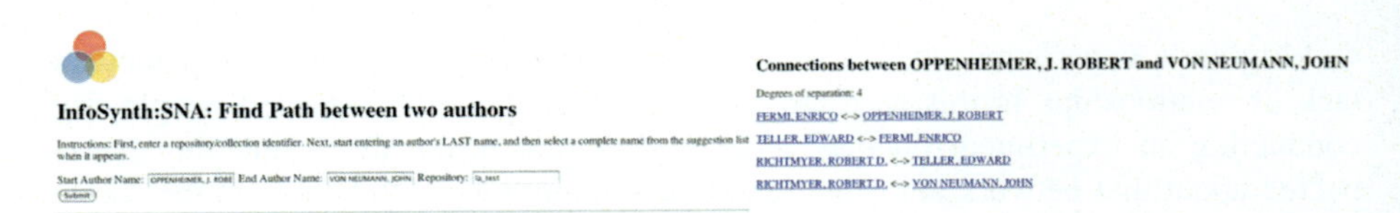

Figure 14.2 SNA in action: Results of a shortest path search in a coauthorship network.

Graph analytic techniques for SNA are broadly concerned with connections, distributions, and clustering. Let's first look at the analysis of connections in a social network. Some terms in SNA are specific to social (human) relationship networks. Nonetheless many SNA techniques are identical to those applied to other types of networks. Here are four connection related terms from SNA: homophily, multiplexity, reciprocity, and propinquity. If you've ever heard the old adage "birds of a feather flock together," well, that's homophily. It refers to the tendency for people to form ties to other people with whom they share some characteristic, which can be as simple as race, gender, or age, or less obvious traits such as educational status, hobbies, or religious beliefs. The concept of agency is also explored through homophily, because agency is the ability of a person to act outside the predicted norm, thus forming ties that bridge groups that might otherwise only exhibit homophily. Multiplexity refers to the potential for multiple different relationships to exist between two people. More generally a graph that captures this characteristic is referred to as a multipartite graph. Reciprocity implies a directionality to a relationship. A reciprocal relationship can be represented by one or two edges, where one edge points at both nodes, or two edges represent the bidirectional nature of the relationship. Thus a social network that reflects reciprocity between nodes is by definition a directed graph. Finally, propinquity is a term that refers to a type of homophily, that is, the tendency of people to form ties when they are geographically close to one another. Another class of pattern of connections that can recur in a network is called motifs. Motifs are small, recurring groups of connections that can be distinctly detected via visual scrutiny or statistical analysis. In a social network, triads tend to be the smallest motif of interest, and as the name implies, a triad is a grouping of three nodes in which all three individuals are connected with one another.

Distribution is another way to analyze a social network. Distribution analysis employs many of the core graph analytic techniques used to analyze all types of graphs, including centrality measures, graph density, strength of connections, path analysis, and identification of hubs. We have explored various centrality measures related to nodes before, but let's recap a few of them in this context. Degree centrality is a measure of the number of connections an individual node has. Someone might be said to be more popular or important if they have high degree centrality. Betweenness centrality reveals the people that bridge disparate groups of nodes. They are the hubs that enable communication between people who are not directly connected.

Eigenvector centrality is a technique for measuring the influence of nodes in a network. It relies on the overlaying of weights onto all nodes in the network, where the weight value is associated with some characteristics of interest, such as expertise in a given field. Influence is apparent when analyzing nodes connected to nodes with high scores, because the cumulative score of a node connected to nodes with higher weights indicates a potentially greater influence. Graph density is a measure of the frequency of connections in the actual graph as compared to a graph in which the maximum possible number of connections could occur. Path analysis, like degree centrality, is concerned with many aspects of the edges between nodes. Recalling six degrees of separation, the value of six reflects the shortest average path between any two nodes—six hops through five nodes. Other path metrics consider things like closed paths (such as those found in a triad motif) versus open paths, disconnected groups of nodes, and directionality, which reveals something about the flow of information, commodities, or some other entity (such as an infectious agent, or popular trend) through a network.

Clustering is a third major area of concern with social networks. As the name implies, a cluster is a tightly connected group within itself, with fewer or perhaps no ties to other parts of the network. At its most extreme, a cluster can be a clique, like a scaled-up triad motif, where everyone is connected with everyone else within the cluster. A social circle is a less highly interconnected cluster. Cluster coefficient is essentially a density measure for clusters, where the actual number of connections within the cluster is compared with the maximal (clique) cluster. Finally, edges within clusters can obviously have an impact on the durability of a cluster. Analysis of the structural cohesion of a cluster is concerned with the nodes within the cluster that act as bridges. These are the nodes with high betweenness centrality within the cluster, which if removed, would cause the cluster to fall apart.

There are many practical applications for SNA. It can be used to analyze and suggest actions to improve the efficiency or communication within a business organization. SNA can be used to explore how an infectious disease might spread through a group of people. It can be used to model traffic patterns, the spread of ideas, how a product or service becomes popular within a given community. Advertisers are particularly keen to understand how something becomes popular and how individuals influence one another in the adoption of products, services, and ideas. Their goal is to turn viral marketing into something that can be understood and can be reproduced, for obvious reasons.

A contemporary, if slightly unsettling application of SNA happens within online social networking sites. Sites such as Facebook and LinkedIn track and analyze the connection patterns among their users. This has many internal applications such as the aforementioned concern regarding a product or service, since online advertising and marketing has become a very large business. SNA has found more recent application in detecting and analyzing terrorist networks. But as one might expect, this application of SNA can ensnare the innocent as well as the guilty. Social networking sites thrive when small-world networks emerge, and so they do whatever they can to encourage their formation such as suggesting you connect with friends or former coworkers. And as we learned earlier, there's an obvious benefit to encouraging users to assemble their own small-world networks within a social networking site: they are resilient and enduring, thus ensuring the relationship of the person to the site is also resilient and enduring!

In the next few chapters we'll revisit RDF graphs. We start by surveying some commonly used ontologies. So we'll end this part of the book with a brief discussion of how social networks can be represented in the Semantic Web. Social networks are of broad interest across many domains, because they can reveal relationships among people. As we saw at the beginning of this section, social networks are of particular interest in the context of libraries. Yet one of the earliest ontologies concerned with people and their relationships is predictably aimed at one of the most basic relationships one human can have to another: the "knows" relationship.

This relationship property resides in an ontology that makes explicit reference to the network effect of the "knows" relationship, the somewhat whimsically named Friend of a Friend ontology. This ontology is used to describe a variety of relationships among people in the real world as well as online. And since people tend to congregate in groups, there are ontologies for describing collections of people. One of these is the Organization ontology, which we will take a closer look at in the next chapter.

Upper ontologies

15

A unifying framework for knowledge

Reading ontologies falls somewhere between reading the dictionary and reading the US Tax code in terms of excitement. Upper ontologies are sometimes prescribed by doctors for insomnia. And yet upper ontologies are an essential component of the Semantic Web because they are concerned with general ideas and cross-domain concepts.

There are many concepts that transcend any domain-specific ontology. If you spend much time exploring published ontologies at the Linked Open Vocabulary site, you will see many ontologies that are composites of other ontologies. Soon you may also note that a few ontologies recur over and over. These are upper ontologies. They are imported and used over and over across various domains and disciplines. Upper ontologies serve as a unifying framework for knowledge across many domains. They are typically intuitively obvious, often relatively small, well organized, and easy to comprehend.

Some ontologies dive deep, describing in some detail a particular knowledge domain. Others attempt to address general topics that have application in a variety of contexts. Many things can be measured, all people have names, and places on Earth exist at some coordinates. You can try to model these concepts in each vocabulary, but a better approach is to extract similar concepts that have broad application and represent them in a separate ontology that can be used directly or imported into others. This is the role of upper ontologies.

You've already encountered a few upper ontologies. People are often a topic of, or have some, relationship with other things. A de facto standard for classes and properties that describe people is the Friend of a Friend (FOAF) ontology. The intent of this ontology is to support the representation of instance data describing a person, their contact information, some of their basic demographic information, and some online identity information and contact information.

Friend of a Friend

FOAF is not an especially deep or intricate ontology but it is clearly defined, widely used, and easy to understand (Figure 15.1). An individual is first declared with a statement using the foaf:Person predicate. The subject of that statement is a unique identifier for that individual. Other triples can specify e-mail (foaf: mbox), foaf:homepage, nickname (foaf:nick), a link to a photograph of the person identified (foaf:depiction), and triples pointing to identifiers which represent

Vocabulary used in **249** datasets (information coming from LOD Stats project)

Occurrences	Dataset
7564093	bibliographica-org-bnb-export.131.nq
7334650	bibliographica-org-bnb-export.133.nq
5858792	bibliographica-org-bnb-export.100.nq
5044301	b3kat.249.rdf
4814525	b3kat.241.rdf
See the full list...	

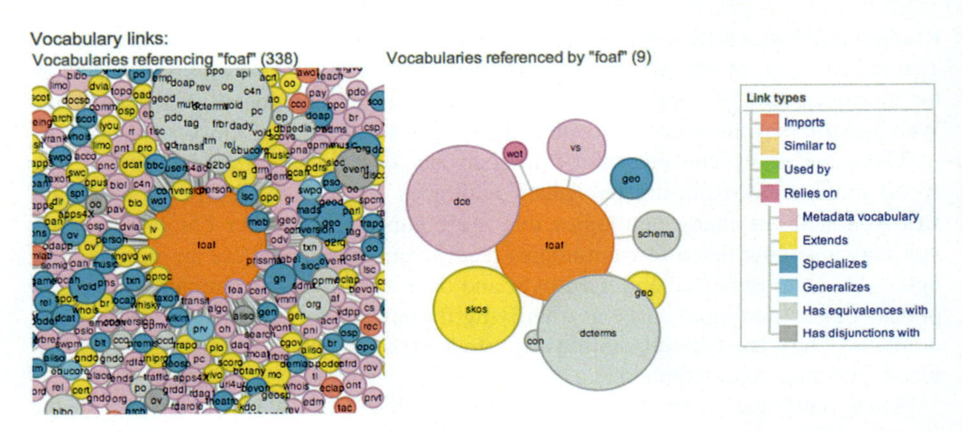

Figure 15.1 Linked Open Vocabulary overview for FOAF.

interests (foaf:interest), among other characteristics. The predicate foaf:knows provides the edge between two people who have a connection. In all FOAF defines 6 top level classes and 37 properties.

FOAF can be used to represent the relationship among researchers. For example, the foaf:knows property is often assumed to be a valid means for representing the relationship between two people when they are coauthors of a research paper. The same would be true for a student and an advisor or mentor and mentoree. The foaf:knows property does not specify the nature of the relationship between two individuals; it merely allows one to state there is such a relationship.

Organization

The Organization ontology (ORG) is an ontology which is suitable for making statements about the structure and makeup of an organization. Like many ontologies, it builds on others. One of the ontologies that ORG uses or extends is FOAF. ORG has a top level class called Organization which is also a subclass of the FOAF ontology Agent class. Whereas an Agent is defined as "things that do stuff," whether it is a person, group, software, etc., an org:Organization is defined as a collection of people that share a common purpose. It is fairly common for ontologies to borrow and extend classes from one another in this way.

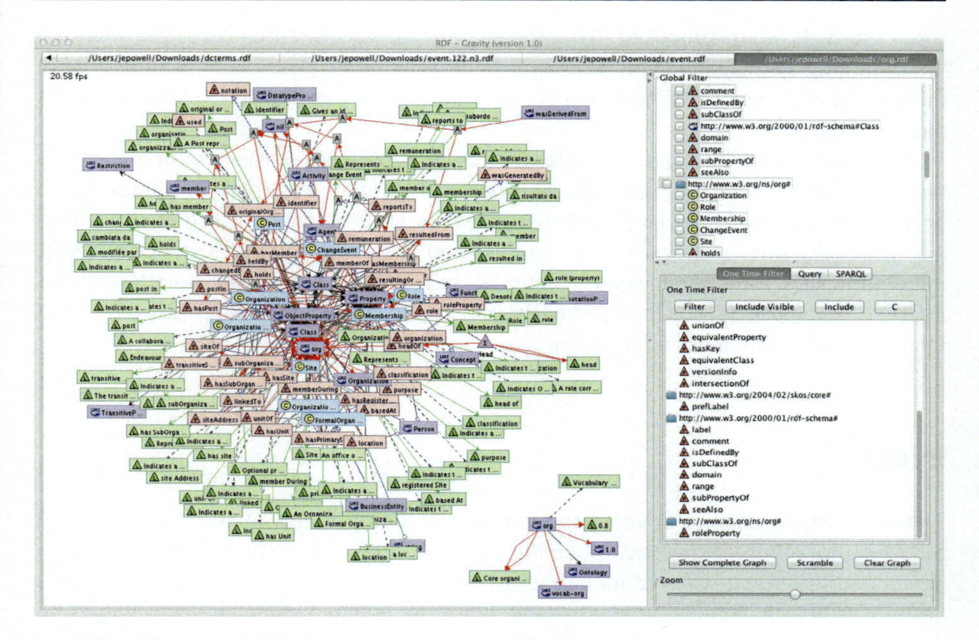

Figure 15.2 RDF Gravity tool used to visualize the ORG.

The ORG is as concerned with organizations as it is with the relationship that people have to those organizations. It is suitable for describing things and properties associated with corporations, universities, schools, religious organizations, charities, and governing bodies. The relationships and roles that people have in these organizations can be expressed with ORG properties, such as org:Posts or have org: Membership or org:Role in organizations and suborganizations. This ontology also includes properties to specify time periods for a statement's validity, such as org: memberDuring, which uses time interval values from the OWL Time ontology (more on this in a moment). ORG has 9 top level classes and 35 properties (Figure 15.2).

As organizations form and disband over time, it is important to be able to represent the time period for which a group existed, or for when an individual had a role, membership or post within an organization. One way to reflect this is with the Time ontology which has existed in some form since the earliest inception of the Semantic Web. A variety of use cases are defined in the Time ontology specification including processing time, delivery duration, validity period, and using Time ontology classes and properties to support scheduling tasks. One of the most important classes in this ontology is the TemporalEntity. A temporal entity is something that specifies some unit of time. The two subclasses of TemporalEntity are Instant and Interval. It is probably apparent from their class names what they represent: an Instant is a point in time, while an interval defines a relationship of an instant with other points in time. It is a more formalized and specific version of what we mean when we talk about things like before and after. Interval properties are based on time intervals first proposed in a paper by James F. Allen in 1983 entitled "Maintaining knowledge about temporal intervals." Allen's ideas about time greatly influenced the way in which many information systems process and represent temporal data.

The paper describes and formalizes ways of representing various time intervals known as Allen's temporal intervals. This paper identified 13 intervals of interest. Each of these intervals is represented as properties in the Time ontology. The property names are intervalBefore, intervalMeets, intervalOverlaps, intervalStarts, intervalDuring, intervalFinishes, and their reverse interval relations: intervalAfter, intervalMetBy, intervalOverlappedBy, intervalStartedBy, intervalContains, intervalFinishedBy, and intervalEquals (which has no inverse).

Event

There's a whole chapter devoted to temporal modeling issues related to graphs and the Semantic Web. Temporal modeling can be tricky, and different domains have developed their own ways of modeling aspects of time. For example, the word circa has no utility in some domains, yet it helps to bound estimated time values in domains such as history and genealogy. That's why chapter 17 is entirely devoted to temporal modeling issues related to graphs and the Semantic Web. Meanwhile, there is one more small ontology that merits mention now, because it is so widely used, and that is the Event ontology (Figure 15.3). The Event ontology was developed for making statements about musical performances. Yet it has found its way into other ontologies and is probably the most popular ontology for expressing facts about various types of events, regardless of the domain. Event builds on several other ontologies, including Time, Geo, and FOAF. It has only three classes of its own: Event, Factor (which is anything used in an event), and Product (anything produced by an event). Here are some Event properties:

Domain	Property name	Range
Event	agent	FOAF:Agent
Event	factor	xs:string
Event	literal_factor	xs:string
Event	place	Geo:SpatialThing
Event	product	xs:string
Event	sub_event	Event
Event	time	Time:TemporalEntity

Provenance

Provenance ontologies are concerned with the who, what, and when regarding changes to data. Provenance has broad application in content authoring, software development, and management of research data. It overlaps with the concept of

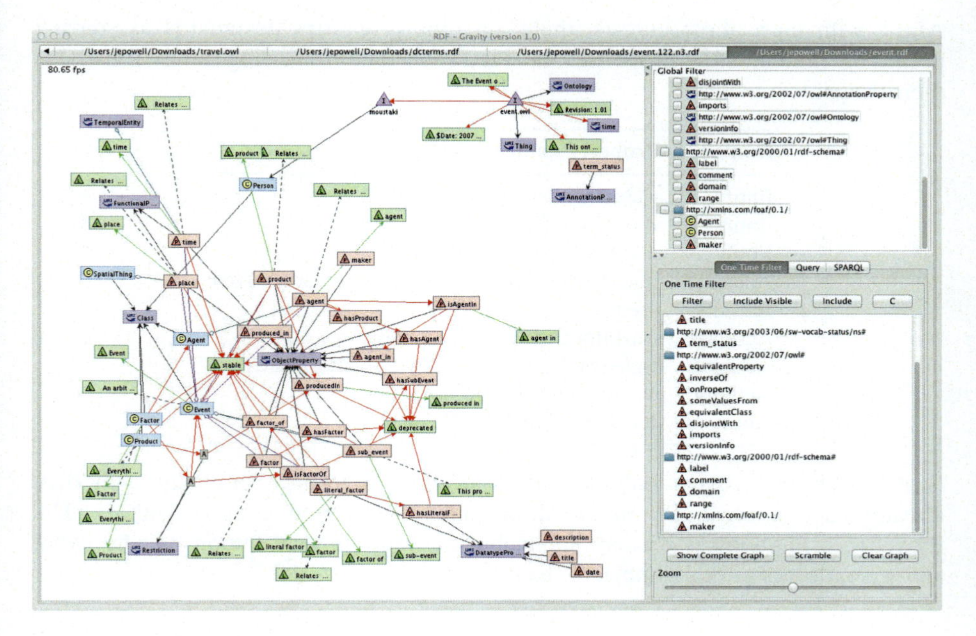

Figure 15.3 Visualization of the Event ontology.

versioning, which is especially familiar to software developers, since there are numerous tools to help with software version control, which is important to the software development life cycle as new features are added and software bugs are corrected. There can be slight overlap between provenance and instrumentation, time, and unit of measure ontologies, but provenance information tends to be more focused on describing aspects of a human-driven workflow and about documenting the changes to a thing over time. Another area that Provenance ontologies sometimes address is scientific workflows. With various workflows it is important to capture provenance information throughout a process.

The W3C PROV-O ontology became a recommendation in April 2013. The namespace for this ontology is http://www.w3.org/ns/prov# and the generally accepted prefix for referring to it in abbreviated form in serialized triples is prov. When introducing the Provenance ontology to new users, the creators group classes and properties into three categories: starting point, expanded, and qualified. Since the starting point classes and properties provide a nice introduction to the ontology and its purpose, we'll focus mainly on those.

The Provenance ontology defines three classes: Entity, Activity, and Agent. An entity is an object about which provenance data is being generated. It is the thing that some Agent is making changes to over time. An agent can be anything that can affect change to an entity, such as a person, a process, or a software application. An activity is something that happened or was done to an entity, things we might refer to as update, merger, add, or delete, for example.

Along with these three classes, there are nine properties designated as starting point, or fundamental properties in PROV-O. The following table illustrates their usage:

Domain	Property name	Range
Entity	wasGeneratedBy	Activity
Entity	wasDerivedFrom	Entity
Entity	wasAttributedTo	Agent
Activity	startedAtTime	XMLSchema#dateTime
Activity	used	Entity
Activity	wasInformedBy	Activity
Activity	endedAtTime	XMLSchmea#dateTime
Activity	wasAssociatedWith	Agent
Agent	actedOnBehalfOf	Agent

Although this covers only a portion of the Provenance ontology, you may already have a sense for the kind of things you could express with it. The Provenance ontology is broadly applicable for capturing attribution of who, what and when details as digital objects change over time.

Aggregations

Many intellectual products are collections of things. Books, journal issues, and data sets are examples of aggregations. A book contains chapters, a journal issue is made up of articles, and a data set might contain data sets arranged by time or locations. Object Reuse and Exchange ontology (ORE) is an ontology for representing aggregations of digital objects. ORE has a relationship to the Dublin Core Collection class by virtue of the fact that one of its core classes, Aggregation, is a subclass of the Collection class. ORE defines four classes: Aggregation, AggregatedResource, Proxy, and ResourceMap. The ORE Aggregation class identifies an aggregation of items and assigns it a unique identifier. AggregatedResource is an optional class that simply indicates an identified resource is part of an aggregation. The Proxy class represents an aggregated resource in the context of an Aggregation. For example, it is not uncommon for a poem or short story to appear in multiple anthologies. A thing identified as a Proxy class points at an aggregated resource (a poem) in a particular anthology. The Proxy identifier is used in various statements about the resource in the context of the aggregation, and is used to reference the resource outside the context of the aggregation (using proxyFor property). Finally, a ResourceMap is used to enumerate the members of the aggregation and it can provide other information about the aggregation such as relationships among the items in the aggregation, relationships to other resources and other aggregations, and metadata for the ResourceMap.

Domain	Property	Range
Aggregation	aggregates	AggregatedResource
AggregatedResource	isAggregatedBy	Aggregation
ResourceMap	describes	Aggregation
Aggregation	isDescribedBy	ResourceMap
Proxy	lineage	Proxy
Proxy	proxyFor	AggregatedResource
Proxy	proxyIn	Aggregation
Aggregation	similarTo	some resource URI

Data Sets

The Data Catalog vocabulary (DCAT) is used to describe various aspects of a set of scientific data. It makes no assumptions about the format of the data, so it can be used to describe spreadsheets, XML encoded data, CSV files, database contents, virtually any data that one wishes to characterize as a set and make statements about. DCAT is defined using RDF and RDFS. It is used in conjunction with an RDF vocabulary based on qualified Dublin Core (DCT) because the required terms to describe a data set overlap with general bibliographic metadata elements. DCAT has four classes: Catalog, DataSet, CatalogRecord, and Distribution. FOAF, SKOS, and DCT provide both properties and classes to compliment and complete a catalog description with concepts and concept scheme information represented with SKOS, publisher, homepage and topic from FOAF, and numerous metadata elements from Dublin Core serve as properties. For example, a dcat:Catalog class can have these Dublin Core properties: dct:title, dct:description, dct:issued, dct:modified, dct:language, dct:license, dct:rights, and dct:spatial. DCAT properties are listed below. In a few cases, the properties are subproperties of external vocabularies, and this is indicated in parentheses next to the property name:

Domain	Property	Range
dcat:Catalog	dcat:themeTaxonomy	skos:ConceptScheme
dcat:Catalog	(dct:hasPart)→dcat:dataset	dcat:Dataset
dcat:Catalog	dcat:record	dcat:CatalogRecord
dcat:Dataset	(dct:subject)→dcat:theme	skos:Concept
dcat:Dataset	dcat:keyword	rdfs:Literal
dcat:Dataset	dcat:contactPoint	vcard:Kind
dcat:Dataset	dcat:distribution	dcat:Distribution
dcat:Dataset	(foaf:page)→dcat:landingPage	foaf:Document
dcat:Distribution	dcat:accessURL	rdfs:Resource
dcat:Distribution	dcat:downloadURL	rdfs:Resource
dcat:Distribution	dcat:byteSize	xsd:decimal
dcat:Distribution	d(dct:format)→cat:mediaType	dct:MediaTypeOrExtent

Thesaurus

Simple Knowledge Organization System (SKOS) is a vocabulary for overlaying a formalized structure onto an existing concept space. In other words, it is an ontology you can use to convert existing thesauri or taxonomies to RDF, or create new ones. SKOS uses RDFS and OWL to define a container vocabulary for structured vocabularies. It defines a way to represent concepts and the relationships between them in a knowledge domain. You could use SKOS to convert a dictionary, thesaurus, or subject headings into triples. Although it is widely used in library RDF data, it can be applied to concepts in any knowledge domain. SKOS is used to express semantic relations (relationship between words based on their meaning), lexical labels (characters used to represent a term), concept schemes (rudimentary description of the overarching relationship among terms), mappings (clues as to how to map between concept schemes), and administrative data such as definitions, examples, and notes. The SKOS classes are Concept, ConceptScheme, Collection, and OrderedCollection. Here's an SKOS example that defines a concept—a type of tree and some of its taxonomic context:

```
Gymnosperm:Agathis rdf:type skos:Concept.
Gymnosperm:Agathis skos:preferredLabel "Kauri"@en;
    skos:atLabel "dammar"@en;
    skos:altLabel "Kauri pine"@en;
    skos:definition "Any tree of the genus Agathis. Fossils of Agathis have
    been found in fossil beds dating back to the Jurassic period. These trees
    are native to New Zealand, Australia, Indonesia, and New Guinea. They
    are among the largest and most long lived trees in the world.";
    skos:inScheme Gymnosperm:trees;
    skos:broaderTerm Gymnosperm:Araucariaceae;
    skos:narrowerTerm Gymnosperm:AgathisAustralis.
```

Here is a comprehensive list of SKOS properties, organized by their use:

- Properties related to ConceptScheme:

  inScheme, hasTopConcept, topConceptOf

- Properties related to lexical characteristics of a Concept:

  prefLabel, altLabel, hiddenLabel, notation

- Administrative details about an instance of any skos class:

  note, changeNote, definition, editorialNote, example, historyNote, scopeNote

- Semantic relationships between Concept classes:

  semanticRelation, broader, narrower, related, broaderTransitive, narrowerTransitive

- Properties applicable to Collection, OrderedCollection class:

  member, memberList

- Mapping between ConceptScheme:

  mappingRelation, closeMatch, exactMatch, broadMatch, narrowMatch, relatedMatch

Measurements

Another group of upper level ontologies that have broad applications in science are unit and measurement ontologies. Some of these tend to be related to or part of sensor or instrument ontologies. These tend to be applicable in hard sciences like biology, chemistry, astronomy, physics, and in other areas where observations are logged and archived (Figure 15.3).

The Quantities, Dimensions, Units, Values (QDUV) model was developed to enable very precise description of measurements. It was developed as part of the Systems Modeling Language by the Object Management Group which works to define and publish open technology standards. This ontology can be used to describe the units of measurement employed in scientific data sets. There is an ontological representation of QDUV with the namespace http://purl.oclc.org/NET/ssnx/qu/qu. QDUV deals with measurement as a concept domain. That means, it doesn't tell you what a mile, gram, or liter is, instead it lets you semantically represent various aspects of such measures which you can then reference from contexts where you have used them, such as observations or scientific data sets. Because it is quite detailed, and perhaps comfortingly precise, it is one of the larger upper ontologies include here, with 21 classes and 33 properties. Since it is so large, we will give you a sense for how it works and what it concerns itself with, and you can review the entire ontology using the namespace URI above. The QDUV documentation separates aspects of the ontology into modules Data, Unit, Scale, Quantity, and Dimension. There are no corresponding classes for these modules; they are just logical groupings of QDUV classes and properties. A companion ontology to QUDV is Quantities, Units, Dimensions, and Types. It illustrates how the classes and properties in QDUV can be used to develop an increasingly specific taxonomy of measurements by specifying subclasses of QDUV elements. http://qudt.org/schema/qudt.

Geospatial

It has been suggested that if you know the time and place that something happened, then you have everything you need to uniquely identify that event. Day to day, these are the dimensions that are most important to most of us as we go about our lives. And they are important in many domains. Birth time and place is a crucial piece of information in genealogy. Landing time and place can ensure the success or failure of a robotic mission to another planet. Credit card companies use time and place to track charges and detect fraud. So we end this chapter with a tour of a few spatial ontologies that deal with "where."

We close with a review of three spatial ontologies. These are used to represent geographic and spatial information semantically. Two of these (Geonames, WGS84) are Earth centric, meaning they are concerned with coordinate systems or locations on Earth. With the classes and properties in these ontologies, you can make a variety of statements about the location of and spatial relationships among things.

Geonames

Geonames publishes an aggregated collection of location information about places around the world. The information is all in the public domain and so it is made freely available in a variety of formats. It is also part of the linked data Web. There is a corresponding geonames ontology which facilitated the publication of this data. The geonames namespace is http://www.geonames.org/ontology#. This ontology can be used to reference or describe places. Some parts of this ontology really only have applications within the context of the geonames data itself, so we won't spend much time on it. Classes of interest include Feature and Code, where feature is vaguely defined as a "geographic feature." If you're familiar with the geonames data set, you know this can include cities, towns, states, rivers, lakes, mountains, and a variety of other named geographic entities. Features can be organized into classes of features, which somewhat confusingly, are of class Class. Code is a subclass of SKOS Concept and refers to the feature code system employed by geonames. Feature codes are 2-4 digit abbreviations that represent things like airports (AIRP), streams (STMS), railroad (RR), and a host of other natural and manmade features. A few properties you may want to consider as you link to geonames data include featureClass, featureCode, locatedIn, nearby, name, historicalName, and geonamesID (which can be used for linking). All of these properties have the domain of class Feature. In many cases, it may be sufficient to simply reference the geonamesID of an identifier that serves as an entry point into their collection of triples about a place. Below is an IRI for New Zealand that targets a Geonames semantic service, and the RDF/XML it returns:

http://sws.geonames.org/2186224/about.rdf

```
<rdf:RDF xmlns:cc="http://creativecommons.org/ns#"
xmlns:dcterms="http://purl.org/dc/terms/" xmlns:foaf="http://xmlns.com/foaf/0.1/"
xmlns:gn="http://www.geonames.org/ontology#"
xmlns:owl="http://www.w3.org/2002/07/owl#" xmlns:rdf="http://www.w3.org/1999/02/22-
rdf-syntax-ns#" xmlns:rdfs="http://www.w3.org/2000/01/rdf-schema#"
xmlns:wgs84_pos="http://www.w3.org/2003/01/geo/wgs84_pos#">
  <gn:Feature rdf:about="http://sws.geonames.org/2186224/">
  <rdfs:isDefinedBy rdf:resource="http://sws.geonames.org/2186224/about.rdf"/>
  <gn:name>New Zealand</gn:name>
  <gn:countryCode>NZ</gn:countryCode>
  <gn:population>4252277</gn:population>
  <wgs84_pos:lat>-42</wgs84_pos:lat>
  <wgs84_pos:long>174</wgs84_pos:long>
  <gn:parentFeature rdf:resource="http://sws.geonames.org/6255151/"/>
  <gn:locationMap rdf:resource="http://www.geonames.org/2186224/new-zealand.html"/>
  <gn:wikipediaArticle rdf:resource="http://en.wikipedia.org/wiki/New_Zealand"/>
  <rdfs:seeAlso rdf:resource="http://dbpedia.org/resource/New_Zealand"/>
</rdf:RDF>
```

WGS84

World Geodetic System 1984 (WGS84) is an ontology for classes and properties associated with the coordinate system defined by this standard. Its namespace is http://www.w3.org/2003/01/geo/wgs84_pos#. The WGS84 coordinate system is used by GPS systems to identify places on Earth. The ontology is defined in RDFS and is quite small. There are four classes: SpatialThing, TemporalThing, Event, and Point. The ontology also defines a set of data properties for specifying a location (see geonames RDF example above for examples of WGS84 properties used in triples):

Domain	Property	Range
SpatialThing	lat	xs:decimal
TemporalThing	time	XMLSchema#dateTime
SpatialThing	location	SpatialThing
SpatialThing	long	xs:decimal
SpatialThing	alt	xs:decimal

Spatial

The Spatial ontology was developed and is published by Great Britain's national mapping agency, called Ordnance Survey. It deals with spatial relationships among any existing thing that can have a location. It defines a small set of simple and readily comprehensible object properties which all share the same domain and range, SpatialObject, which is a class from the GeoSPARQL ontology. The GeoSPARQL ontology is a very generic ontology for referencing spatial features that overlaps or is incorporated into the spatial ontologies we've already covered. All you need to know about that ontology to understand the spatial ontology is that a SpatialObject is the class of anything that can have a spatial representation.

Domain	Property	Range
SpatialObject	containedBy	SpatialObject
SpatialObject	contains	SpatialObject
SpatialObject	disjoint	SpatialObject
SpatialObject	equals	SpatialObject
SpatialObject	touches	SpatialObject
SpatialObject	partialOverlaps	SpatialObject
SpatialObject	within	SpatialObject

Library metadata ontologies

16

Where are the books?

For centuries, a library was thought of as a place that contained books organized in some fashion with the goal of facilitating knowledge discovery and sharing. This notion is enshrined in the various words used in different languages to refer to a library. In the romance languages, the word for library incorporates the root of a Greek word for book which is *biblion*. Thus in Italian and Spanish, a library is called *biblioteca*, while in French, it is essentially the same word: *bibliotheque*. Japanese and Chinese kanji for library are similar in form and consist of two characters that together means "books" or "documents" and a third which means building or place: *toshokan* or *tushuguan*. In Arabic, the word for book is *kitabu*. This word serves as the root for other words related to books, including the Arabic word for library, which is *makitaba*.

Human knowledge has been captured in books, papyrus, scrolls, stamped clay tablets as ideograms, that is, images that represent discrete concepts, and in phonetic alphabets which preserve the spoken word. These are the two primary writing systems we know of, both of which are in use today. There may well have been others as evidenced by enigmatic carvings and petroglyphs found in the American southwest, for example. There have certainly been languages in human history for which no system of writing was devised. Now, books, articles, databases, and other sources of information are being deconstructed. Bits and pieces of data are being interconnected in ways that weren't previously possible, and at a level of granularity that hasn't been attempted on such a large scale before in history.

An individual graph segment is a pretty simple construct. It's not difficult to write a triple and add to the graph. Presumably there is a collective belief, or hope, that the resulting network of knowledge will have value, perhaps even hope that it will exhibit some unanticipated emergent properties as we find uses for the graph. After all, there's no central authority, just a few simple rules. But like an ant moving a grain of sand, do we know what it will become? Will it become a new language? A new way of communicating? A vast memory for a yet-to-be built artificial super-intelligence? Is this Semantic Web thing a crowd-sourced Manhattan Project for information technology? Are we collectively building the Artificial Intelligence equivalent of a hydrogen bomb?

It wouldn't be the first time that a graph model led to a seismic shift in our lives. Not the second, not even the third. In just the last 20 years, two examples come to mind. You could think of Google search as the consequent to the antecedent of the World Wide Web. The Web is a vast directed graph, a worldwide network of content and services. Google modeled this graph, used the relationships among its nodes to rank Web pages, hid this immense complexity behind an input field and a button, and forever changed how we seek information.

It's ironic that a network model for online exploration challenged the libraries' supremacy. Libraries had been building information discovery networks before anyone else. The problem was, some of these networks tended to be scale free, and users were getting lost in the long tail. The information users needed to find an item were the nodes that had relatively few connections, or worse yet, didn't exist at all. If a cataloger didn't create an authority record for a concept, the concept may as well not exist.

In libraries, metadata is a first-class object. Metadata doesn't just describe a library resource, it also connects that resource to entities such as people, places, events, and to other resources. Existing metadata formats don't necessarily hide this network, they're just awkward at representing it. RDF promotes these relationships to first-class objects. In this chapter, we'll look at some vocabularies for library metadata, and some projects that have pioneered the migration of bibliographic metadata and authority data onto the Semantic Web.

Migrating descriptions of library resources to RDF

Dublin Core

To date, most bibliographic Semantic Web efforts are based on Dublin Core and Dublin Core Terms vocabularies, which are basic taxonomies defined using XML schema and RDFS. DCTerms has properties, classes, and subclasses, but lacks richer logical characteristics and relationships which could be defined using OWL. These metadata standards were developed to facilitate simple data exchange such as via OAI-PMH, and they were intended to be used by nonlibrarians who, it was thought, would use them to embed basic metadata into their Web pages. Early Semantic Web adopters repurposed them for use with RDF. They used DC elements as properties for RDF representations of mapped metadata.

The Library of Congress publishes an XSLT stylesheet that will transform a MARC XML file into an XML representation that was close to an RDF/XML representation. The transformation uses most of the 15 original Dublin Core metadata elements. Many who were concerned with cataloging and the quality of metadata were alarmed at Dublin Core, and the lossy MARC to DC mappings that were used by various projects, including Semantic Web projects.

Dublin Core was conceived of as a simple metadata model that could be used by the masses to embed supplemental discovery information into Web pages, and as a lowest common denominator exchange model between object repositories. A richer model was subsequently developed called the DCMI Abstract Model or qualified Dublin Core, which is another product of the Dublin Core metadata initiative. It incorporates the original 15 Dublin Core metadata elements as properties and goes on to define a formal RDF representation for a more detailed metadata vocabulary. As you are already familiar with Dublin Core since we covered it earlier, there are aspects of this vocabulary which will be familiar to you. The original 15 elements are often referenced in various other ontologies and even in OWL vocabulary specifications by their original Dublin Core XML schema namespace (Figure 16.1).

The original 15 element set was subsumed by an ontology that defined a larger Dublin Core vocabulary for the Semantic Web, called dcterms. Dcterms expands on Dublin Core and provides an ontological description of the expanded metadata version of this metadata encoding standard. The existing 15 elements actually became properties in dcterms, thus solidifying their common use in the Semantic Web as predicates. An additional 39 properties were added which in many cases represent refinements of the original 15 elements. The dcterms ontology has 21 classes of objects which these properties can be used to annotate. The classes for dcterms are:

> *Agent, AgentClass, BibliographicResource, FileFormat, Frequency, Jurisdiction, LicenseDocument, LinguisticSystem, Location, LocationPeriodOrJurisdiction, MediaType, MediaTypeOrExtent, MethodOfAccrual, MethodOfInstruction, PeriodOfTime, PhysicalMedium, PhysicalResource, Policy, ProvenanceStatement, RightsStatement, SizeOrDuration, Standard*

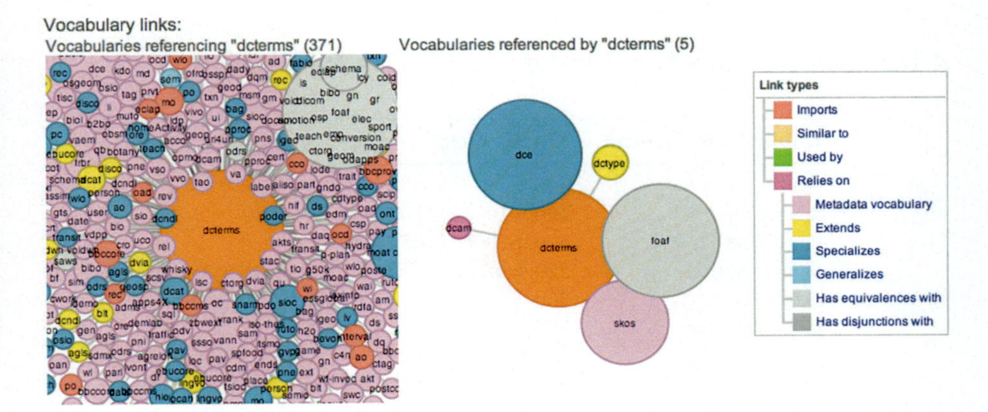

Vocabulary used in **327** datasets (information coming from LOD Stats project)

Occurrences	Dataset
50035396	jiscopenbib-bl
26346007	hebis-bibliographic-resources.315.rdf
19503702	hebis-bibliographic-resources.241.rdf
12476820	hebis-bibliographic-resources.132.rdf
9141736	b3kat.241.rdf
See the full list...	

Figure 16.1 Dublin Core Terms vocabulary overview from http://lov.okfn.org/.

MARC and the Semantic Web

There's a lot of data in a MARC record. If you have a way to convert or already have XML representations of your MARC data, you can use an extensible stylesheet transformation to extract some of the data from a MARC record and map it into an RDF that uses the 15 original Dublin Core metadata elements as predicates. Library of Congress publishes an XSLT stylesheet that will transform a MARC XML file into an RDF/XML file which uses the 15 Dublin Core metadata elements. It's a path from MARC to the Semantic Web but the data conversion is lossy, and the resulting RDF graph is pretty skimpy on details and relationships.

The goals of mapping bibliographic metadata to the Semantic web are to make the data open, integrate it with linked data, and to facilitate alternate forms of resource and information discovery. Depending upon the tools that are built to explore this data, RDF can be a good way of recapturing some of the serendipitous discovery that was possible in physical libraries and other catalog systems, all the way back to the card catalog. The card catalog lent itself to browsing. You could flip to adjacent cards and they might give you an idea of other relevant resources, albeit in a very limited fashion. Likewise, when you went to the shelves to look for a physical item, you could scan the shelf for related items.

Today, browsing is almost forgotten. Library systems may support it, but the user has been trained by systems like Google that search is the way to find something. If a search fails, then the user will try another. Depending on their query formulation skills, they may arrive at a results set. In the Google world, once you have some results, the assumption is typically that you have all of the results you need. It's almost never true. And the results set itself is a static, neglected entity. There's usually no effort to provide any sort of context for the results. Semantically mapped bibliographic data can be used to augment search with reasonable suggestions, to provide context for results sets, and to provide links out into the linked data Web. In this model, bibliographic metadata becomes embedded into a larger distributed, crowd-sourced knowledge representation environment, with all the risks and rewards such an environment provides.

A Library of Congress mapping of MARC to Dublin Core

Dublin Core Element	MARC Field
dc:title	245
dc:creator	100, 110, 111, 700, 710, 711, 720
dc:subject	600, 610, 611, 630, 650, 653
dc:description	520 subfield a, 521 subfield a, other 5xx
dc:publisher	260
dc:contributor	N/A
dc:date	260 subfield c
dc:type	From MARC leader, 655
dc:format	856 subfield q

(*Continued*)

(Continued)

Dublin Core Element	MARC Field
dc:identifier	856 subfield u, 020 subfield a
dc:source	N/A
dc:language	Control field 008,36,3
dc:relation	760, 762,765, 767, 770, 772, 773, 774, 775, 776, 777, 780, 785, 786, 787
dc:coverage	752, several subfields of
dc:rights	506 subfield a, 540 subfield a

The OCLC Schema Model

Both OCLC and the Library of Congress are interested in increasing the visibility of library resources in major search engines, and in the Web of Linked Open Data. Both organizations have been exploring potential uses for Semantic Web technologies for a few years. One of OCLC's more public efforts has been to develop a model for bibliographic information based heavily on classes and properties from Schema.org.

Schema.org is a set of schemas that Web masters can use to add useful metadata to their Web pages. When it's embedded in a Web page, it's usually represented as RDF using the RDFa serialization, which is embedded in the HTML of a Web document. Schema.org was created with the goal of establishing vocabularies to describe entities such as people, places, movies, and restaurants. Some key classes related to bibliographic metadata include CreativeWork, Event, Organization, Person, and Place. There are many subclasses associated with these core classes. Book, Article, DataCatalog, DataSet, MediaObject, Movie, MusicRecording SoftwareApplication, and WebPage are all subclasses of the CreativeWork class. Many of these classes have child classes that more specifically identify an entity. Many search engines including Google and Yahoo! extract and store this metadata so that it can be incorporated into results pages to give users more and better information for evaluating and selecting items from search results.

Schema.org has attracted quite a bit of attention in the library community. It is a shallow, easy to use vocabulary that covers a variety of topics and offers a rich collection of properties which can be associated with the various entity classes it defines. It also has support from the private sector. In a report that compared the BIBFRAME effort to the OCLC Schema Model based on schema.org, OCLC explained their motivation for considering this vocabulary:

> *OCLC researchers have tried to make the case that Schema.org is a suitable foundation for the description of library resources. The most important argument is that the library community cannot afford to ignore Schema.org because it has been defined by Google, Yahoo!, Bing and Yandex to be the standard of choice for the publication of structured data and intelligent consumption of web resources that the major search engines commit to recognizing.*

Motivated to use open community and industry supported standards, they investigated Schema.org and found that

> *the [Schema.org] ontology defines a reasonably coherent commonsense model with classes and properties that are important for simple descriptions of bibliographic resources managed by libraries—including* creative work, person, author, director, place, organization, publisher, copyright date, book, ISBN, *and so on. These concepts can be serialized in a variety of forms and are compatible with the modeling philosophy promoted by the Semantic Web community.*

OCLC's RDF model for bibliographic metadata makes extensive use of schema.org classes and properties. OCLC developed an experimental "library" extension vocabulary that extended schema.org entities to accommodate more descriptive information for library holdings. This vocabulary add a few properties and a number of new classes, including:

> *Carrier, ComputerFile, Game, Image, InteractiveMultimedia, MusicalScore, Newspaper, Periodical, Thesis, Video, VideoGame, VisualMaterial, WebSite*

OCLC has been working on several fronts related to Schema.org and BIBFRAME. They have been working through a W3C community, "Schema Bib Extend" to share ideas for enhancing Schema.org support for describing library content, such as elements contained in their experimental library extension vocabulary. They have also proposed some steps that could be undertaken to better align the OCLC Schema Model with the Library of Congress' major Semantic Web project, called BIBFRAME.

BIBFRAME

Many decades after its invention, most library catalogs are still based on MARC records. As XML became increasingly important for representing data for archiving and exchange, an XML schema was developed for MARC. This schema faithfully mapped MARC elements to XML tags and attributes. Unlike some vocabularies encoded in XML, MARC XML is utterly unsuitable for use in RDF graphs. Could you imagine using <marc:650> as a predicate in a triple?

MARC and Dublin Core are not native Semantic Web vocabularies. Indeed MARC seems uniquely ill-suited for use in the Semantic Web. The Semantic Web is a graph model, not a record oriented model. That's why the Library of Congress has been working for several years on an RDF model for describing library resources called BIBFRAME (http://bibframe.org).

BIBFRAME is intended to eventually replace MARC as a standard for library metadata. It consists of four core classes: Creative works, Instances, Authorities, and Annotations. There is a single BIBFRAME vocabulary, which defines these entities and their properties. There are also lots of white papers and slideshare presentations about BIBFRAME. But the best way to get a sense for how it works

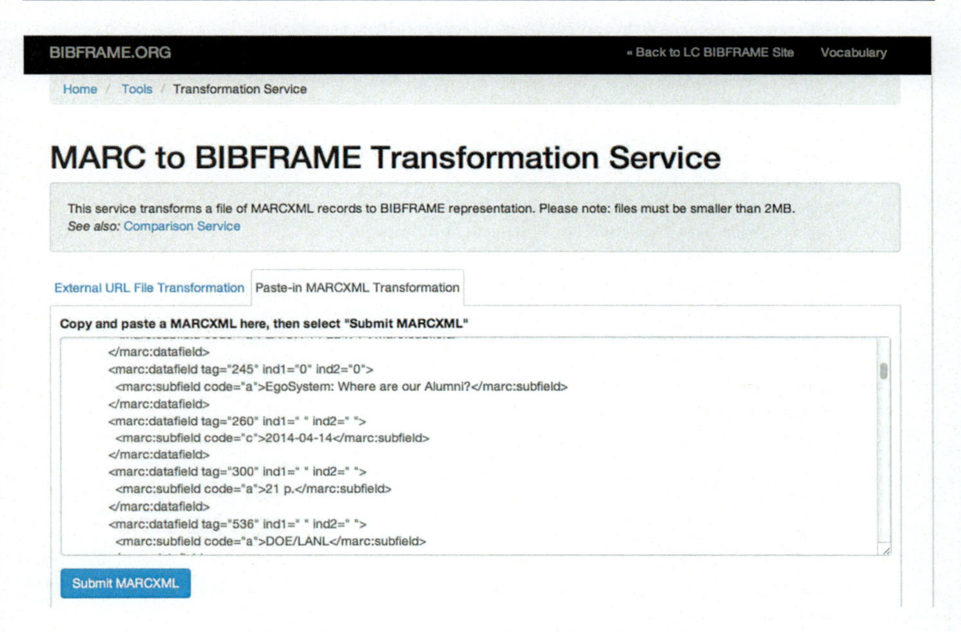

Figure 16.2 Library of Congress' MARC to BIBFRAME transformation tool.

is to see how it transforms and represents actual metadata. The Library of Congress anticipated this and they created an opensource tool which can transform MARC/XML to BIBFRAME RDF. There are several versions of this tool, including one based on XQuery and one written in Python, which are freely available on GitHub. They host a Web-accessible version of the tool into which you can paste MARC/XML for conversion at http://bibframe.org/tools/transform/start (Figure 16.2).

We tested the tool with a MARC/XML record to see how its contents would be mapped to RDF. There's no question that BIBFRAME provides a vastly more descriptive model for library resources than what could be achieved by mapping elements into Dublin Core. The tool, and the BIBFRAME vocabulary, seemed to do a terrific job of preserving all of the MARC data in RDF. Some excerpts of the BIBFRAME RDF are included below, starting with an excerpt which illustrates the Work and Instance classes. The original source data was MARC/XML which described a paper published in the journal Code4Lib (Figure 16.3):

```
<bf:Work xmlns:bf="http://bibframe.org/vocab/" ...>
...
  <bf:title>Journal Code4Lib</bf:title>
  <bf:authorizedAccessPoint>Journal Code4Lib</bf:authorizedAccessPoint>
</bf:Work>
<bf:Instance   ...   rdf:about="http://bibframe.org/resources/qwX1416863487/LA-UR-14-22471instance28">
```

```
    <rdf:type rdf:resource="http://bibframe.org/vocab/Monograph"/>
    <bf:instanceTitle    rdf:resource="http://bibframe.org/resources/qwX1416863487/LA-UR-14-
         22471title31"/>
    <bf:publication>
      <bf:Provider>
         <bf:copyrightDate>2014-04-14</bf:copyrightDate>
      </bf:Provider>
    </bf:publication>
    <bf:modeOfIssuance>single unit</bf:modeOfIssuance>
    <bf:extent>21 p.</bf:extent>
    <bf:titleStatement>EgoSystem: Where are our Alumni?</bf:titleStatement>
    <bf:providerStatement>2014-04-14</bf:providerStatement>
    <bf:note>DOE/LANL</bf:note>
...
    <bf:reportNumber>
      <bf:Identifier>
         <bf:identifierScheme>reportNumber</bf:identifierScheme>
         <bf:identifierValue>LA-UR-14-22471</bf:identifierValue>
       </bf:Identifier>
    </bf:reportNumber>
    <bf:derivedFrom rdf:resource="http://bibframe.org/resources/qwX1416863487/LA-UR-14-22471.
          marcxml.xml"/>
    <bf:instanceOf rdf:resource="http://bibframe.org/resources/qwX1416863487/LA-UR-14-22471"/>
  </bf:Instance>
```

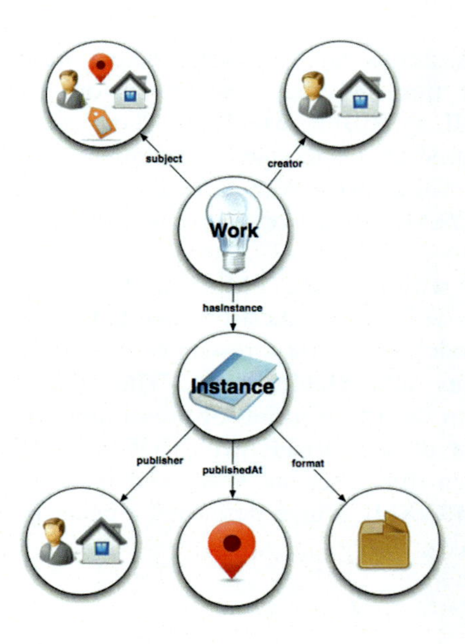

Figure 16.3 The BIBFRAME model.
Source: Library of Congress. <http://commons.wikimedia.org/wiki/File:BIBFRAME_model.png>.

Here is an RDF/XML excerpt from BIBFRAME related to Authority information for an author's name. Note how MADS vocabulary elements are used with BIBFRAME elements:

```
<bf:Person xmlns:bf="http://bibframe.org/vocab/"
xmlns:rdfs="http://www.w3.org/2000/01/rdf-schema#"
xmlns:madsrdf="http://www.loc.gov/mads/rdf/v1#"
xmlns:relators="http://id.loc.gov/vocabulary/relators/"
rdf:about="http://bibframe.org/resources/qwX1416863487/LA-UR-14-22471person7">
    <bf:label>Powell, James E. Jr.</bf:label>
    <bf:authorizedAccessPoint>Powell, James E. Jr.</bf:authorizedAccessPoint>
    <bf:hasAuthority>
      <madsrdf:Authority>
        <madsrdf:authoritativeLabel>Powell, James E. Jr.</madsrdf:authoritativeLabel>
      </madsrdf:Authority>
    </bf:hasAuthority>
  </bf:Person>
```

Both BIBFRAME and the OCLC Schema Model show great promise. The most exciting aspect of these two projects is that it is apparent that the people behind the efforts really get it. These are genuine efforts to reimagine how to represent and share descriptions of library resources. Just as exciting are the models for authority data, which have even broader applications in the Semantic Web, since so much effort went into matching and disambiguating these entities. The Semantic Web would benefit tremendously if these became part of the Web of Linked Open Data. Anything that can be done to make descriptions of library resources and authority data more widely available will be good for libraries, for library patrons, and for anyone seeking quality information sources on the World Wide Web.

Pioneering Semantic Web projects in libraries

If you want to make use of and contribute to the Web of Linked Open Data, look at some pioneering efforts. The British Library, which is the national library of the United Kingdom, has undertaken an ambitious effort to map MARC data into RDF. We'll look briefly at some of the ontologies and linked data sources they've used. Then we'll look at a project out of University of California at San Diego (UCSD) which relies heavily on a homegrown ontology to represent its data as triples. Both efforts are well-documented projects that have elected to share their design documents and various other materials that describe the projects. The British Library additionally provides their complete collection of data for download in various RDF serialization formats including RDF/XML, N-Triples, and Turtle.

The British Library

The British Library, which is the national library of the United Kingdom, publishes RDF that represents 2.8 million bibliographic records described by over 9 million triples and made this data set available in the public domain. They provide a detailed overview of how they mapped MARC into RDF. Beyond that, they publish exhaustive models of how they describe a book and a serial publication using RDF. Their models use a variety of existing ontologies. Here is a complete list of the ontologies used in the British Library model to describe a book:

British Library Terms	<http://www.bl.uk/schemas/bibliographic/blterms#>
Dublin Core Terms	<http://purl.org/dc/terms/>
ISBD	<http://iflastandards.info/ns/isbd/elements/>
SKOS	<http://www.w3.org/2004/02/skos/core#>
BIBO	<http://purl.org/ontology/bibo/>
RDA	<http://rdvocab.info/ElementsGr2/>
BIO	<http://purl.org/vocab/bio/0.1/>
FOAF	<http://xmlns.com/foaf/0.1/>
Event	<http://purl.org/NET/c4dm/event.owl#>
Org	<http://www.w3.org/ns/org#>
WGS84	<http://www.w3.org/2003/01/geo/wgs84_pos#>

We've reviewed many of these ontologies in the previous chapters, as they have broad application in a variety of Semantic Web contexts. But several are specific to library data. The International Standard Bibliographic Description (ISBD) is an RDF vocabulary for a set of rules for organizing and describing an item. The Bibliographic Ontology (BIBO) is a vocabulary for describing citations and bibliographic references. The Biographical ontology (BIO) is an extensive vocabulary for describing biographical data regarding people. RDA is a vocabulary based on a set of cataloging rules called Resource Description and Access. RDA vocabularies were originally organized into groupings, and RDA group 2 is concerned with people and corporate entities. RDA relates to another standard, an abstract data model called FRBR (Functional Requirements for Bibliographic Records), which is concerned with modeling search and access of bibliographic data from a user's perspective. In other words, patron use cases guide this particular model, rather than the metadata the users interact with. Finally, there's the British Library Terms ontology, which is a small homegrown ontology that provides some classes and properties that were not reflected in any of the other ontologies they used:

	Classes
PublicationEvent	subclass of an Event:Event
PublicationStartEvent	subclass of an Event:Event
PublicationEndEvent	subclass of an Event:Event
FamilyTopicDDC	Dewey Decimal Classification (DDC) number
TopicLCSH	Library of Congress Subject Heading (LCSH)
PersonConcept	SKOS Concept subclass for Person
OrganizationConcept	SKOS Concept subclass for an Organization
FamilyConcept	SKOS Concept subclass for for a family
PlaceConcept	SKOS Concept subclass for for a place
	Properties
bnb	British National Bibliography Number
hasCreated	inverse of dcterms:creator
hasContributedTo	inverse of dcterms:contributor
publication	has range PublicationEvent
publicationStart	has range PublicationStartEvent
publicationEnd	has range PublicationEndEvent

The British Library provides more documentation about their data model, links to the ontologies they use, and links for downloading their data sets at http://www.bl.uk/bibliographic/datafree.html.

UCSD Library Digital Asset Management System

The UCSD Library system developed an RDF-based application called the Digital Asset Management System, or DAMS. A major difference between the British Library effort and DAMS is that DAMS is concerned with born digital content. Their model revolves around three core classes: Object, Component, and Collection. A Component is a means to subdivide an Object. An Object or a Component can be associated with a File class, which, as the name implies, describes a stored electronic manifestation of a digital asset. DAMS allows descriptive metadata to be associated with instances of the core classes, and this metadata is modeled after MODS: the Metadata Object Description Standard, from the Library of Congress.

MODS has the following top level elements, which should give you a sense for what it is concerned with describing:

abstract, accessCondition, classification, extension, genre, identifier, language, location, name, note, originInfo, part, physicalDescription, recordInfo, relatedItem, subject, tableOfContents, targetAudience, titleInfo, typeOfResource

UCSD developed an extensive homegrown ontology (also called DAMS) to represent their data model. DAMS is based heavily on MODS, but at the time UCSD started this project, there was no MODS ontology. The DAMS project uses an ontology for authority data called Metadata Authority Description Schema (MADS) for representing subject and person authority data. MADS (http://www.loc.gov/standards/mads/rdf/) is used by the Library of Congress in conjunction with SKOS to represent authority data that they make available through a prototype linked data service at id.loc.gov.

Here is a MADS geographic authority example:

```
<madsrdf:Geographic rdf:about="http://id.loc.gov/authorities/sh85072887"
xmlns:madsrdf="http://www.loc.gov/mads/rdf/v1#">
  <rdf:type rdf:resource="http://www.loc.gov/mads/rdf/v1#Variant"/>
  <rdf:type rdf:resource="http://www.loc.gov/mads/rdf/v1#DeprecatedAuthority"/>
  <madsrdf:variantLabel xml:lang="en">Kona (Hawaii Island, Hawaii)</madsrdf:variantLabel>
  <madsrdf:elementList rdf:parseType="Collection">
    <madsrdf:GeographicElement>
      <madsrdf:elementValue>Kona (Hawaii Island, Hawaii)</madsrdf:elementValue>
    </madsrdf:GeographicElement>
  </madsrdf:elementList>
  <madsrdf:useInstead>
    <madsrdf:Geographic rdf:about="http://id.loc.gov/authorities/names/n2010027753">
            <rdf:type rdf:resource="http://www.loc.gov/mads/rdf/v1#Authority"/>
      <madsrdf:authoritativeLabel xml:lang="en">Kona (Hawaii :
District)</madsrdf:authoritativeLabel>
    </madsrdf:Geographic>
  </madsrdf:useInstead>
  <madsrdf:isMemberOfMADSScheme
rdf:resource="http://id.loc.gov/authorities/lcsh"/>
  <madsrdf:isMemberOfMADSCollection
rdf:resource="http://id.loc.gov/authorities/collection_LCSH_General"/>
  <owl:sameAs rdf:resource="info:lc/authorities/sh85072887"
xmlns:owl="http://www.w3.org/2002/07/owl#"/>
```

More information about the UCSD DAMS data model and ontology is available at their github site: https://github.com/ucsdlib/dams/tree/master/ontology.

Linked data services

OCLC provides an authority data service called the Virtual International Authority File (VIAF). VIAF provides comprehensive access to the world's major name authority files. Triples associated with individual authority entries can be downloaded as RDF. Some VIAF data is available for bulk download as linked data (http://viaf.org/viaf/data/). OCLC also provides a tool called "Linked Data Explorer" for Worldcat (http://oclc.org/developer/develop/linked-data/linked-data-exploration.en.html). This tool returns RDF for URIs that point to entries in Worldcat. If you access an OCLC Worldcat URI through a Web browser, a stylesheet is applied to generate a Web page. RDF serializations include Turtle, N-triple, JSON-LD, and RDF/XML.

- http://schema.org/Article
- http://schema.org/Book
- http://schema.org/CreativeWork
- http://schema.org/Enumeration
- http://schema.org/Event
- http://schema.org/Map
- http://schema.org/MusicRecording
- http://schema.org/Organization
- http://schema.org/Person
- http://schema.org/Place
- http://schema.org/Review
- http://schema.org/Thing

OCLC also supports an experimental linked data service that maps the Dewey Decimal Classification system into resolvable URIs which return linked data of details for each classification as well as the divisions within a classification. The service is at http://dewey.info.

The Library of Congress provides a variety of linked data authority and vocabulary services at http://id.loc.gov. Authority collections include LC Children's Subject Headings, LC Genre/Form Terms, LC Name Authority, LC Medium of Performance Thesaurus for Music, and LC Subject Headings. Vocabularies include an ethnographic thesaurus, cultural heritage organizations, and vocabularies related to languages and geographic regions. You perform a search against a collection and you can download the RDF data associated with an authority entry. There are also bulk downloads available at http://id.loc.gov/download/.

Where to go from here?

Leverage the graph topology

Studies show that people are good at finding paths through small-world networks. Yet, when we organize data, we tend to favor hierarchical trees. There are relatively few top level nodes, and more nodes with fewer connections as specificity increases. Small-world networks have only two requirements: local regularity and random shortcuts. How might a subject heading graph be reconstructed as a small-world network? First, reduce the hierarchical relationships in the graph and build connections directly among related terms. Then, use the concepts that are common to multiple disciplines to build shortcuts between clusters. This will decrease the path length through the network.

Incorporate graph visualizations

There are a wealth of lightweight tool kits for presenting graphs on the Web. In a later chapter we'll explore some specific toolkits. The challenge isn't drawing graphs on the Web, but rather making a determination about what portion of a graph to show a user. There are also many information visualizations that use graph-based data, but represent it in such a way that it no longer looks like a graph. A Sankey diagram is one example. One way it is typically used is to illustrate the volume and flow of information through a system over time. In fact, it is ideal for rendering graph data, but it is unrecognizable as a graph. You can also use graph analytics to highlight particular aspects of the graph that might be of interest.

Use inferencing

Inferencing uses the logical structure of statements to deduce new information. Inferencing over descriptions of library resources could aide in a variety of user interactions. From a basic initial keyword query, a reasoner could suggest potential query refinements based on what it found in the graph. Semantically enhanced search has existed for a long time in various forms. Linked Open Data provides a wealth of opportunities for inferencing over RDF representations of library resource metadata. This inferencing could occur at query time, or it could be an ongoing process which uses big data technologies to explore large amounts of data and continually infer new facts.

Use rules and reasoning

In Artificial Intelligence, building an expert system has been a long-standing goal. An expert system would accept questions as input and use custom sets of rules to deduce what information might be relevant. With Semantic Web data, a great deal of knowledge has already been encoded into the graph. By incorporating custom rules and a reasoner, a library could templatize some fundamental aspects of an expert system, and then add specific rules appropriate for the topic and discipline. Imagine if the entire interaction were like a conversation. Information seekers might collaborate with an information savvy version of Alan Turing's simulated question game participant.

Time

17

Time flies

A chapter about time may seem a bit of an outlier in a book about graphs. But so much of what we do, what we know, and the dynamics of the world we live in depend upon measuring and thinking about time. A model is a static snapshot largely devoid of meaning unless it is coupled with or allowed to evolve over time.

An event makes no sense without the notion of time. So many processes we observe and concern ourselves with are a function of time. Most areas of science incorporate temporal data whether it is observations of a forest over time, steps in a chemical reaction occurring in a particular sequence, the decay of one element into another, the spread of a disease, or the predicted arrival of a solar storm after a violent eruption on our sun. Our social networks evolve over time, weather erodes terrain, organisms change over time, satellite orbits decay, trees grow, we age. Time is often an integral component of the data we value. Reasoning about time is intuitive to us. We understand the passage of time, time intervals, overlapping events, and the concept of now.

And yet, there is no universal model for representing time in any arbitrary information system. Even the units of time and the notion of using a local time value versus a universal time value are not applied uniformly across systems. Time continues to be a big challenge for information representation and retrieval, no matter what form it takes and no matter what technologies or standards are employed. But because graphs and Semantic Web technologies are relatively recent inventions, their developers have had to revisit time.

Standard time

Before we examine how graphs and the Semantic Web work with time, it might be helpful to review some of the fundamentals with respect to data and time. It wasn't all that long ago that we all got into trouble because of some of our assumptions about how best to represent and store time data. Some day in the far future, perhaps our descendants will have to content with a Y10K problem. Since our own Millennial issues, however, some steps have been taken to time-proof our technologies. Nevertheless, dealing with time can still be a challenge for information systems.

There are unique usability considerations with respect to representing time. Different regions of the world represent components of time differently. A few even use calendars that present a chronology of years radically different than the Gregorian calendar. Time zones allow for us to manage the effects of time to a modest degree on our daily activities. They also make it possible for us to have a uniform concept of morning and afternoon, which varies based on a person's location on the earth.

A Librarian's Guide to Graphs, Data and the Semantic Web.

The standard ISO 8601 concerns itself primarily with documenting various alternate ways of representing time as a string value. In the United States, it is common to specify the calendar month before the calendar day, followed by the year. In Europe, day occurs before month. There are numeric alternatives and abbreviations for months, and even (still) accepted abbreviations for year. Humans expect to see time information separated by delimiters such as spaces, commas, colons, and/or forward slashes. Time data stored in an information retrieval system might omit most or all delimiters and rely largely on position to represent point in time in a string. Here are some formats specified by ISO 8601:

Time Point	Example	Format
A calendar date	12/23/14	YYYY-MM-DD or YYYY/MM/DD
Date and time	2014-12-23: 16:30 + 00:00	YYYY-MM-DD: HH:MM + SS
Date and time as coordinated Universal time UTC value	2014-04-29T13: 16:30Z	As above with Z to indicate UTC

ISO 8601 does not concern itself with representations of time that use calendar month names or dictate a uniform calendar. This would be problematic since there are different words for months in different languages. Another standard, RFC 3339, overlays some requirements onto specifying time that are used by Internet software such as web servers, e-mail systems, and time synchronization systems like the Network Time Protocol (NTP). Time stamps and time synchronization can be important in many applications, especially communications systems and online business transaction systems.

Assuming we all have a shared model for representing time, or at least a mechanism for mapping between different representations, what do we use time for in information retrieval systems? Well, time is obviously important for e-commerce and online banking. Transactional time stamps should be based upon an agreed-upon method of tracking time, and to the extent possible, synchronized time keeping between the systems involved in the transaction. E-mail, texts, and chat conversations have a chronological flow which should be preserved by time stamps. Posts and comments in social networking applications likewise have a chronological component. An online experience in a social networking application that ignored time stamp information would be frustrating as it would bear no resemblance to face-to-face or other forms of real-time communication. It would have no discernible intervals, durations, or comprehensible history.

Allen's Temporal Intervals

In the early 1980s, a researcher at the University of Rochester, James F. Allen, wrote a landmark paper entitled "Maintaining knowledge about temporal intervals."

He proposed a model for temporal reasoning that is often referred to as Allen's Temporal Intervals or Allen's Temporal Algebra. This model is explicitly replicated in some ontologies and rules systems for the Semantic Web, including the time ontology and Semantic Web Rules Language (SWRL). It starts by making a distinction between time points and time intervals. He then defines 13 possible relationships that can occur with temporal data and events. Two time points or intervals can be said to be equal, meaning that two events or actions occurred simultaneously, or during exactly the same time period. The other 12 intervals are similarly distinct and intuitive.

Allen's Temporal Intervals:

- before, after
- during, contains, overlaps, overlapped by
- meets, met by
- starts, started by, finished, finished by

Allen went on to describe how time intervals can be compared using this nomenclature, and he also suggested mathematical operators that could be used in programming languages to represent these interval comparison operations. In the Semantic Web, support for Allen's Temporal Intervals can be found in various rules engines and ontologies. For example, SWRL provides a suite of temporal built-ins for reasoning about time. Other rules engines such as Euler offer sets of rules that build on functional primitives such as equivalency, greater than, and less than operators. These rules can be used to reason about time values and events which use XML schema date or dateTime literal values to define time points:

SWRL built-ins	Euler eventTime rules
equals	hasSameTimeAs
before	before
after	after
meets	beginsSameAsEndOf
metBy	endsSameAsBeginningOf
overlaps	overlaps
overlappedBy	overlaps
contains	includes
during	during
starts	begins
startedBy	hasSameBeginningAs
finishes	end
finishedBy	hasSameEndAs

For example, this SWRL rule uses a temporal built-in (http://swrl.stanford.edu/ontologies/built-ins/3.3/temporal.owl) to evaluate two date values to determine if the first is earlier than the second:

```
temporal:before("2013-11-02T09:00", "2014-01-01T10:00")
```

Here's an example which uses Euler event time rules (http://eulersharp.sourceforge.net/2003/03swap/eventTime_rules.html) to compare two events bound to variables ?event1 and ?event2:

```
time:hasSameBeginningAs(?event1, ?event2)
```

Rules engines include other temporal functions for convenience, such as functions to compare durations and functions which add or subtract from time points. SWRL has a special function for designating that a time point corresponds to the current moment of the operation temporal:now.

Allen's intervals work well enough with precisely defined time values, but there are many instances when time values are indeterminant. We might say something happened before 1840, and it may not be possible to be any more precise about an historical event. Time granularity doesn't always match from one representation to another. We might know that someone was born in March 1872, and that they died on April 4, 1907. Or we may have an interval with a defined starting point but lack information about its end point. Indeterminant time values are a fact of life. All we can do is record as much data as we have and represent it in a uniform way. If we don't have good temporal data, then temporal queries and temporal reasoning will only be as effective as the data allows.

Relational database developers and database schema modelers have grappled with time. Databases have a date data type for representing time, but that's just a field type which does not address the larger temporal comparison issue. In databases, there's often interest in both a transactional record of time, and a record of time as a component of a row. Of course a point in time can be handled with a single date column, and an interval can be represented with two date type fields. But there are some challenging exceptions to points and intervals. For example, what do you do if one of the values is indeterminant, until changed, currently valid, or an until now values? Different systems (and programmers) tend to come up with their own solutions to this problem.

Semantic time

How are these standards and models applied in Semantic Web and graph databases? Well you must first consider what temporal aspect you need to represent. A statement or an edge between two nodes may be valid for a specific time period and invalid for others. So generally speaking, some sort of time stamp (a time point) is necessary at a minimum, and if it is possible you could even express the temporal period (interval) for which a statement or an edge is valid. For example, the population of New York City was 3.4 million people in 1900. Second, the thing you are making statements about may have temporal characteristics. Charles Dicken's "Great Expectations" was first published in 1860. A property graph is generally superior to RDF for modeling time, as the relationship (edge) can have arbitrary properties associated with it. Time points and time intervals can be associated with nodes and edges throughout the graph. Because of their inherent flexibility, it is usually easier to add time stamps and time interval information to a property graph, because you can add properties to a graph element without changing the graph's structure.

Making statements about a relationship expressed in another triple in RDF is more difficult. W3C documentation about RDF describes it as "*atemporal*." It does not deal with time and does not have a built-in notion of temporal validity of information. Since RDF is atemporal, time representation is not an intrinsic part of RDF modeling. There's no standard way for a triplestore to assign time stamps to statements. There's no built-in model for representing temporal points or intervals.

This can be problematic because so much value associated with information is expressed or represented with temporal information. We often want to know when a given fact was determined to be true. The temporal ordering of information is frequently crucial to understanding it. Facts can also later be invalidated, or called into question, and the time at which this happened may have value. Even mundane temporal data such as the date that a triple was added to a triplestore can be useful.

The W3C offers some guidance regarding time and RDF graphs. They note that RDF graphs can incorporate temporal data using the appropriate vocabularies. However, they also note that doing so changes the graph. If that matters to you, then you could create a new RDF graph to contain temporal information about another graph and its entities. Here's some additional guidance and comments about RDF and changes over time:

- Never change an existing IRI to point to a different thing
- Literals as expressed in a triple are constants and shouldn't change
- A relationship between two things can be true at one point in time but not true at another
- An RDF graph can change over time
- You can use snapshots of RDF graphs to preserve their structure at a certain point in time

Given these considerations, how do you add time data to RDF graphs? One approach uses a technique called reification. Reification involves decomposing a statement into its components, minting a new identifier for the decomposed statement, and then asserting triples about the components. It can be used within or outside of an RDF graph to express details about temporal characteristics of a triple or its components. You could, for example, use reification to express when a predicate was valid for a triple. Or you could use the provenance ontology which has properties and classes for expressing version information (including date/time) about things.

Events ontologies might work in cases where the thing that has a temporal aspect can be considered to be an event. And there are time ontologies which are useful for expressing temporal information about things as a distinct characteristic. Is this a failure of the RDF model, or is it the case that representing time in information retrieval systems is an incompletely solved problem? The truth is probably a little bit of both. RDF graphs were conceived of as a way to represent a static snapshot of information. That doesn't preclude their use with dynamic data but it does make that more challenging.

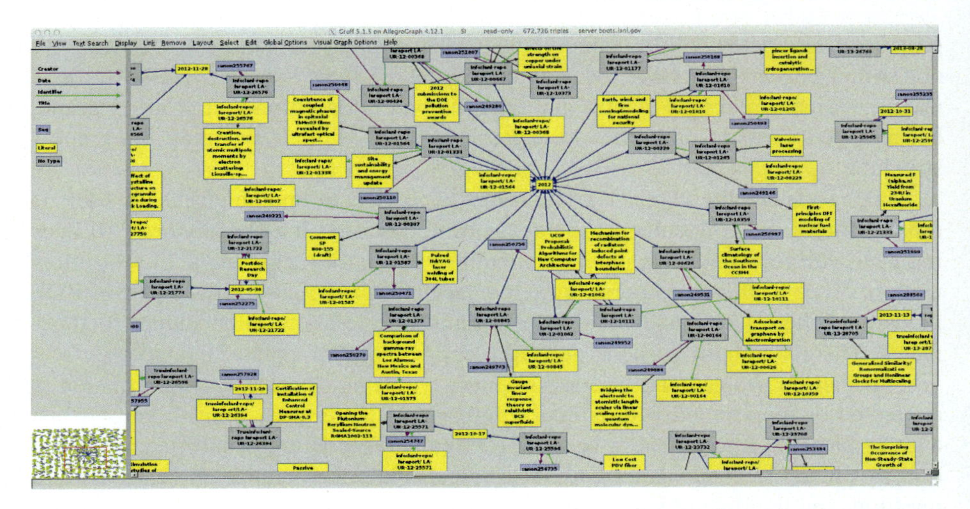

Figure 17.1 Allegrograph's Gruff triples visualization tool illustrating one way that RDF resources can be associated with temporal information.

As with other literal data, RDF supports typing of temporal data (Figure 17.1). There are a number of XML schema types for time and date information, including xsd:date, xsd:time, xsd:dateTime, and xsd:dateTimeStamp, for example,

```
<some paper> dcterms:issued "2014-04-29"^^xsd:date.
```

There are also types for partial temporal information: xsd:gYear, xsd:gMonth, xsd:gDay, xsd:gYearMonth, and xsd:gMonthDay, and for recurring temporal data: xsd:duration, xsd:yearMonthDuration, and xsd:dayTimeDuration.

Linked Open Vocabularies list 50 different ontologies that have something to do with the concept of "when." A brief tour highlighting classes and properties from some of these ontologies may give you an idea of what kind of temporal artifacts have been modeled in various ontologies and how they were handled.

The Observation ontology has a TemporalObservation Class which is a subclass of Observation and is defined as "[an] Observation whose result is a temporal object, such as a time instant or period."

The Nepomuk Calendar Ontology (NCAL) is an ontology for modeling calendar data and calendar events such as meetings. The Event class is a central class in this ontology, although, interestingly enough it is a subclass of many other classes, rather than the other way around. The reason for this is that there are a number of Union classes which combine an Event with some other thing that occurs in the calendar domain such as a Todo, Alarm, or Freebusy class. An NCAL Event is defined as "Provide a grouping of component properties that describe an event."

The Geologic Timescale model is an ontology adaptation of a previously defined markup language for representing information about various temporal aspects of geological formations and data. Its classes include GeochronologicEvent, GeologicTimescale, and StrategraphicEvent. Instance data that uses this vocabulary isn't concerned with defining calendar points or intervals for things, but rather relating geological formations to one another in a temporal sequence. For example, it could be used to express a statement about the fact that the KT boundary (a StrategraphicPoint) occurs at the end (boundary) of the cretaceous period (GeochronologicEra).

The Geographic Information Temporal Schema (temporal) is an ontology representation of a preexisting standard that provides temporal context for places (ISO 19108). Two important classes in this ontology are temporal#ReferenceSystem and temporal#Primitive. ReferenceSystem is a parent class for various means of tracking time including Clock, Calendar, and timelines (Coordinate) or contextual models (Reference). Two subclasses of the temporal#Primitive ought to be familiar: temporal#Instant and temporal#Period (for defining intervals).

The Event ontology represents a very simple model for a thing called an Event, which it defines as "An arbitrary classification of a space/time region, by a cognitive agent." The only other classes in this ontology are Factor and Product, which can be thought of as what things are inputs of the event, and what are its results. The time property is used to associate a time object with an instance of an Event. The range of the time property is the TemporalEntity from the time ontology.

The Linked Data Event Ontology is a small ontology that builds on the Event ontology and many others to provide a vocabulary for describing historical events using RDF. The only class in this ontology is Event, which is equivalent to the Event ontology Event class. The atTime property relates an Event to a TemporalEntity. There is also a circa property for expressing that an approximate time value has a "nearness" relationship with a known time interval.

The Time ontology (or OWL Time) defines a general-purpose ontology for temporal concepts and relationships. It defines an Instant and Interval class, and as mentioned above, a TemporalEntity class, which can be a collection of Instants and Intervals. All of Allen's Temporal Intervals are defined as properties in the Time ontology, generally of the form intervalBefore, intervalAfter, intervalMeets, etc. Various temporal durations are defined as data properties, including years, months, weeks, days, hours, and minutes.

Graph time

In graph theory, there is a great deal of interest in what are referred to as dynamic or temporal graphs. A timeline makes an obvious and intuitive directed graph. In that model, points along the timeline are nodes that other nodes sharing a temporal relationship with that time point would have an edge with. Something that has a relationship with a temporal interval might have edges with two points along the timeline (Figure 17.2).

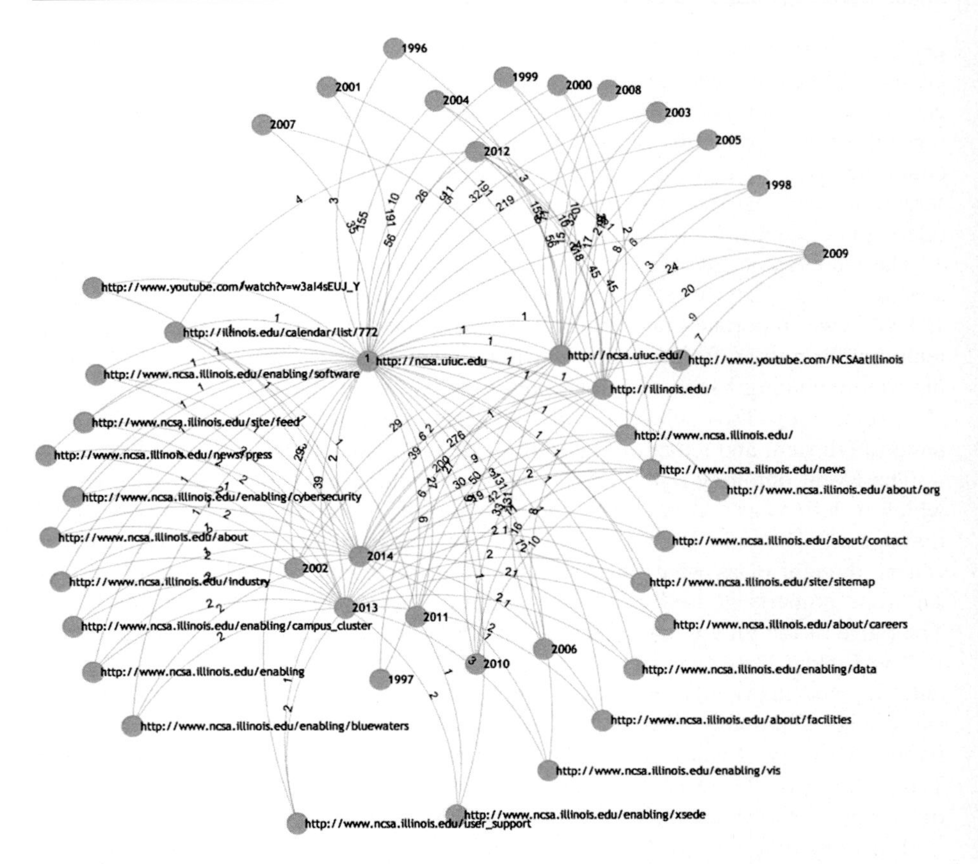

Figure 17.2 A graph visualization of Memento (Time Travel for the Web http://timetravel.mementoweb.org) TimeMap data for several Web resources. Resources and years are nodes; edge values indicate the number of archived versions for that year.

Time can be more directly associated with a graph. For example, in a bipartite or multipartite graph, nodes and edges can each have their own time properties. Movies, books, and music become popular with an increasing number of people starting at a certain point in time and continuing for some duration of time, before leveling off or falling. Theaters fill seats and book sellers sell books via network effects, whether through marketing or word of mouth. A blockbuster movie typically experiences a burst of attention in its first weeks of release. The spread of disease through a population can exhibit similar characteristics over time. A super-spreader, that is, someone who either has many contacts or exhibits extreme symptoms during the most contagious phase of a disease can cause a burst of new infections. Burstiness is an effect that can be observed, measured, and at times, leveraged in various ways using temporal networks.

Time can be an integral part of a graph model as graph element properties, an overlay where time nodes point at other graph elements, or time values can be used to aggregate and compare multiple graphs. In a dynamic graph, clusters may form and disappear over time, and paths may cease to exist as edges disappear. It may be sufficient to know that two people know each other, or to also know when they met, or how long they've known each other. Again, a fundamental question to consider is, are you interested in a temporal point or in a temporal interval? Answering that question will help you determine how best to represent time in your graph model. Then, consider how the measures of the graph may change as time passes. Degree centrality in a model of people attending summer movies will change over time. If two friends have moved away from one another, one of them may not be the best person to contact in order to quickly reach the other, because what was once a strong connection is now weak, or the path between them may no longer exist at all.

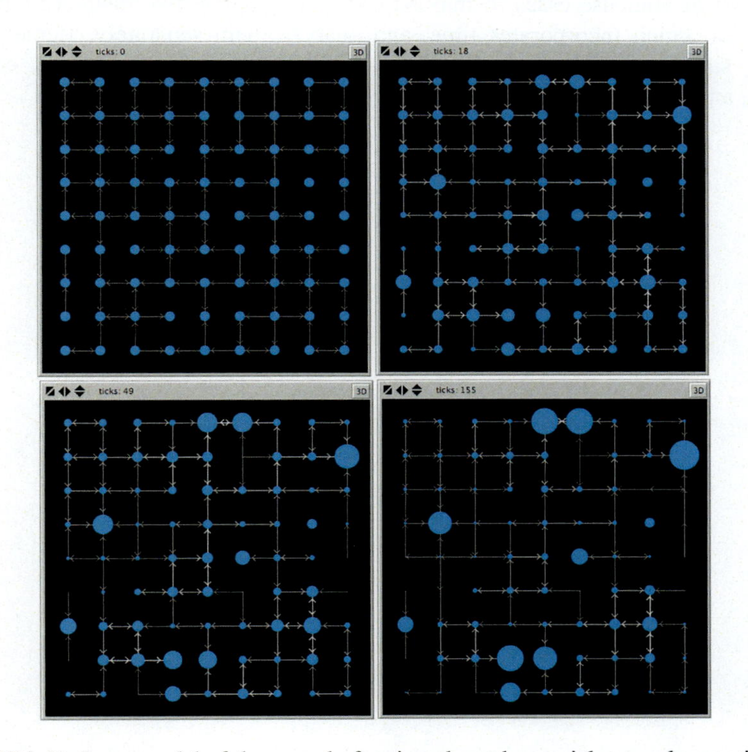

Figure 17.3 NetLogo model of the spread of a virus through a social network over time. *Source*: Attribution: Stonedahl, F. and Wilensky, U. (2008). NetLogo Virus on a Network model. <http://ccl.northwestern.edu/netlogo/models/VirusonaNetwork>. Center for Connected Learning and Computer-Based Modeling, Northwestern Institute on Complex Systems, Northwestern University, Evanston, IL.

There is no one correct way to model time in a graph. It depends entirely upon the relationship or phenomena of interest. It may be the case that it happens instantaneously or that the duration of the phenomena does not matter. Or the start and end time may be of interest, for purposes of measuring duration or comparing intervals. Time can be a property, a relationship, or a node. Depending on how you represent it, time can modify the structure of a graph. Some processes and systems change the graph structure to the extent that the entire graph state must be captured at discrete intervals (Figure 17.3).

Many systems and processes which cannot be modeled without including a time dimension. In many cases, you will probably need to incorporate time into your graph model in some fashion. Once you've incorporated a preliminary temporal model, it can be helpful to test your model against Allen's 13 Temporal Intervals. If you cannot determine the temporal relationships among things in your graph using the model you came up with, then you probably need to rethink how you've modeled time in your graph. Iterate and adjust your model until you can effectively address all of your use cases. It may be easier to generate two distinct graph models, one of which incorporates time, and analyze them separately. Remember, in general, simpler graphs tend to be computationally easier to visualize, compare, analyze, and explore.

Drawing and serializing graphs 18

The inscrutable hairball

Visualizations of data are popular because a good data visualization can convey so much information to the viewer. Creating good visualizations of graph data is inherently challenging because a graph is typically a large data set representing a complex system. One of the first graph visualizations most of us master is the "inscrutable hairball."

The steps for creating an inscrutable hairball are as follows: find a really large graph data set, load it into a graph visualization tool, click a button to draw it. After a few minutes, the results are, well, an inscrutable hairball. There were so many nodes and edges in the data set that the screen is soon filled with hints of circles and shadows of lines. The results convey no more information than would a handful of gravel and a fist full of grass clippings.

Graph drawing is hard. Edward Tufte could just as well have been referring to graph drawing as to any effort to visualize a complex data set when he said "What is to be sought in designs for the display of information is the clear portrayal of complexity. Not the complication of the simple; rather the task of the designer is to give visual access to the subtle and the difficult—that is, the revelation of the complex." Tufte, a widely recognized expert in data visualization, offers up several graph visualizations as examples of good data visualizations in his series of books. Interestingly enough, these graphs were hand drawn in many cases decades before the advent of computers. One could argue that these graphs are so good because the person who created them was intimately familiar with the data, and they had clear goals for how they imagined others would use the depiction.

One of Tufte's guiding principles for design is "clutter and confusion are not attributes of data—they are shortcomings of design." The challenge for any automated graph drawing tool is that there's no easy way to encode a design principle like this into software. Thus graph visualization tools provide interactive refinement of visualizations. They offer different strategies for laying out graph elements, visual cues for emphasizing aspects of the graph, and filtering mechanisms for reducing clutter and focusing in on specific features of a graph. A graph drawing tool is unlikely to generate a beautiful visualization on its own. Software provides an environment and tools to make it possible for a person to make visual sense of graph data and share the results with other.

Graph visualization tools strive to reveal both the subtle and complex. There are graph visualization tools that specialize in rendering particular types of graphs such as biological networks, social networks, and RDF graphs. Different tools employ different strategies for drawing and laying out graph elements. Some incorporate

A Librarian's Guide to Graphs, Data and the Semantic Web.

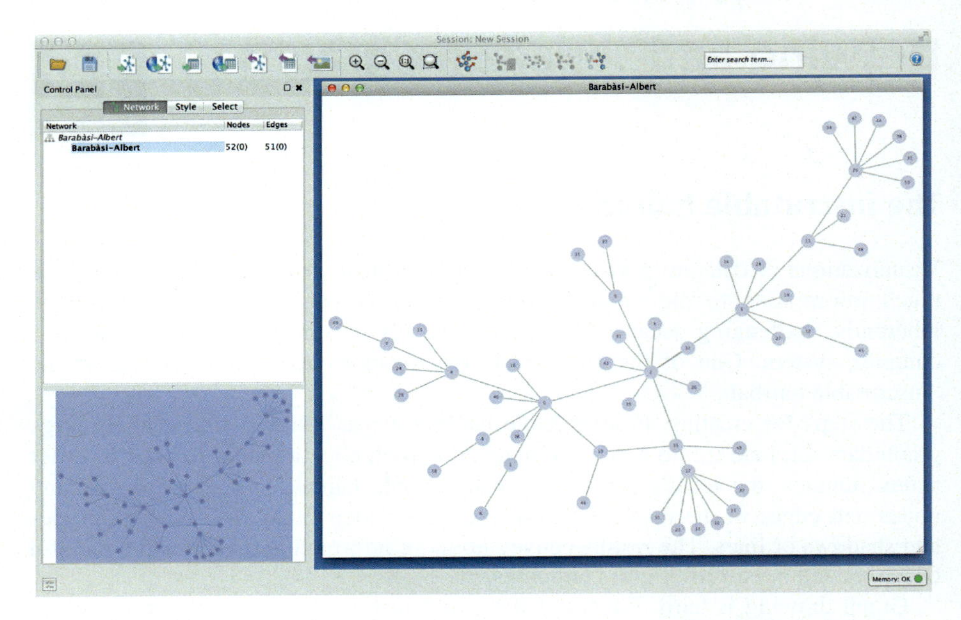

Figure 18.1 A scale-free network visualized using Cytoscape and the organic layout.

3D effects or they animate the graph visualization simulating natural forces such as gravity or magnetism. Others offer graph analytic and graph element filtering options (Figure 18.1).

Graph Data Formats

The first challenge is getting your graph data into a graph visualization tool. There are quite a few standard formats for representing graph data. The simplest representation of a graph is an adjacency or association matrix. This is a table where all the nodes are listed as row headings and the same nodes are listed again as column headings. When there's a connection between two nodes, you can indicate this by finding the row or column for the first node, and the row or column that corresponds to the node it is connected to and put a value of 1 in the table where they intersect. For a directed graph, each axis represents a different direction, so if row B, column C has a 1, but row C, column B has a 0, then B's edge points at C. If there is no connection between a node, that cell would contain a value of 0. You can also use this model to represent a weighted graph. Instead of 1, the weight representing whatever criteria you use to indicate the strength of the connection can be inserted as an integer or floating point value. You can create an adjacency matrix in Excel or using any text editor (Figure 18.2).

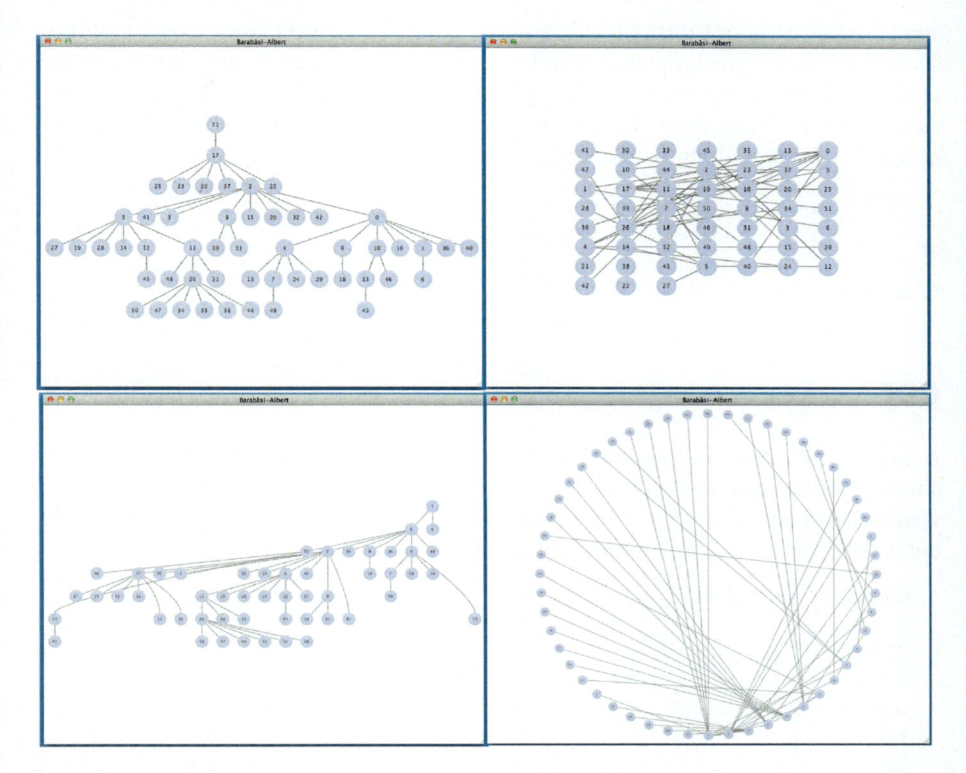

Figure 18.2 The same network that appears in Figure 18.1 rendered with Cytoscape using, from top left, tree, grid, hierarchical, and circular layouts.

Here are two examples, one for an unweighted graph, and the other illustrates an alternate version where weights have been assigned to edges.

	A	B	C	D
A	0	0	1	0
B	1	0	0	1
C	1	0	0	1
D	0	1	1	0

	A	B	C	D
A	0	3	1	0
B	3	0	4	2
C	1	4	0	7
D	0	2	7	0

Note the diagonal. In the first example, it is filled with 0s. When the diagonal contains anything other than a zero value, it indicates that there is a loop (recall that a loop is an edge that is connected at both ends to the same vertex). If you use spreadsheets, it is not difficult to create an adjacency matrix from existing spreadsheet data. Some graph databases and visualization tools can load a CSV file representing an adjacency matrix. You could either create a list of comma separated values, one per row, from the data above, or you could have one entry per row for each pair of nodes along with an edge value like this:

```
A, 0, 0, 1, 0
```

or

```
A, B, 0
```

GDF

A Java-based graph visualization tool for the Web called GUESS supports an even simpler format called Graph Data Format (GDF). GDF optionally supports some visualization and data type attributes as do many graph data representation formats, but a GDF file can be as simple as this:

```
nodedef> name, label
1, Jon
2, Anne
3, Pat
edgedef> node1, node2
1,3
2,3
```

One interesting thing to note about this format is the node1, node2 designation for edge values. This can be used to give the visualization software a clue about directionality, if that's important in your visualization. It is also implicit in the ordering of the pair of nodes listed for an edge in the first example (e.g., node1 is connected to node3 because the order is 1, 3). Directionality is not always explicitly represented in graph visualizations even when it is known, since it tends to overload the viewer. But the capability is there in case you want to incorporate it into a small graph or a graph which explicitly illustrates the path between a set of nodes. And now you know how to represent it!

XML and graphs

Unlike RDF, where there's a single XML serialization that's widely used (RDF/XML), there are several XML-based graph serialization formats. They are all quite similar. XML graph serializations serve two purposes: as textual representations that can be loaded into analysis and visualization tools, and as graph exchange data formats that allow graphs to be saved and loaded to the filesystem and exported from one graph database into another. We will look at examples of three formats: XGMML, GraphML, and GEXF.

XGMML

XGMML stands for eXtensible Graph Markup and Modeling Language. It is primarily used by a visualization tool called Cytoscape, which is popular in the bioinformatics community. An XGMML document, as with any XML document, starts with a declaration of the namespace for the format description. An XGMML document root element is <graph>. This element is followed by a list of <node> elements. Each node element has an id attribute and optionally a label attribute. No additional elements or data are required to define a node. Nodes are followed by a list of edge elements. As with the node element, an edge has an id attribute, an option label attribute, and a source and target attribute. The key here are the values assigned to the source and target attribute—these values should correspond to the id attribute for a previously defined node. Here's an example:

```
<graph id="graph" graphic="1" label="Twitter friends"
      xmlns="http://www.cs.rpi.edu/XGMML">
    <node id="1" label="Jon" />
    <node id="2" label="Anne" />
    <node id="3" label="Pat" />
    <edge id="node" label="node" source="1" target="3" />
    <edge id="node" label="node" source="2" target="3" />
</graph>
```

GraphML

GraphML is a general-purpose graph description language supported by various tools. The intent of GraphML was to establish a graph interchange format. At first glance, it looks quite similar to XGMML, even sharing its graph, node, and edge elements. But the root element of a GraphML document is graphml, and there can be multiple graphs contained within a single document. Here's a simple example:

```
<graphml xmlns="http://graphml.graphdrawing.org/xmlns/1.0/graphml.xsd">
  <graph id="graph1" edgedefault="undirected">
    <key id="name" for="node" attr.name="name" attr.type="string"/>
     <node id="1">
          <data key="name">Jon</data>
     </node>
     <node id="2">
          <data key="name">Anne</data>
     </node>
     <node id="3">
          <data key="name">Pat</data>
     </node>
```

```
      <edge id = "4" source = "1" target = "3" label = "knows" />
      <edge id = "5" source = "2" target = "3" label = "knows" />
   </graph>
</graphml>
```

GEXF

GEXF (Graph Exchange XML Format) is yet another XML graph description format. It is supported by a few visualization tools, most notably the Sigma JS library, which is a Javascript library that can be used to embed a graph visualization into a Web page. A basic graph defined in GEXF looks almost exactly like GraphML representation:

```
<gexf xmlns = "http://www.gephi.org/gexf">
  <graph type = "static">
    <meta>
      <description>Twitter friends</description>
    </meta>
    <nodes>
      <node id = "1" label = "Jon" />
      <node id = "2" label = "Anne" />
      <node id = "3" label = "Pat" />
    </nodes>
    <edges>
      <edge id = "4" source = "1" target = "3" />
      <edge id = "5" source = "2" target = "3" />
    </edges>
  </graph>
</gexf>
```

JSON for D3

Many Javascript Web-embedded graph visualizations use the D3 data visualization library. Graph visualizations that have been built with D3 include forced directed networks, sankey diagrams, dendrograms, hive plots, flare diagrams, and many others. Since D3 natively supports JSON, graph data is usually supplied to these visualizations in JSON (Figure 18.3). One common JSON serialization has an object labeled "nodes" which is associated with an array of vertex objects, followed by an object labeled links, which is associated with a list of edge objects. Edge

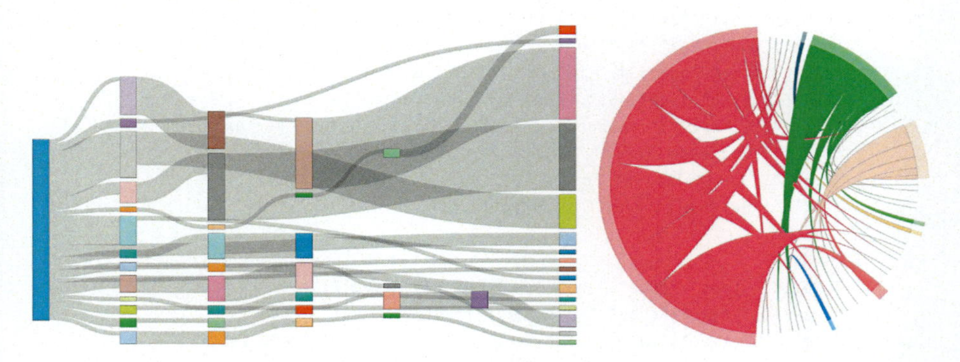

Figure 18.3 D3 visualization examples: Left – Sankey diagram illustrating change in a network over time. Right – Chord diagram revealing strength of relationships.

objects use a 0-based indexing scheme to reference objects in the node array. Each link entry is a source and target key value pair as shown below:

```
{
  "nodes": [
      {"name": "Santa Fe Depot Station"},
    {"name": "South Capital Station"},
    {"name": "Zia Road Station"},
  ],
  "links": [
    {"source": 0, "target": 1},
    {"source": 1, "target": 2},
    {"source": 2, "target": 3},
  ]
}
```

GraphSON

GraphSON is a more comprehensive graph serialization and interchange format, also based on JSON. It is vertex-centric and comes in two variants: typed and non-typed. Nodes and edges are represented in a manner similar to the JSON format shown above, but there's also support for serializing properties associated with nodes and edges. Here is an example of GraphSON:

```
{
  "graph": {
    "mode":"NORMAL",
    "vertices":[
```

```
      {"name":"Scott","age":36,"_id":1,"_type":"vertex" },
      {"name":"Bob","age":47,"_id":2,"_type":"vertex"},
      {"name":"Anne","age":34,"_id":3,"_type":"vertex"},
      {"name":"Susan","age":45,"_id":4,"_type":"vertex"},
      {"title":"Solaris","category": "novel","_id":5,"_type":"vertex"},
      {"title":"Roadside Picnic","category":"novel","_id":6,"_type":"vertex"},
      {"title": "Annihilation","category":"novel","_id":7,"_type":"vertex"},
      {"title":"Brief History of Time","category":"nonfiction","_id":8,"_type":"vertex"}
    ],
    "edges":[
      {"_id":9,"_type":"edge","_outV":1,"_inV":7,"_label":"read"},
      {"_id":10,"_type":"edge","_outV":1,"_inV":8,"_label":"read"},
      {"_id":11,"_type":"edge","_outV":2,"_inV":6,"_label":"read"},
      {"_id":12,"_type":"edge","_outV":2,"_inV":7,"_label":"read"},
      {"_id":13,"_type":"edge","_outV":3,"_inV":5,"_label":"read"},
      {"_id":14,"_type":"edge","_outV":4,"_inV":5,"_label":"read"},
      {"_id":15,"_type":"edge","_outV":1,"_inV":2,"_label":"friend"},
      {"_id":16,"_type":"edge","_outV":1,"_inV":3,"_label":"friend"},
      {"_id":17,"_type":"edge","_outV":2,"_inV":3,"_label":"friend"}
      ]
  }
}
```


Graph exchange formats exist for several reasons. Mainly they are used to exchange data between graph visualizations and graph database tools. Or you could take data from a nongraph application and convert it, for example, create a macro in a spreadsheet application to export data in a JSON or XML graph serialization.

Most tools simply render the nodes and edges by default, and leave other visual clues to be defined elsewhere, perhaps by another process or some optional configuration parameters adjusted by the user.

Graph visualization

Graph visualization, or graph drawing tools are desktop or Web-embedded applications for converting graph data into a 2D image that you can see and interact with. These tools use typical conventions such as circles for nodes, lines for edges, and arrows to indicate edge direction. Some offer additional visual clues as they draw the graph, such as larger circles for nodes with higher degree values, thicker edges for weighted edges, and so on. Some graph serialization data formats let you include some rendering information with your data. More sophisticated tools will let you filter by node and edge characteristics, or assign colors or size values to groups of graph elements. And of course, they usually offer multiple strategies for drawing a graph, called layouts.

The layout of graph elements as it is drawn is major challenge, especially with larger graphs. A graph visualization first and foremost must accurately represent the nodes and connections between them. With a small graph, scattering nodes randomly on the screen and then drawing edges between them as appropriate may result in a usable rendering, where few or no nodes obscure one another and it is readily apparent which nodes are connected to which. But most graphs of interest are large and complex, as graphs are frequently used to represent complex systems. Visualizations of complex graphs inevitably result in overlapping nodes and a tangle of edges among them. So most visualization tools offer strategies, called layouts, which can be employed to position nodes as the graph is drawn.

Graph layouts

Before we look at specific graph visualization tools, let's look at a few of the most common layout algorithms you will encounter, and the rules that govern their behavior. Generally speaking, graph layout algorithms look for ways to minimize node overlap, minimize edge crossover, and group interconnected nodes in such a way that clusters are visually apparent. To do so, an algorithm might employ rules that determine how the nodes are positioned in relation to one another on a plane or in three dimensional space, rules that govern the interactions among nodes according to some simulated force, or both. Layout rules can take graph element characteristics into account such as edge weights or direction, degree metrics, etc. In the literature on graph layout, there is a general consensus around these requirements:

1. Distribute the vertices evenly in the frame
2. Minimize edge crossings
3. Make edge lengths uniform
4. Reflect inherent symmetry
5. Conform to the frame

Layouts that use complex rules based on natural forces (force-based layouts) tend to be computationally more intensive than layouts that focus on positioning nodes in space (topological layouts).

Force-directed layout

Most visualization tools support a force-directed layout, which draws the graph and then attempts to attain a good separation between nodes with minimal edge crossover. Crossover occurs whenever an edge intersects with another edge. Ideally intersections should only occur between nodes and the edges that connect to them, but in practice that's hard to achieve with large graphs. In force-directed layouts, after the initial rendering, nodes will move away from one another until whatever uniform degree of separation that is possible given the density of the graph is achieved. Disconnected nodes move farther apart, while nodes that share an edge are placed closer together. Various force models from nature are simulated as the graph is drawn, including gravitational attraction, electromagnetic attraction/repulsion, and mechanical spring/weight interactions. Force graph layouts may offer you the option of specifying maximal distance between nodes and length of edges. This kind of layout usually allows the user to select and drag nodes around in order to affect the layout. Many layout algorithms are derived from the force-directed layout algorithm.

Fruchterman–Reingold layout

Fruchterman–Reingold layout is another force layout, named for its co-developers Thomas M. J. Fruchterman and Edward M. Reingold. In their 1991 paper entitled "Graph Drawing by Force-Directed Placement," the authors identify two requirements that this layout model had to address:

1. Vertices connected by an edge should be drawn near each other.
2. Vertices should not be drawn *too* close to each other.

The algorithm treats nodes as particles with some mass, and edges function as springs between them. As the energy in the springs dissipates, the graph achieves a sort of "energetic equilibrium." This again attempts to make as many nodes visible as possible with as few edge crossovers as possible.

Topological layouts

Other graph layout strategies are primarily focused on how the nodes are positioned in respect to one another. The following layouts render graph data using a topological model such as a circle, tree, or lattice.

Circular layout

A circular layout positions all the nodes around the perimeter of a circle, with the nodes sometimes ordered by degree, and then draws the edges among the nodes. The inner part of the circle can become quite dense if there are a lot of edges in the graph.

Tree layout

A tree layout positions nodes with lower degree connectivity as the root of a branching tree of node—edge connections that expand as it progresses from a given root node. This works best with a graph that has hierarchical characteristics.

Lattice layout

A lattice layout positions all the nodes in a grid and then adds edges. If there are lots of edges, this tends to result in a lot of edges crossing one another and so it works best with a particular type of graph called a planar graph. Planar graphs are

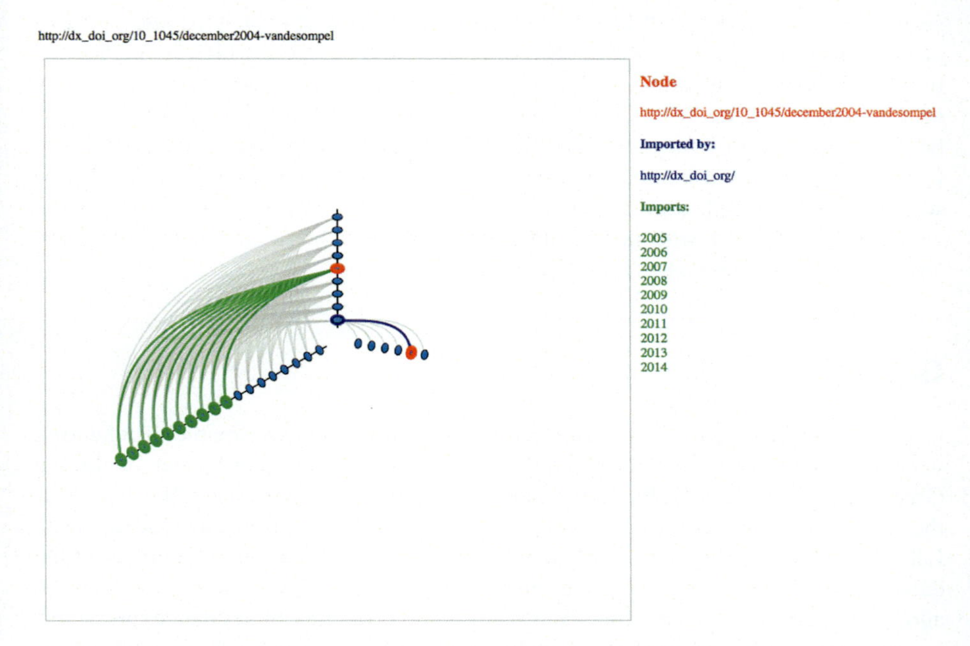

Figure 18.4 A hive plot of Memento data also portrayed in chapter 17, Figure 17.2.

graphs that can be drawn in 2D space such that their edges only intersect at the nodes to which they are connected. Think lots of squares or lots of triangles.

Hive plot

A hive plot is a visualization which uses multiple axes to position nodes based on simple rules. For example, given three axes, you might define three rules based on node degree such that nodes with a degree value of 3 or less fall on one axis, nodes with a degree of 4 to 7 fall on another, and nodes that have a degree greater than 7 fall on the third axis. Edges are then drawn as appropriate between these nodes. You can vary the number of axis, the rules for placing nodes and other details to further refine the visualization (Figure 18.4).

Cytoscape

Cytoscape desktop is a Java-based graph visualization package that runs on many different platforms. It was first developed for visualizing biological networks, and some of its functionality is specific to that domain. Cytoscape is modular and its functionality can be extended with plug-ins. There are data parsing and retrieval plug-ins for data sources that supply proteonomic interaction data and gene sequences, and many well-known biological data services such as the services offered at the National Center for Biotechnology Information, which is maintained by the US National Institutes of Health. Cytoscape can load graph data in a variety of formats, including SIF, GML, XGMML, comma delimited text, Excel workbooks, and several formats specifically for describing biological networks. Cytoscape provides a number of basic default layouts, including circular, degree sorted, edge weighted, grid, and hierarchical. You can zoom in and out on a graph visualization, interact with nodes and edges, search for particular nodes or edges, and export a visualization as a PDF or image file.

Gephi

Gephi is a desktop graph visualization package written in Java capable of rendering very large networks. It supports a variety of common graph data formats including GraphML, GEXF, and GML. One feature which makes Gephi especially flexible is the Data Laboratory. Once a graph description file has been loaded, Data Laboratory will display node and edge data, as well as any properties defined in the data file in a tabular form. You can then manipulate this data in a variety of ways, add, merge or delete data, filter data using simple queries or regular expressions, and duplicate columns of data. It includes some basic layout options and allows you to manipulate visual aspects of the graph such as node, edge, or background colors. Gephi also supports a large collection of graph metrics algorithms. For example, you can compute and see a plot of node degree distributions. It comes with a few default layouts, but there's also a large library of layout plug-ins available for Gephi as well as a number of good tutorials (Figure 18.5).

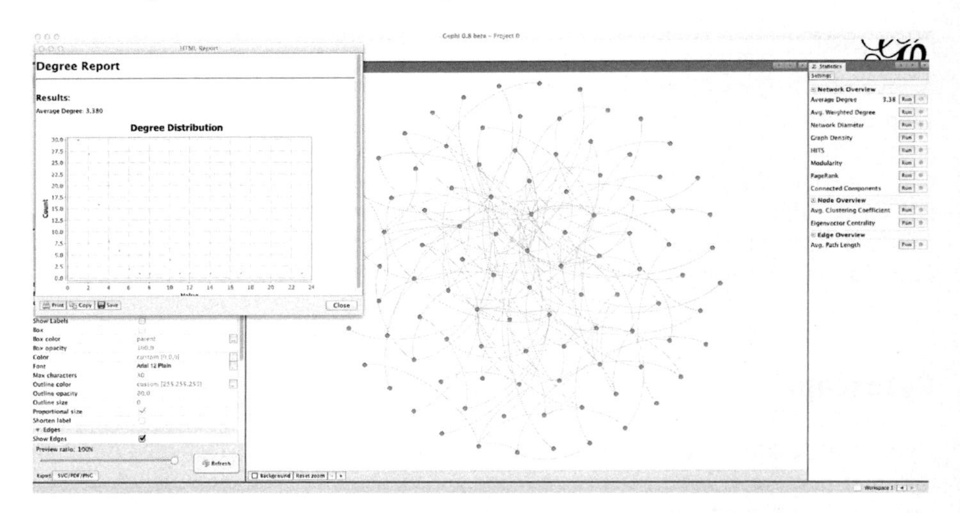

Figure 18.5 Gephi graph visualization and analysis application.

GUESS

GUESS, which stands for Graph Exploration System, is a Java applet for rendering graphs on the Web. It supports GraphML and Pajek, and its own format called GDF, which is a simple text format for describing nodes, edges, and some optional visual characteristics. When GUESS loads a graph, it stores the graph data in an in-memory SQL compliant database, so you have the option of explicitly defining the field type and size, for example, VARCHAR(32) for a 32 character string. Obviously you sacrifice cross-tool compatibility if you use the GDF format to leverage the database-like capabilities of GUESS. Since GUESS is a Java applet, its developers have incorporated support for the Jung graph analysis toolkit, so it is possible to use Jung to affect the visualization by taking into account things like degree or betweenness centrality. GUESS is very flexible, but ensuring Java applet support is available can be problematic as some users disable Java applet support in their Web browser (or never enable it), or simply don't have a Java runtime environment installed on their computer.

Javascript libraries for graphs on the web

Sigma.js is another graph visualization library for the Web. Once the library is installed on a Web server, you can embed the Sigma.js client into a Web page using the script element and add a small amount of additional code to load a graph data file and initialize the graph. The graph data must be published on the same Web server that hosts the Sigma.js library and the Web page in which the graph is embedded. Graph data can be supplied in gephi, GEXF, or JSON. Developers can implement functions to modify aspects of the visualization (e.g., change color, edge thickness, node size) depending on characteristics of each node or edge.

Cytoscape has a Web-based companion library of the same name called Cytoscape Web. Since it is a library and not an application, you will have to install additional client libraries and write some Javascript code to embed it in a Web page and load your data. Cytoscape Web lacks many of the features found in the Cytoscape desktop application. It's also important to remember that Cytoscape Web library runs inside a Web browser and must retrieve the graph over the network. So it may perform slower and not be capable of rendering larger graphs. In some cases, you may want to consider extracting a meaningful subgraph for Cytoscape Web.

D3, which stands for Data Driven Documents, is a general-purpose data visualization library for the Web. The language provides functions for loading and iterating through a set of data. With D3, you can interact with the parent Web page that embeds D3 to add, update, or remove HTML, CSS, and SVG elements dynamically, as your D3 application runs. This allows user input and events to affect the visualization. D3 also supports animated transitions which allow you to present different aspects of a data set over a period of time or in response to user interactions.

Since it is implemented in Javascript, D3 is especially well suited for working with JSON data. DOM support makes it relatively straightforward to load and access graph data in any XML format, such as XGMML, GraphML, or GML.

It's important to note that there's no specific support for graph visualizations in D3. But like bar charts and scatter plots, graph visualizations consist of simple elements available in SVG. So the base D3 library is fully capable of rendering a network using SVG circle element to draw nodes and the SVG line element to draw edges between nodes. Many developers have contributed code for rendering specific types of visualizations, some of which can be adapted to display graph data. These are often referred to as plug-ins. This makes D3 one of the better environments to explore alternate methods of visualizing graphs. For example, you could adapt a D3 Sankey diagram to show the relative connectiveness of any given node in a graph at some point in time, assuming you had temporal properties associated with your graph data. You could also generate line or bar charts to illustrate relative degree values for nodes in your graph. The D3 Gallery on github allows you to browse various types of visualizations and access contributed code that can produce them. Typically this code will include sample data which will give you some idea of the data elements and format you need to supply it with in order for it to render your data.

Graph analytics techniques

19

Linux and food poisoning

In one part of the country, a developer is busy putting the finishing touches on his customized Linux operating system. In another part of the country, someone is fighting for their life after ingesting a tainted cantaloupe. What does one thing have to do with another?

As we previously mentioned in chapter 11, a 2010 paper entitled "Comparing genomes to computer operating systems in terms of the topology and evolution of their regulatory control networks" attracted a bit of attention in the popular science press. The paper compared internals of the Linux operating system (representative of a human-generated, and presumably designed, network) with a biological network, the transcription network of *Escherichia coli*.

E. coli is a common bacteria most people have heard of or become painfully aware of at some point in their life, since some strains cause food poisoning. A transcription network manifests and controls a cell's biological processes accordingly by utilizing applicable sequences in its DNA. It enables a cell to utilize enzymes and create proteins specified in DNA in a dynamic manner that takes into account environmental conditions. Like the organism itself, the transcription network has evolved over billions of years in reaction to environmental factors and competition for energy. The Linux call network is a collection of functions that are used by other software running in the operating environment. These include various input/output functions, higher level filesystem and memory management, device control, and networking capabilities. The Linux call graph has been refined over several decades by humans. Over time much of the system has been reworked to improve reusability and performance.

One of the end products of their research, visualizations of the respective networks, appeared in several popular summaries of the paper including Wired and Discover Magazine. The authors had found a roughly hierarchical structure in both networks and found a way to represent them visually, that didn't result in an inscrutable hairball. The networks were structurally quite a bit different, and this was apparent in their respective renderings. The Linux call graph has a roughly hierarchical, top heavy tree-like structure, with many higher level functions connected to a smaller number of lower level functions. This graph had over 12,000 nodes and more than 33,000 edges. There were fewer nodes at the bottom, with a lot of incoming edges, functioning as hubs. This was interpreted to be a function of a cost-effective design, to produce a small number of extensively reusable components. But because so much of the system depends on a relatively small number of components, a failure in one of these components has a significant effect on the system as a whole. It is efficient but not resilient.

A Librarian's Guide to Graphs, Data and the Semantic Web.

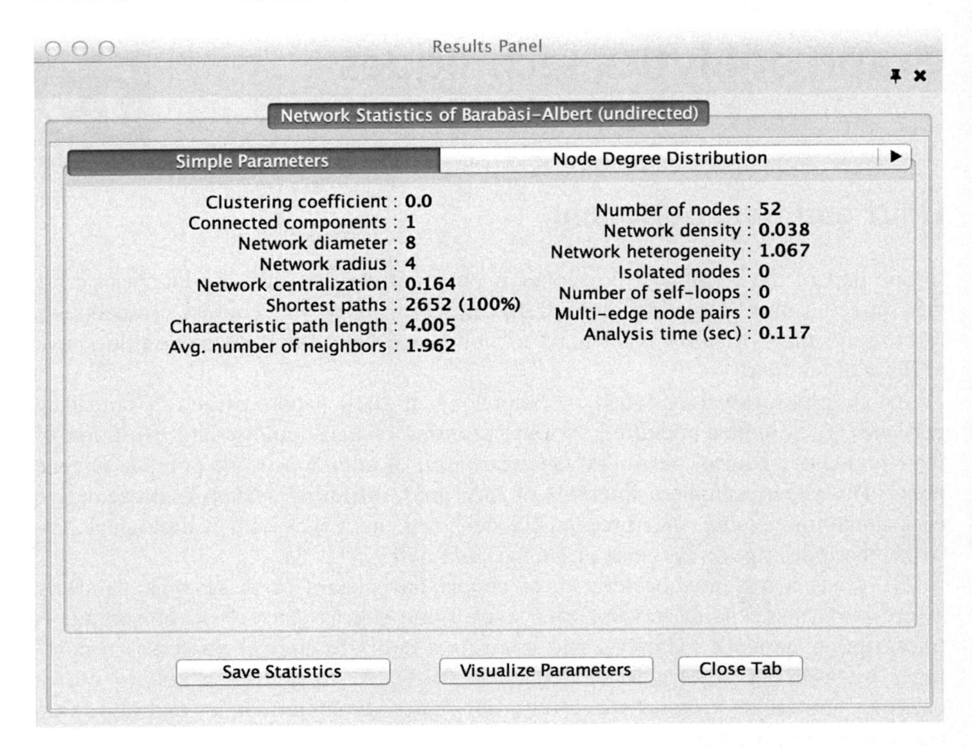

Figure 19.1 Cytoscape graph statistics report for a scale-free network.

The *E. coli* transcription is quite a bit smaller than the Linux call graph, with about 1300 nodes and 2900 edges. This network favors nodes that perform unique tasks to general-purpose nodes. Intuitively this makes sense for a system that has evolved in response to environmental challenges. Were the network to depend too heavily on generic nodes, it would be increasingly vulnerable to complete failure in response to a challenge. Rather than putting all its eggs in one basket, the transcription network that persists has done so by spreading functions among distinct sets of nodes, rarely relying on one node to do more than one thing, thus greatly reducing the likelihood of any single point of failure. When those did emerge over time, they were likely eliminated when the organism that carried those traits failed to survive and reproduce.

To learn more about these networks, researchers represented them as directed networks and applied some basic graph analytic techniques in an effort to characterize them. Several had to do with quantifying aspects of the graph such as the number of nodes and edges, the number of incoming and outgoing edges, the frequency with which a path extended through a given node. They also analyzed the overall degree distribution of nodes in the graph. This can yield evidence of characteristic degree distributions such as a power-law distribution, that would indicate the presence of hubs. Collectively the results of these various analyses are sometimes called graph statistics (Figure 19.1). Analysis of these graphs revealed clear evidence that they developed under radically different circumstances. The Linux network reflected a modular design, with many upper level functions depending on a few lower level functions. The *E. coli* transcription network exhibited characteristics of something that had developed over time and in response to many challenges. Their differences also provided clues for how a complex system might be structured to achieve higher levels of resilience in response to challenges. The research also dealt a blow to intelligent design advocates, if any of them were paying attention.

Why analyze entire graphs?

For dynamic networks, connectedness and information flow can tell us a lot about a system. With a small graph, you might be able to comprehend these factors by simply looking at a visualization. But as the graph gets bigger, it becomes harder and harder to make sense of it by just looking at it. Some visualization tools can help by allowing you to filter out some nodes, color, or change the size of others, based on certain criteria in addition to providing different layout options. But there comes a point where you may need to analyze bigger graphs or analyze your graph in ways that visualizations and visualization tools just can't support. This is where graph analytics can help.

Graph analytics is a generic term for techniques for equations and heuristics for analyzing aspects of graphs. Different graph theorists tend to categorize graph analytics in different ways. In this chapter we organize graph analytic techniques by

- node degree measures
- path analysis and metrics
- clusters, communities, and motifs
- graph structure and metrics.

Node degree measures

In some networks you might be interested in who has the most connections. You might want to know who has coauthored lots of papers, who has the most friends, or who might be the source of that office cold that spread around so quickly. Node metrics can help.

Node degree measures are all based on counting. Degree centrality is the term used for this concept, where degree is equivalent to the edge count. Often the interest is in the node with the highest number of connections. Sometimes, it's important to weed out nodes with high degree values because they really don't tell you anything. Barack Obama has a high degree centrality in twitter's network because so many people follow him, but if you are looking at the social network of your friends because you want to know what they are interested in, Barack Obama becomes just so much noise in that network. Conversely, if you want to know who among your friends is the most popular on twitter, then you are very interested in identifying the highest degree node because that will reveal the answer to your question.

Node metrics may be calculated differently depending on whether the graph is directed or undirected, and whether the edges have been assigned any weights. The degree of a node in an undirected unweighted graph is simply a count of the number of edges connected to each node in the graph. A high degree centrality score simply means that a node has a larger than average number of connections for that graph. For directed graphs, there can be in-degree and out-degree measures. As the names imply, this is a count of the number of edges that point toward and away from the given node, respectively.

For weighted networks, the degree measure for a node not only counts the edges, but sums the weights of the edges. Regardless of how it is arrived at, a node with higher degree centrality is telling you something important about that particular node. It's up to you to look at the nodes and edges involved to determine what that something might be. An often valuable measure of centrality is betweenness centrality. This is a measure that indicates which node or nodes are between clusters of other nodes. Again, betweenness centrality is revealing that something is special about the node or nodes with high or highest betweenness centrality, but the meaning is contextual. There are other centrality measures but it's often sufficient to measure degree and betweenness centrality to get a sense for relative importance of nodes in the graph.

Path analysis

In some graphs, especially networks, there is keen interest in how things move through the network. You might be interested in the flow of information, electricity, or products in a supply chain. This is where path analysis can be useful.

Path analysis, or when it is performed interactively, graph traversal, is concerned with paths between nodes. Let's say you are looking for a new job, and you know someone who knows someone who works at Google. This network involves a small number of nodes, and you can quickly identify who you need to talk to in order to get your resume to the right person. But let's say the network was bigger, and there were multiple paths to employees at Google. Maybe you want to identify all of those paths and decide for yourself who you feel most comfortable asking for help. Or maybe you want to find the shortest path, that is the route with the least number of edges, to someone at Google. Path analysis can help you do that (Figure 19.2).

Path length is a quantity representing the number of edges between two nodes. There are various situations when the shortest path between two nodes is useful. The shortest path is the path that traverses the least number of edges. With a directed graph, paths often take into account directionality. Paths through directed graphs represent the flow of information within an organization, the process of gene expression, or the relationships among concepts in a taxonomy or ontology.

Sometimes it is useful to identify special paths called cycles. A cycle is a path that ultimately leads back to the starting node. Sometimes you may want to identify

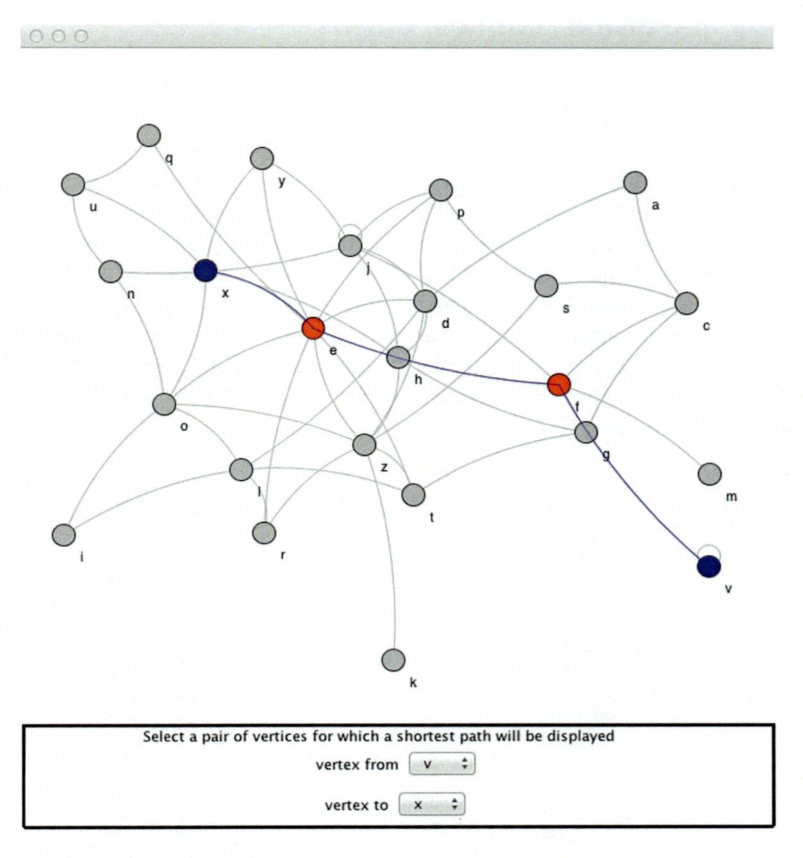

Figure 19.2 Shortest path detection between nodes x and v.

multiple paths that start and end with the same node, but do not incorporate the same nodes along the way. In other cases you want all paths, or or in other instances you may want to set a threshold and just see the first five or ten shortest paths. It turns out that path analysis is a hard and computationally intense problem. Path analysis can tell you the diameter of a graph, which is defined as the longest nonrepeating path between two nodes in the graph. Path analysis algorithms are provided in some visualization tools and in most graph analysis libraries. Implementation characteristics vary such that some algorithms favor speed over completeness, for example. Finally, weights can factor into path analysis. If your edges have weights, you can sum these values to determine the weight of that path.

A graph database usually offers some kind of interactive graph traversal support. Since edges and nodes are both first-class objects in graphs, it follows that finding paths would be as important as finding nodes. In a graph database, these can both be thought of as search tasks, and providing some kind of search capability is fundamental to any type of data storage software.

Clusters, partitions, cliques, motifs

In some graphs, it's useful to know about clusters of things. A tightly knit community of people might all know one another through a shared hobby or because their children attend the same school. A food web might have recurring connection patterns representing predator–prey interaction. You can discover these groups through cluster analysis.

A cluster is a collection of nodes with relatively few connections to other groups of nodes, but a fairly high number of connections among themselves. Clusters tell you something about the similarity of a group of nodes, at least with regard to the edges that connect them. The prevalence of clusters, along with the distribution of node degree values within the graph, can tell you something about the overall graph itself, and how it compares to reference graphs like random, scale-free, and small-world graphs. When large group of nodes are connected, they are referred to as a partition or a community (Figure 19.3).

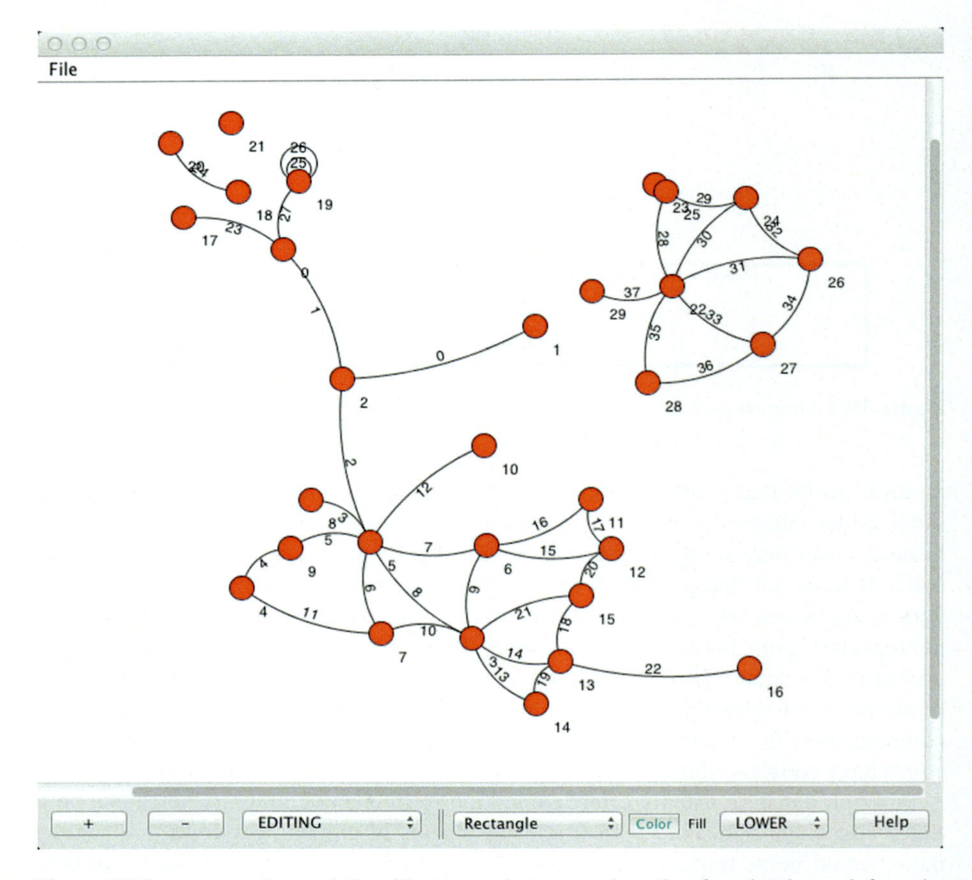

Figure 19.3 An example graph that illustrates clusters, such as that found at lower left, and motifs, in this case, a triangular pattern of connectivity that recurs nine times.

Cluster coefficient is a useful measure for determining whether there are clusters in a network, or a subgraph. The cluster coefficient of a node is a ratio of how many edges it actually has divided by the maximum number of edges that it could have. Clusters are groups of nodes that have a significantly higher number of edges among them than compared with the graph as a whole, or with other subgraphs within the graph. How does cluster analysis differ from node degree, for example? Because it involves statistical analysis of the entire graph. The focus is not on individual nodes. This technique can also help you determine what type of graph it is, in cases where you want to know this. Remember that types of graphs include random, small-world, and scale-free network. Cluster analysis can also help you identify things like homophily in graphs, that is, instances where there is a regular preferential pattern of connectivity among nodes (all boys like baseball, for example).

Closely related to cluster analysis is finding cliques. Everyone has some idea of what a clique is because we've all encountered the social example of it—a tight knit group within which everyone knows everyone else, but one that is also hard to penetrate from the outside. In graph theory, the definition is a bit more explicit and basically says that a clique is a subset of a graph where every two vertices in the subset share an edge. If you recall, a complete graph is one where every node shares an edge with every other node. So, a clique is a subgraph that exhibits this characteristic. Cliques overlap with another category of substructures within graphs, called motifs. A motif is any sort of distinct, recurring pattern of nodes and edges. These three concepts provide a cross section of patterns of interest that can occur within a graph.

Graph structure and metrics

There are at times remarkable similarities between networks that represent very different things. People tend to exist within networks that have small-world characteristics, where paths are typically short between any two points. Scale-free networks show up a lot in biology. To get at these characteristics of a network, you often have to evaluate all the nodes or paths in a graph.

Distributions reveal statistically significant aspects of the graph, with respect to both nodes and edges. Distribution analysis builds on centrality measures, graph density, strength of connections, path analysis, and identification of hubs. Graph density compares node connectivity across the graph. Distribution analysis can also compare the graph of interest to random, small-world, and scale-free networks to see if it has similar characteristics to any of these well-known types of graphs.

Graph statistics can be used to elucidate a graph's overall structure. These measures can be used to determine how similar a graph is to a known graph type or to compare it with other graphs. A graph's diameter is the longest average path in a graph. The diameter of a small-world graph is smaller than for other graphs such as a lattice or random graph. Calculating the diameter of a graph is based on path analysis but the result is a value that characterizes the entire graph. Node distributions across a graph can determine how similar it is to other graphs. For example, a scale-free network has a node distribution that conforms to the power law: there are a few nodes that have high degree values, and a lot of nodes that have low degree values.

Various graph analysis functionality can be found in software libraries, graph visualization tools, and graph databases. Recall that Gephi, a graph visualization tool, incorporates some graph analytic capabilities. These capabilities can be used to filter nodes or edges based on certain criteria, to change visual aspects of nodes or edges based on things like degree measure, or this information can be presented alongside a graph as tables or plots. There are several interactive graph pattern matching and traversal languages for graph databases.

Finally there are times when you might want to integrate graph analysis into a custom software application. This is the role of graph analysis software libraries. These are typically implemented in a particular programming language such as Java or Python, with distinct types of functionality grouped into programming constructs such as functions, objects, or class libraries. They each tend to have their own internal way of representing a graph. Some offer multiple algorithms for doing the same thing. You can use them to extract subgraphs from larger networks. You can generate reference examples of common types of graphs such as random or small-world graphs and compare them to your graph. You can import and export common graph data representations such as GraphML or GraphSON. Some libraries include implementations of well-known algorithms such as Google's pagerank algorithm, which you can apply to your own graphs. The next chapter looks at several graph analysis libraries and their capabilities.

Graph analytics software libraries 20

One of the remaining mysteries of science is understanding the nature of human consciousness. A theory that attempts to explain the emergence of conscious is called the Integrated Information Theory (IIT) which is described in a paper entitled "Consciousness as Integrated Information: A Provisional Manifesto" by Giulio Tononi. IIT suggests that consciousness is a function of the degree to which a system is able to integrate information. The author introduces IIT by means of a pair of thought experiments. The first involves a sensor that can detect whether a light is off or on. A light is shown periodically on a screen. A person and the sensor report when the light is on or off. The two perform equally well, so why isn't the sensor considered conscious? The answer lies in the possible states that a human can discern verses what the sensor is able to determine. And this is a function of the amount of information a human is able to integrate and consider when performing this observation task.

Claude E. Shannon developed a theory of communication in 1948 that included a mathematical definition of information. Shannon was considering the various characteristics of what we called information in the context of electronic communications. Unsurprisingly in 1948, electronic communications were conveyed over noisy transmission lines subject to voltage fluctuations due to various external factors. But what is noise and what constitutes the message? To answer this question, he developed a theory of information that took into account the relative entropy within a defined means of representing a message, such as the characters that could be sent and received via a teletype. This has been described in layman's terms as the degree of uncertainty about the content of a message or the extent to which the message itself comes as a surprise.

The sensor in Tononi's consciousness thought experiment can only discern two states: the light is on or off. A human would be able to tell if the light were different colors, if it formed a geometric pattern, or if it were in fact the opening sequence of 2001: A Space Odyssey. In a haze of connections and probabilities about the nature of a thing we perceive, we're leveraging integrated information to consider and discard a myriad possible explanations for what's being shown on the screen. By Shannon's definition of information, it is apparent that even a single frame of a movie projected onto a screen contains much more information than the glare from the usher's flashlight. Tononi's second thought experiment involved a digital camera. A digital camera has a dense matrix that contains millions of sensors. It can detect many millions points of light simultaneously. But there is no integration of the various states detected by its sensors. Each sensor acts independently of all others and neither the sensors nor the camera integrates this information in any way. So IIT says the digital camera also fails to meet the threshold of consciousness.

IIT has inspired more research into the nature of consciousness, what portions of the brain might be crucial to consciousness, and the extent to which connections

A Librarian's Guide to Graphs, Data and the Semantic Web.

within the brain are responsible for it. Olaf Sporns at MIT coined the term "connectome" which is a name for a map of connections within a brain. He suggests a cross-disciplinary effort to map the "Human Connectome" would yield significant results in understanding cognition and mental disorders. Other researchers maintain that consciousness is an emergent property of the connectome. A paper entitled "Spectral Signatures of Reorganised Brain Networks in Disorders of Consciousness" describes an approach to evaluating consciousness by using EEGs to characterize the network in a human brain. The authors compared these networks among people who are observably conscious and those who seem to be in a vegetative state, and found some comatose patient's brain networks exhibited a degree of consciousness far beyond what was expected. It would appear that, even though we don't fully understand what consciousness is, we can analyze the network of connections in a human brain over time and say whether or not a person is conscious.

This chapter looks at software libraries for performing graph analytics. Software libraries are collections of application code written in a particular programming language that do a particular set of things. You can't necessarily load and run these as they are and do anything useful. They are building blocks. Someone has to add some additional program code to make use of them. In this chapter, we introduce two Java libraries: Jung and JGraphT, and one python library called NetworkX. We also look at a library for computing Graph Edit Distance which is useful for comparing graphs. Among these libraries, there is much overlap in terms of functionality. As you investigate further, you might find functionality that you need in one that isn't available in the others. Another common selection criteria is to select a library that is actively being developed and has a large user base. It is also perfectly valid to choose one over the other because your staff has experience with that particular programming language.

A note about RDF and graph analytics

You can use these libraries with RDF graphs, albeit with a bit more effort. An RDF graph is a multi-partite graph, that is, there are many different types of nodes and a variety of relationships expressed as predicates within a semantic graph. Many graph analytic techniques are intended for use with unipartite graphs. So for example if you want to analyze a coauthorship graph that's part of an RDF graph, you need to extract that subgraph. For example, an RDF graph that expresses coauthorship relationships may do so through a shared edge to an identifier for the paper that two individuals coauthored. You might want to reduce this relationship to an edge that directly links the two authors in a subgraph so you can analyze the coauthorship relationships. Graph analysis and visualization tools often provide support for generating subgraphs.

Jung

Jung is a collection of graph algorithms implemented in Java. It includes libraries for generating graph representations suitable for processing with the algorithms library, visualization libraries which can be used as stand-alone applications or as building blocks for custom graph visualization tools, and a small library of input–output classes for reading existing graphs represented in GraphML or Pajek, and outputting graphs in those formats. The algorithms library contains implementations for a variety of graph analytic techniques. There's extensive online documentation for the Jung library. We're going to illustrate how Jung represents graphs and give you an idea of the implementations of graph analytics Jung includes.

Let's first look at the graph representation library. In the Java programming community, it is common for programmers to publish a sort of Web guide to a software library. This documentation is called Javadocs and it is generated from the actual program code, but is often amended so that it can be read by nonprogrammers. Each software library is identified by a package name. The full Java package name for the Jung library is edu.uci.ics.jung.graph. The typical package naming convention for Java libraries is to use the inverse of the fully qualified name that represents the organization that originally developed the library, followed by the library name and package libraries that are named for the functionality they provide.

Since all of the libraries provided by Jung share the same root (edu.uci.ics.jung), we'll abbreviate that portion of the library name to jung, so edu.uci.ics.jung.graph becomes jung.graph. For all these libraries, you have to convert your graph data into a form the library understands. Jung has a library that's concerned with representing and manipulation of a graph, called Graph.

A Jung Graph corresponds to the mathematical representation of a graph mentioned in the introduction to this book: G = {V,E}. That says a graph is a set of vertices and edges. Across the Jung libraries, this is represented as G <V,E> using a syntax in Java that defines a collection that contains two types of things, vertices and edges. In Java, program code is organized into classes. A class defines some variables (fields) and some things you can do to those variable (methods). A simple kind of graph in Jung is called Hypergraph. Here are some Jung Hypergraph methods:

addEdge, addVertex, containsEdge, containsVertex, degree, findEdge, findEdgeSet, getDefaultEdgeType, getEdgeCount, getEdges, getEdgeType, getIncidentCount, getIncidentEdges, getIncidentVertices, getNeighborCount, getNeighbors, getVertexCount, getVertices, isIncident, isNeighbor, removeEdge, removeVertex

Sometimes classes are arranged in hierarchies, very much the same way Class and subClass work in ontologies. Hypergraph is the most basic kind of Graph in Jung. Most of the time you want to use the Jung graph class, which builds on Hypergraph and adds some rudimentary node and path analysis methods, some are intended for use with directed graphs:

getDest, getEndpoints, getInEdges, getOpposite, getOutEdges, getPredecessorCount, getPredecessors, getSource, getSuccessorCount, getSuccessors, inDegree, isDest, isPredecessor, isSource, isSuccessor, outDegree

All of these methods create or perform some action on one or more nodes or edges.

Here is a list of some of the more commonly used Jung packages. We've grouped these by the analysis categories identified in Chapter 19. In some cases, a library may combine analysis techniques from multiple categories. For example, some classes you would use to analyze graph structure and generate graph-wide metrics fall into the shortest path and scoring libraries.

Node degree measures

- jung.algorithms.scoring—a library for calculating a variety of graph node metrics which also contains some more advanced algorithms such as an implementation of Google's pagerank.

Path analysis and metrics

- jung.algorithms.shortestpath—a collection of algorithms for performing path analysis, primarily finding shortest paths.

Clusters, communities, and motifs

- jung.algorithms.cluster—a few techniques for identify clusters in a graph.
- jung.algorithms.metrics—a library for calculating cluster coefficients, structural holes in graphs, and counting triad motifs.

Graph structure and metrics

- jung.algorithms.generators.random—a package that can generate representative examples of scale-free, small-world, as well as random graphs.
- jung.algorithms.importance—various ways of calculating betweenness centrality and a few algorithms for ranking nodes in some fashion.

Other useful libraries

- jung.graph—the core Jung graph library.
- jung.algorithms.filters—several ways of filtering a graph to generate a subgraph.
- jung.io—a library that supports outputting a graph to a file (serializing it) as GraphML, Pajek, or an ASCII text file of a graph's adjacency matrix.
- jung.samples—a large collection of code samples that use various Jung packages to demonstrate how to do graph analysis, visualizations, etc.
- jung.visualization—a set of graph drawing packages that can be used in Java desktop applications and applets.

At some point you might want to apply Jung to an RDF graph. As we noted earlier, to do this you may first need to extract a subgraph and then analyze it. You can do this with the jung.algorithms.filters library. It contains several classes you could use to filter an RDF graph, including VertexPredicateFilter and EdgePredicateFilter. The use of the word predicate in the class names may be a bit confusing. This is not the same as a predicate in a semantic triple. It simply means these classes perform a test on input data. A programmer defines their test in a custom method called evaluate. It performs a test on some input values and returns true or false. The results from this process are written to a new graph, which can be analyzed just like any other graph (Figure 20.1).

Some graph measures, such as various degree centrality measures, are performed by the Graph on the object of interest, either a vertex or an edge. All graphs have an edge field and a vertices field which contain all the edges and vertices for that graph. Since the Graph includes various vertex and edge measures such as degree, getEdgeCount, inDegree, outDegree, you have to examine each node or edge in the graph and call the appropriate method (e.g., degree for an undirected graph) to calculate these values.

Other measures must be calculated in the context of the entire graph. You can only calculate betweenness centrality based on how connected the graph is and how important a given node is to connecting different parts of the graph. Distance centrality is similar. It is a measure of a given node's distance to all other nodes in the graph. The DijkstraShortestPath class can evaluate all the paths in the graph or measure the path length between two specified nodes.

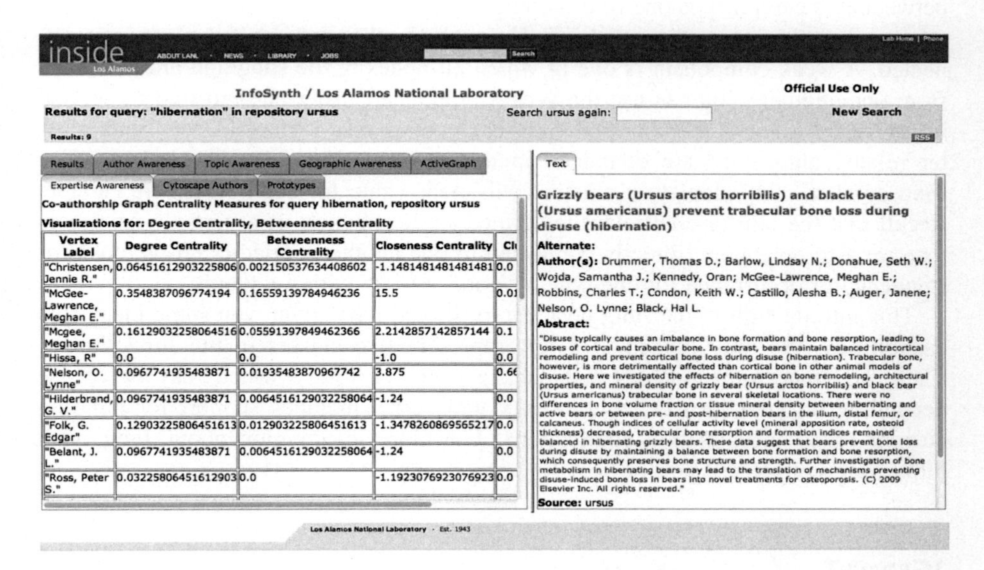

Figure 20.1 A summary of several centrality measures for a coauthorship graph, generated by the JGraphT graph analysis library.

Here's an excerpt of Java code that uses the Jung libraries to load a GraphML file containing coauthorship graph data, and compute degree for all the nodes in the graph:

```
// First, create a graph and populate it with data from a GraphML file
final UndirectedGraph coauthGraph = new UndirectedSparseMultigraph();
GraphMLReader, node, edge> gmlr = new GraphMLReader, node, edge>(new VertexFactory(),
new EdgeFactory());
String filename = "coauthors.graphml");
gmlr.load(filename, coauthGraph);
// Now, compute degree for each node in the graph
System.out.println("Computing degree for each coauthor node...")
DegreeScorer degreeRanker = new DegreeScorer(coauthGraph);
for (java.lang.Object authorNode : coauthGraph.getVertices()) {
  Double nodeScore = degreeRanker.getVertexScore(authorNode)
  System.out.println("Degree Centrality for\t" + authorNode.name+ "\t" + nodeScore);
}
```

Jung has quite a few ways to explore clusters within a graph. EdgeBetweennessClusterer examines the relative "edgebetweenness" of an edge between nodes in the graph. We haven't seen edge betweenness before. It evaluates each edge to determine if it lies along the shortest path between any two nodes in the graph. Remember that a small-world network has a few rewired nodes that greatly reduce the distance between any two nodes in the graph. An edge with high betweenness centrality is one of those edges.

A component is a portion of the graph in which all nodes in a group are interconnected. A weak component is one in which all nodes in the subgraph are reachable from one another. You can use the WeakComponentCluster class to find these, and it will return a list of member nodes for each component it finds. A few other cluster related algorithms are contained in the jung.algorithms.metrics package. The Metrics class can calculate a cluster coefficient value for each vertex in a graph. Recall that the cluster coefficient is defined as the fraction of a vertex's neighbors that are also neighbors (directly connected to one another). TriadicCensus looks for frequency of occurrence for one type of motif, a triad, within a graph.

This introduction to the Jung java library should have given you some idea of its capabilities. We only looked at a few representative classes in the Jung library. There are many other classes and packages in the library which may be of use depending on your project requirements. Jung even includes support for building custom graph visualization applications. For more information about Jung, visit http://jung.sourceforge.net.

JGraphT

There is another open source Java library that provides much of the same functionality as Jung, called JGraphT. Like Jung, it has a Graph interface that essentially defines a template for a graph object. Here are the methods it specifies. These are the things you can do to, or with a Graph object:

> *addEdge, addVertex, containsEdge, containsEdge, containsVertex, edgeSet, edgesOf, getAllEdges, getEdge, getEdgeFactory, getEdgeSource, getEdgeTarget, getEdgeWeight, removeAllEdges, removeEdge, removeAllVertices, removeVertex, vertexSet*

Does this list look familiar? It ought to, because it is very similar to the things you can do with a Jung Graph object. This library has classes for generating special types of graphs including RandomGraphGenerator, RingGraphGenerator, ScaleFreeGraphGenerator, CompleteGraphGenerator, StarGraphGenerator, and others. It can export graph data in several formats including DOT, GraphML, GML, an adjacency matrix, or in a format compatible with a popular desktop diagram drawing tool called Visio. It has a variety of path traversal and path analysis classes, as well as several connectivity inspector classes for identifying sets of strongly connected nodes. Unlike Jung, JGraphT does not provide support for building graph visualization applications. More information about JGraphT can be found at http://jgrapht.org.

Here is a small program which uses the JGraphT libraries to generate and output a random graph as a list of adjacent edges and also in the DOT graph serialization format:

```
import java.io.*;
import org.jgrapht.*;
import org.jgrapht.graph.*;
import org.jgrapht.generate.*;
import org.jgrapht.ext.*;
public final class rg {
  public static void main (String args[]) {
    RandomGraphGenerator<String, DefaultEdge> randomGenerator = new
RandomGraphGenerator<String, DefaultEdge>(35, 95);
    Graph<String, DefaultEdge> randomGraph = new SimpleGraph<String, DefaultEdge>
(DefaultEdge.class);
    VertexFactory<String> vertexFactory = new VertexFactory<String>()
        {
            int n = 0;
            @Override
            public String createVertex()
            {
                String s = String.valueOf(n);
                n++;
                return s;
            }
        };
    randomGenerator.generateGraph(randomGraph, vertexFactory, null);
    System.out.println(randomGraph.toString());
    try {
      DOTExporter de = new DOTExporter();
      PrintWriter pf = new PrintWriter("rg.dot");
```

```
        de.export(pf.randomGraph);
    } catch (Exception e) { System.out.println(e); }
  }
}
```

NetworkX

NetworkX is a python library which includes implementations for a great many graph analysis algorithms. It is implemented as a module, so any python application that needs to use any part of the networkX library must import the module, for example, import networkx as nx. From that point on, functions within NetworkX are addressable using whatever prefix you specified in the import statement, followed by a period and the name of the function. As with Jung, the first step for using NetworkX is to create a graph. A graph is an object created with the networkx.Graph() method, or with a method corresponding to the type of graph you need to generate, such as a DiGraph, which is a NetworkX directed graph. Networkx includes functions for reading data in a variety of formats and converting it to graphs. Networkx can read and write a variety of graph formats including Pajek, GraphML, JSON, GEXF, and GML to name a few.

Here is a brief example that uses a built-in sample graph generator library. It calculates and prints the degree centrality measures for all nodes in the graph.

```
from networkx import *
G = lollipop_graph(4,6)
print(G.nodes())
print(G.edges())
dg = degree_centrality(G)
for v in G.nodes():
print('%s %s' % (v,dg[v]))
```

When the program is executed, it produces the following output which consists of a node list for the graph, followed by an edge list, and finally the degree centrality values for all nodes:

```
[0, 1, 2, 3, 4, 5, 6, 7, 8, 9]
[(0, 1), (0, 2), (0, 3), (1, 2), (1, 3), (2, 3), (3, 4), (4, 5), (5, 6), (6, 7), (7, 8), (8, 9)]
0 0.333333333333
1 0.333333333333
2 0.333333333333
3 0.444444444444
4 0.222222222222
5 0.222222222222
6 0.222222222222
7 0.222222222222
8 0.222222222222
9 0.111111111111
```

Once you have created an instance of a NetworkX graph and populated it with data, there are a variety of classes and functions which can be used to visualize and analyze the graph. As with Jung, for the purposes of this overview, we are primarily interested in the graph analysis algorithms provided by NetworkX. Here are a few examples of connectivity algorithms available in NetworkX:

degree_centrality(), in_degree_centrality(), out_degree_centrality(), betweenness_centrality, pagerank(), shortest_path(), has_path(), dijkstra_path_length()

Distribution measures include:

diameter(), radius(), center(), all_shortest_paths(), all_pairs_shortest_path(), all_pairs_dijkstra_path()

There are also numerous cluster analysis functions:

triangles(), clustering(), find_cliques(), edge_betweenness_centrality()

As you can see, there is tremendous overlap between capabilities provided by the Jung java library and the NetworkX python module. Deciding between the two libraries is typically a choice made based upon the knowledge and skills of the individuals that would develop your graph application. Of the two, the learning curve for NetworkX is probably not as steep, assuming you know Python! There is extensive documentation and tutorials are available online for NetworkX, if you want to explore it in more detail.

Graph Edit Distance

There is one final graph library that may be of interest, if you want to compare graphs. Graph Edit Distance is a notion modeled after string edit distance, which is an analysis of two strings which determines how many changes would be necessary (additions, edits, or deletes) to convert string a to string b. Usually a string edit distance algorithm assigns a penalty to each type of edit, and the resulting score reflects that. Graph Edit Distance applies a similar notion to the comparison of graphs. It evaluates the number of node and edge adds, edits, and deletes which would be necessary to convert graph a to graph b, where penalty values are assigned to the edit types. This analysis is computationally intense, so it best used on smaller graphs, and obviously only makes sense when comparing "like" graphs, such as two coauthorship graphs, excerpts of gene sequences from closely related species, or short textual content such as blog posts.

There is an opensource Java implementation of a Graph Edit Distance algorithm called the Graph Matching Toolkit. This toolkit computes the Graph Edit Distance for two graphs represented in an XML format called GXL (Graph eXchange Language). Comparison of graphs can be useful in the study of social networks, biological networks, food webs, aligned subgraphs from semantic networks, and citation networks, to name a few.

Here is an example of the sentence "the quick brown fox jumped quickly" represented as a directed graph using GXL. Words are defined as noded and directed edges connect the words together in the order that they occur:

```
<!DOCTYPE gxl SYSTEM "http://www.gupro.de/GXL/gxl-1.0.dtd">
<gxl xmlns:xlink="http://www.w3.org/1999/xlink">
<graph id="SEN_002" edgeids="false" edgemode="directed">
  <node id="_0"><attr name="word"><string>the</string></attr></node>
  <node id="_1"><attr name="word"><string>brown</string></attr></node>
  <node id="_2"><attr name="word"><string>fox</string></attr></node>
  <node id="_3"><attr name="word"><string>jumped</string></attr></node>
  <node id="_4"><attr name="word"><string>quickly</string></attr></node>
  <edge from="_0" to="_1"/>
  <edge from="_1" to="_2"/>
  <edge from="_2" to="_3"/>
  <edge from="_3" to="_4"/>
</graph></gxl>
```

This toolkit allows you to assign a specific penalty for node edits and a penalty for edge edits. You may decide that the absence of a node is a much greater indicator of difference between two graphs than the absence of an edge between two nodes. The toolkit allows you to specify a list of graphs to which a source graph is to be compared. Here is an excerpt from a configuration file that assigns a penalty of 3.0 if a node is missing from one of the graphs, and a penalty of 2.0 if an edge exists between two nodes in one graph but not the other:

```
##############################################################################
# graph matching paradigm (possible choices are: AStar, Beam, Hungarian, VJ)
# if "Beam" is chosen, maximum number of open paths s has to be defined
##############################################################################
matching=Beam
s=10
##############################################################################
# cost for node/edge deletions/insertions (both cost values have to be > 0)
##############################################################################
node=3.0
edge=2.0
##############################################################################
# number of node attributes and the individual names of these attributes
##############################################################################
numOfNodeAttr=1
nodeAttr0=word
```

GraphMatching has a variety of applications. The example above uses graph matching to compare the graph representation of two documents. Each document is converted to a directed graph, where every word in each sentence is converted to a set of nodes connected by a set of directed edges that point to the next word node until the end of the sentence is reached. A stopword list can be employed to omit frequently occurring words, if desired, when generating a graph representation of the document. However, using a stopword list in this situation may yield unexpected results, since the words that occur to either side of the omitted word will now have a directed edge between them. Once the data has been converted to graphs, you can use this toolkit to compute the Graph Edit Distance between the GXL representations of the directed document graphs.

Since we modeled text as a directed graph, the context of words is effectively taken into account when two document graphs are compared. This approach to comparing textual documents may be of use in some situations where word order within entire sentences, and not just word order or frequency of co-occurrence, is an important aspect of text analysis. This Graph Matching Toolkit could be used with RDF graphs. It could be used to compare two named RDF graphs representing the same knowledge space at different points in time. Their respective graph edit scores would indicate how much the two have diverged over time.

Semantic repositories and how to use them

21

VIVO

VIVO is an open source Semantic Web data integration and discovery project aimed at connecting researchers within and across disciplines. The VIVO project was started at Cornell University (and incidentally, VIVO is not an acronym). Its goal is to be discipline neutral and leverage the terminology common to each scientific discipline to associate researchers with their topics of research. The VIVO environment, typically deployed within a university environment, makes all of this information available in a linked open data environment with Web interfaces, search, and visualizations. The aim is to expose outward facing researcher profiles with links out to linked data that exposes fine-grained information about research and association among researchers. VIVO highlights an often overlooked use for Semantic Web technologies—the potential for better integration of heterogeneous data sources. In fact many VIVO users will tell you that one of the things it is really good at is making system of record data inconsistencies very apparent.

VIVO combines many types of data. A university, like most large organizations, maintains Human Resource data about when an individual was hired, their past job experience, and their current employment history within the organization. Libraries are good sources of information about researcher publications. A huge win for any organization that employs researchers is to simply merge those two data sets. VIVO attempts to do more. VIVO supports links out to Open Researcher and Contributor ID (ORCID), which hosts globally unique researcher identifiers. VIVO supports relationships from people and publications to linked data sources such as DBPedia. In VIVO, a user can assume ownership of their profile and contribute to it. VIVO uses many ontologies we've discussed previously, including Geonames, FOAF, the Org ontology, and can accommodate new domain ontologies as needed. VIVO uses Jena as a software interface to a triplestore. In every conceivable way, VIVO is a pure Semantic Web application.

Triplestores

A semantic repository, or triplestore, is a specialized database to store and query triples. In some cases, the word triples is a misnomer, as some semantic repositories use extra data elements to describe or identify discrete triples. Most commonly, there is an internal unique identifier associated with each triple statement, which is especially useful when a triplestore supports transactions such as updates for triples, but these values are also used in some indexes for triples to facilitate rapid retrieval of statements that match a given query. Under the hood, some triplestores use

A Librarian's Guide to Graphs, Data and the Semantic Web.

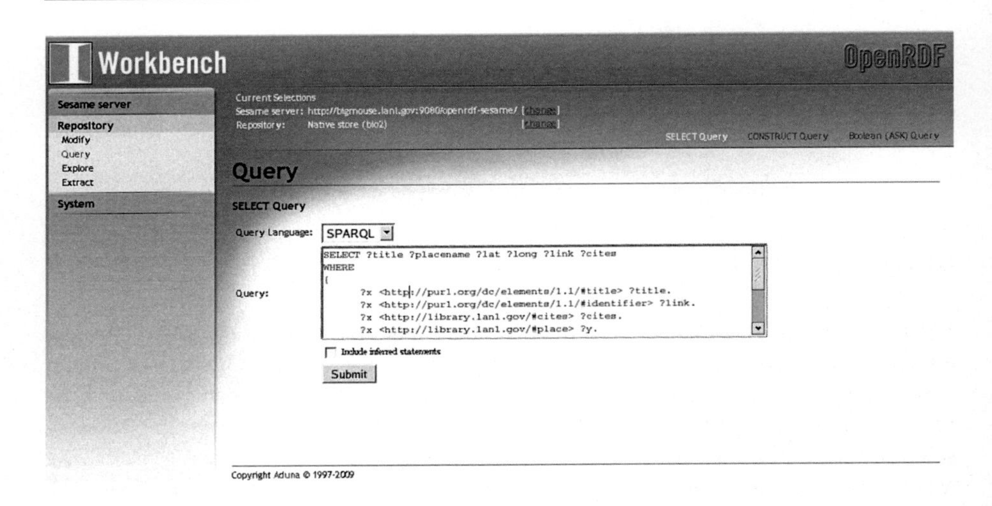

Figure 21.1 OpenRDF Workbench SPARQL query interface.

relational databases to store their data. This sometimes results in a mind-numbing and nearly incomprehensible database schema, which fortunately, you never have to know about, since the software that makes the database look like a triplestore handles all aspects of interacting with the underlying database. There are also "native triplestores" which are designed from the ground up to support triples.

It is also possible to store semantic data in a graph database. As with triplestores and relational databases, there are software layers that make a general-purpose graph store look like a triplestore. Since RDF data is graph data, you can store RDF data directly. If you chose this route, you need to map the subject, predicate and object information to nodes and edges, and retain IRIs as graph element identifiers or as properties. The problem with this approach is that you have to do a lot more work yourself. A general-purpose graph database probably won't be able to parse and import RDF data serializations such as RDF/XML. On the plus side, you won't need to come up with a graph model for RDF data, but you will need to specify a mapping scheme for the components of RDF triples into graph elements and properties.

For Semantic Web data, it's best to use a specialized database for RDF graph data. Triplestores offer functionality specific to RDF graphs. A triplestore has special indexing schemes for the components of triples. Triplestore indexes include at least three types of indexes: subject, predicate, object; predicate, object, subject; and object, predicate, subject.

The standard search language for triplestores is SPARQL. A triplestore that supports SPARQL will offer a Web-based query interface and may also accept SPARQL queries through a SPARQL endpoint. With the SPARQL query endpoint, you submit the same SPARQL query, URL-encoded so it is safe to transmit across the Web, to a Web address that hosts the SPARQL endpoint. Results are returned as an XML-formatted document that contains the data according to a pattern you specified in the SPARQL query select clause (Figures 21.1 and 21.2).

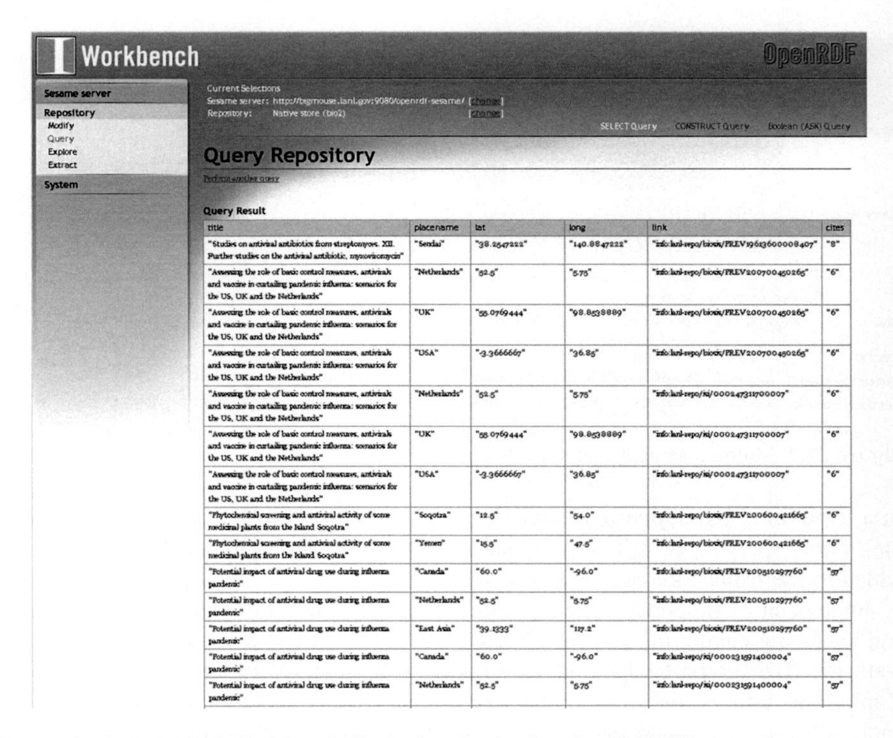

title	placename	lat	long	link	cites
"Studies on antiviral antibiotics from streptomyces. XII. Further studies on the antiviral antibiotic, myxoviromycin"	"Sendai"	"38.2547222"	"140.8847222"	"info:lanl-repo/biosis/PREV19613600008407"	"8"
"Assessing the role of basic control measures, antivirals and vaccine in curtailing pandemic influenza: scenarios for the US, UK and the Netherlands"	"Netherlands"	"52.5"	"5.75"	"info:lanl-repo/biosis/PREV200700450265"	"6"
"Assessing the role of basic control measures, antivirals and vaccine in curtailing pandemic influenza: scenarios for the US, UK and the Netherlands"	"UK"	"55.0769444"	"98.8538889"	"info:lanl-repo/biosis/PREV200700450265"	"6"
"Assessing the role of basic control measures, antivirals and vaccine in curtailing pandemic influenza: scenarios for the US, UK and the Netherlands"	"USA"	"-3.3666667"	"36.85"	"info:lanl-repo/biosis/PREV200700450265"	"6"
"Assessing the role of basic control measures, antivirals and vaccine in curtailing pandemic influenza: scenarios for the US, UK and the Netherlands"	"Netherlands"	"52.5"	"5.75"	"info:lanl-repo/isi/000247311700007"	"6"
"Assessing the role of basic control measures, antivirals and vaccine in curtailing pandemic influenza: scenarios for the US, UK and the Netherlands"	"UK"	"55.0769444"	"98.8538889"	"info:lanl-repo/isi/000247311700007"	"6"
"Assessing the role of basic control measures, antivirals and vaccine in curtailing pandemic influenza: scenarios for the US, UK and the Netherlands"	"USA"	"-3.3666667"	"36.85"	"info:lanl-repo/isi/000247311700007"	"6"
"Phytochemical screening and antiviral activity of some medicinal plants from the Island Soqotra"	"Soqotra"	"12.5"	"54.0"	"info:lanl-repo/biosis/PREV200600421665"	"6"
"Phytochemical screening and antiviral activity of some medicinal plants from the Island Soqotra"	"Yemen"	"15.5"	"47.5"	"info:lanl-repo/biosis/PREV200600421665"	"6"
"Potential impact of antiviral drug use during influenza pandemic"	"Canada"	"60.0"	"-96.0"	"info:lanl-repo/biosis/PREV200510297760"	"57"
"Potential impact of antiviral drug use during influenza pandemic"	"Netherlands"	"52.5"	"5.75"	"info:lanl-repo/biosis/PREV200510297760"	"57"
"Potential impact of antiviral drug use during influenza pandemic"	"East Asia"	"39.1333"	"117.2"	"info:lanl-repo/biosis/PREV200510297760"	"57"
"Potential impact of antiviral drug use during influenza pandemic"	"Canada"	"60.0"	"-96.0"	"info:lanl-repo/isi/000231591400004"	"57"
"Potential impact of antiviral drug use during influenza pandemic"	"Netherlands"	"52.5"	"5.75"	"info:lanl-repo/isi/000231591400004"	"57"

Figure 21.2 OpenRDF Workbench displaying the results of a SPARQL query.

A triplestore also provides at least some data management capabilities such as the ability to create and delete RDF graphs, which some triplestores refer to as repositories. They provide a mechanism for adding triples in bulk, indexing triples, and some provide fine-grained transactions such as updating and deleting individual statements. The commands and interface for managing triples and the triplestore tend to vary from one system to another. There are standards such as SPARQL 1.1 Update, for managing triplestores and triples, which some systems support.

Most triplestores can parse and load triples represented in at least a few different RDF serialization formats. The two most commonly supported formats are N3 and RDF/XML. For some serializations, there are RDF validation tools which can determine the correctness of N3 or RDF/XML representations of triples. Character encoding issues and malformed statements can halt the import process, but data validation can reduce or eliminate most of these problems (Figure 21.3).

Inferencing and reasoning

Inferencing is a process whereby new information can be deduced or inferred from existing triples. Here's a plain English example: if John is Todd's uncle, and Bill is Todd's dad, and John and Bill have the same father, then John and Bill are brothers.

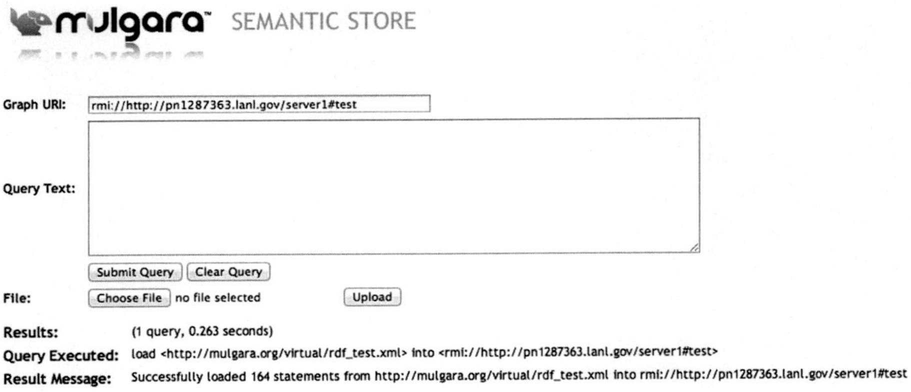

Figure 21.3 Mulgara semantic repository interface.

In a triplestore that supports inferencing, it is possible to dynamically infer new triples either at load or when someone performs a search. Inferred triples can be added to the triplestore as new statements.

Inferencing is supported by some triplestores, sometimes through an integrated rules and reasoning engine (as with KiWi and the sKWRL reasoner). Rules can be used to walk the RDF graph to discover new relationships implied by existing relationships. Triplestores usually use forward chaining inferencing, evaluating rules against existing data. When data is found that causes a rule to evaluate to true, then new data can be inferred and included in search results or added to the triplestore. Sometimes reasoning functionality is exposed through the triplestore or through an add-on rules engine. Other triplestores may simply support inferencing over property and sub-property, class and subclass relationships defined with RDFS. Others may not support inferencing at all due to its complexity and its potential to become computationally intensive.

There are software libraries for triplestores, for building custom Semantic Web driven applications. The purpose of a defined database API as opposed to a simple query mechanism is to provide a mechanism for interacting with the database that maximizes performance in various ways, defines a structured way of interacting with the database, and offloads as much of the routine aspects of interacting with the database as possible to code in the API. We will look at three APIs here briefly: Jena, Sesame, and a generic REST interface example. Of the three, the REST interface is the simplest and illustrates the problem all three are trying to solve, so we will look at it first.

SPARQL 1.1 HTTP and Update

As of SPARQL 1.1, there are a pair of new standards for triplestore data transactions and for a REST API for triplestores. They are called SPARQL 1.1 Update and SPARQL 1.1 Graph Store HTTP. These are World Wide Web Consortium standards that extend the original SPARQL standard. The KiWi triplestore, which is part of the Apache Linked Data Platform called Marmotta, supports SPARQL 1.1. The SPARQL protocol uses existing HTTP operations for verifying the existence and capabilities of a graph in a triplestore, as well as adding, updating, or deleting data in a graph. The HTTP GET request is used to inquire about a particular graph. A GET request is what a browser issues whenever you access a URL. For example, when a Web browser requests this URL:

```
http://triplestore.server.org/rdf-graph-store?graph=books
```

the server triplestore.server.org understands it as being an HTTP operation of the form:

```
GET /rdf-graph-store?graph=books
```

If this is a URL for a triplestore that supports the SPARQL 1.1 Graph Store HTTP, the server will reply with a header that indicates what kind of RDF serializations it supports, if the graph exists:

```
Accept: text/turtle; charset=utf-8
```

Now we know two things, that the RDF graph named "books" does exist, and that we must use the Turtle syntax when we send requests to add, update, or delete data in this repository.

There are three HTTP operations that this protocol uses to support triplestore data transactions: PUT, DELETE, and POST. If you send RDF data serialized as TURTLE using the POST operation, it will be added to the RDF graph you specify:

```
POST /rdf-graph-store?graph=books
```

Data that will be added:

```
@prefix owl:          <http://www.w3.org/2002/07/owl#>.
@prefix dbpedia:      <http://dbpedia.org/resource/>.
@prefix dbpedia-owl:  <http://dbpedia.org/ontology/>.
@prefix dbpprop:      <http://dbpedia.org/property/>.
dbpedia:The_Road  rdf:type  dbpedia-owl:WrittenWork,
            yago:PsychologicalFeature100023100,
            yago:PhysicalEntity100001930,
            owl:Thing.
@prefix bibo:         <http://purl.org/ontology/bibo/>.
dbpedia:The_Road  rdf:type  bibo:Book,
      dbpprop:author  dbpedia:Cormac_McCarthy.
```

You can also combine the HTTP with SPARQL 1.1 Update to submit update requests: SPARQL 1.1 Graph Store HTTP operation:

```
POST /rdf-graph-store?graph=books
```

with this SPARQL 1.1 Update request:

```
PREFIX dbpprop:  <http://dbpedia.org/property/>
INSERT DATA {
  dbpedia:The_Road dbpprop:author  dbpedia:Cormac_McCarthy .
}
```

Jena

Jena is an opensource Java project from Apache, and it is a core component of the VIVO architecture. It has evolved to include its own implementation of a triplestore, a SPARQL query endpoint, and other libraries. The component of Jena that we're interested in is the RDF API. This is a well-defined and mature library for interacting with a triplestore to query semantic graphs (repositories). The RDF API encapsulates Semantic Web constructs and triplestore functions with Java objects. Here is a list of classes from the RDF model class in Jena:

> *Alt, Bag, Container, InfModel, Literal, Model, NodeIterator, NsIterator, Property, RDFList, RDFNode, RDFReader, RDFWriter, ReifiedStatement, ResIterator, Resource, Statement*

There are classes for various RDF model constructs such as lists containers, literal values, resources, and namespace identifiers. There are also classes for reading and writing serializations of triples.

Jena has a graph class that contains most of the functionality associated with an RDF graph. At this level of abstraction, classes deal with the RDF graph itself, with triples, and nodes in triple graph segments:

- GetTriple, Graph, GraphAdd, GraphMaker, NodeVisitor, TransactionHandler, TripleIterator, TripleMatch
- Node, Node_Blank, Node_Literal, Node_URI, Node_Variable, NodeFactory
- Triple, Triple.Field, TripleMatchFilter, TripleMatchIterator

There are other Jena libraries for ontologies, vocabularies, reasoners, and for working with RDF/XML data. Here are some highlights from the ontology library. If you remember our overview of OWL from Chapter 5, you'll see there's a one-to-one correspondence between the OWL language and Jena's API for ontologies:

- FunctionalProperty, SymmetricProperty, TransitiveProperty, InverseFunctionalProperty
- DatatypeProperty, ObjectProperty
- AllDifferent, AllValuesFromRestriction, AnnotationProperty, CardinalityRestriction, HasValueRestriction, MaxCardinalityRestriction, MinCardinalityRestriction, QualifiedRestriction, SomeValuesFromRestriction
- UnionClass, IntersectionClass, EnumeratedClass, BooleanClassDescription, ComplementClass

The Jena library provides a great deal of functionality. As with any code library, there is a steep learning curve. One has to have the conceptual knowledge surrounding triples and the Semantic Web before the API makes much sense. At the highest level, Jena has a Graph abstraction, where a named graph is a collection of triples that reside within a repository. Graphs are created by a Factory class. Graph is not actually a class, but rather a code template that has the ability to perform certain tasks. Other classes implement the Graph class, and so they know how to behave like a Graph. The Graph interface specifies how to open and close a graph, to report its size, to delete all its contents, to add a triple to itself, to delete a triple, and to find triples it might contain.

To create a new triple in a triplestore, you use the ResourceFactory class. Among other things, ResourceFactory can create a triple with its createStatement method. As you might expect, the method accepts three parameters, for the subject, predicate, and object of the triple to be created. Each of these parameters is represented by a Jena class, which in turn encapsulates variables and methods appropriate to it. Since a predicate always has a namespace, it should come as no surprise that the class that represents a predicate in Jena has a method called "getNameSpace()," whereas the template for creating an object in a triple has additional methods for evaluating the type of the object value and, if it is a literal value, a toString() method that can output it as a string value.

If you haven't figured it out yet, Jena is big and complex. On the plus side, a great deal of functionality is available out of the box with Jena. But Jena can be daunting to use. Often you can develop a Web application against a triplestore that performs queries against a SPARQL query endpoint or with a simpler API like OpenRDF Sesame or an REST-based API.

OpenRDF Sesame API

Another Java library for the Semantic Web is the OpenRDF Sesame API. This library is actually more extensive in many areas than Jena, but it is broader and less deep. A quick scan of the OpenRDF API provides a good overview for what it can do and which libraries provide a given capability. The server package is concerned with, as its name implies, things like establishing and managing connections with a server. It also defines classes for interacting with a repository, an entire library that not only supports an HTTP, but exposes one when used in conjunction with a supported triplestore. The Model library provides all the interfaces that define methods for statements and their subcomponents. The query libraries provide an extensive array of interfaces and classes for querying a repository. But the nice thing about OpenRDF is that you don't have to dig too deeply into the API to find capabilities that you can use in your own Java applications. The following examples illustrate a few common tasks and how they are performed using this API.

Connect to a remote semantic repository with OpenRDF API:

```
String sesameServer = "http://rdfserver.somewhere.org/openrdf-sesame/";
String repositoryID = "my-rdf-db";
Repository repo = new HTTPRepository(sesameServer, repositoryID);
repo.initialize(); // connect to named repository on specified server
```

Next, add data to this repository from an RDF/XML file which is published on a Web server:

```
try {
    RepositoryConnection con = repo.getConnection(); // make repository
      connection
    URL url = new URL("http://example.org/data/my-rdf-data.rdf");
    con.add(url, url.toString(), RDFFormat.RDFXML); //add method adds data
    con.close();
}
```

Perform a SPARQL query:

```
String queryString = "SELECT ?s ?o WHERE { ?s ?p ?o } "; // simple SPARQL query
TupleQuery tupleQuery = con.prepareTupleQuery(QueryLanguage.SPARQL,
  queryString);
TupleQueryResult result = tupleQuery.evaluate(); // perform the query
try {
    while (result.hasNext()) { // iterate over the result
        BindingSet bindingSet = result.next();
        Value subjectValue = bindingSet.getValue("s");
        Value objectValue = bindingSet.getValue("o");
    }
}
```

These examples barely scratch the surface of the Sesame API. There are extensive IO libraries for various RDF serializations as well as libraries to parse, construct, and perform SPARQL queries. There are also a collection of libraries (called Sail) for connecting to various backend data stores including native in-memory and disk-based triplestores, and for both MySQL and Postgres, two widely used open-source relational database systems.

Java APIs provide extensive functionality and tighter coupling with the underlying triplestore. Once you are familiar with a given Java RDF API, then building a new application is quicker and less prone to bugs. Tighter coupling can also yield performance benefits, for example when you can use a Class to carefully manage the connection with a triplestore, you can keep that connection alive for the duration of all the transactions you want to perform, and then close it when you are done. A REST API like the SPARQL HTTP is simpler, and thus easier to learn. But it provides less functionality, code written for it is more prone to bugs since there aren't classes for wrapping RDF, queries, triples, etc. There's also a performance penalty for this ease of use.

A simple request-response API like REST doesn't always have the facilities to maintain state between the requester and the server. In that case, the server has to figure out who you are and what you want every time you visit. Then it has to open the triplestore, parse your request, submit it, gather the results and format them appropriately, close the triplestore, and return results to you. It's doing a lot of work behind the scenes and there's little to no opportunity for you to optimize that process. All of these approaches have their strengths and weaknesses. We hope this brief overview of the various triplestore APIs may help you make a more informed decision about what would be involved with building your own Semantic Web applications in-house.

Graph databases and how to use them

22

Thinking graphs

We all have an intimate relationship with an unimaginably large network, without which we would not be who we are. That network is contained within our brain. There are roughly a hundred billion nodes (as neurons) and a thousand trillion edges (axons) in this network. Some portions of the network merely serve to convey information, for example from sensory organs or to muscles or to other parts of the body to regulate essential functions. Other parts assimilate and form associations with information, assist in the conversion of thoughts to spoken words, locate information, and store memories. And yet this network, from all outward appearances seems fairly undifferentiated, since neurons, like the dots in a graph visualization, all work pretty much the same way and thus all look pretty much the same.

So if the most complex living structure we're aware of in the universe is essentially a giant network, can we download and store the contents of a brain in a graph? Not yet. We'd be hard-pressed to store a static snapshot of a brain's contents. The brain is a dynamic system that accepts volumes of sensory input in real time while it juggles autonomous body functions, balance, muscle movements, breathing, thought, and speech. You may fret about whether you can pat your head and chew gum at the same time, but that's a cheap parlor trick compared to what your brain is actually able to do every second.

Can my graph achieve consciousness? As the magic 8 ball says, "all signs point to no." Perhaps consciousness is an emergent property of some kind of informational network, we just don't know. Integrated Information Theory (see chapter 20) suggests that consciousness happens in networks that house highly integrated information. But it's safe to assume that a graph model of your Facebook social network will never achieve consciousness. Most neuroscientists agree that consciousness is not solely a function of our memories or even associations we form among memories. After all, those things persist between states of unconsciousness. Memories play a supporting role, but they are not the seat of consciousness.

Can my graph model think? This is the best question of the three, and the answer is, after a fashion it can, but not merely by virtue of the fact that it is a graph. We discussed at length reasoning and the role that rules can play in processing RDF graph data, deducing new knowledge and making decisions based on criteria matching. A graph is not itself able to perform these actions but computing over a graph can result in the same sorts of fundamental information processing activities that involve logic, reasoning, and deduction that we all use every day to figure things out. Now thinking

A Librarian's Guide to Graphs, Data and the Semantic Web.

over a graph is less flexible than human thought, because like any computational task, we have to come up with rules to govern it. But the interesting thing about applying heuristics such as path traversal rules to a graph is that sufficiently flexible steps will follow whatever paths are appropriate for as long as the rules hold true. As the path is traversed, you can accumulate, filter, and sort the information you encounter along the way, make note of recurring path patterns that may implicitly represent additional information that isn't explicitly represented by adjacent nodes. When you recommend movies to a friend, are you thinking? You can generate movie recommendations using a property graph and a few simple traversal steps.

There's a lot more going on in the network that we call the brain than in a property graph model of some system. In order to manifest any functionality remotely similar to human cognition, our graph database would have to be expansive, malleable, able to process real-time information, able to locate "memories," and build associations at speeds which are for all practical purposes instantaneous. We all experience "deer in headlight" moments, where our thought processes lag, but most of the time the brain is humming along as a real-time information processing system ensuring we don't fall down, say the wrong thing, drive off a cliff or eat a poisonous mushroom. Part of the magic is in various dynamic processes that occur within that network that manifest as remembering, forgetting, seeing, hearing, speaking. The brain is not a static network of immortal connections. The flow of information through the network in real time and the information processing this enables is where the magic happens. Our graph models exist to augment these processes, although that is not to say that someone will someday figure out how to build a graph and accompanying graph computation model that will in every way mimic the human brain. Any living being that can determine the nature of the universe down to the energy fields that exist in a vacuum and dissect invisible particles called atoms down to subatomic resolution of electrons, neutrons, and protons, and further still will likely someday decipher the secrets of its own mind. We're just not there yet.

This thought exercise may seem like a bit of a digression but actually it isn't. It's been an attempt to introduce you to the notion of graph computation. Graph computation makes a distinction between creating and populating a graph (storing data), and searching or traversing a graph in order to apply heuristics or algorithms to some graph data (reasoning over the data). It enlists path traversals over property graphs in conjunction with various other activities such as selecting particular paths to follow based on node or edge properties or counting the steps followed or following a path in a particular direction other criteria that governs traversal, accumulating information about nodes and edges encountered along the way, and using this accumulated information in various ways. So much of the Semantic Web information retrieval model eschews path traversal in favor of pattern matching, but supporting path traversals are an essential function of graph databases. Path traversals are the foundation for some fundamental computational processes that can occur over a graph. For a more in-depth and thoughtful overview of how graph databases can emulate brain activity, see Marko Rodriguez' excellent essay entitled "Graphs, Brains and Gremlin" at http://markorodriguez.com/2011/07/14/graphs-brains-and-Gremlin/.

Graph databases

A graph database uses a graph structure to store data. So there's no intermediate format between the graph you load and the model that's stored. If a node has an edge to another node, then those nodes point at each other in the graph database. A graph database provides persistence, create/update/delete (CRUD), path traversal, indexing, search, and query capabilities for graphs. In addition to these core capabilities, graph databases are often tightly integrated with or directly support graph analytic algorithms for graph computation tasks. Because of this, it is easier to tease out and work with subgraphs, find clusters and motifs, identify hubs and nodes with high degree or betweenness centrality, evaluate graph-wide metrics and compare an instance graph to reference models like random graphs and small-world networks, explore paths in the graph, and investigate characteristics of dynamic graphs such as those that change over time.

Property graph databases augment the graph model with properties. A set of properties is basically a mini-database table that helps to define various characteristics of the thing to which it is attached. Properties can include unique identifiers, labels, weights, temporal data such as timestamps, and pretty much anything else that categorizes or uniquely identifies the graph element with which they are associated. Properties support some core concepts in graph theory such as multipartite graphs, edge weighted graphs, and directed networks. But you can use properties in

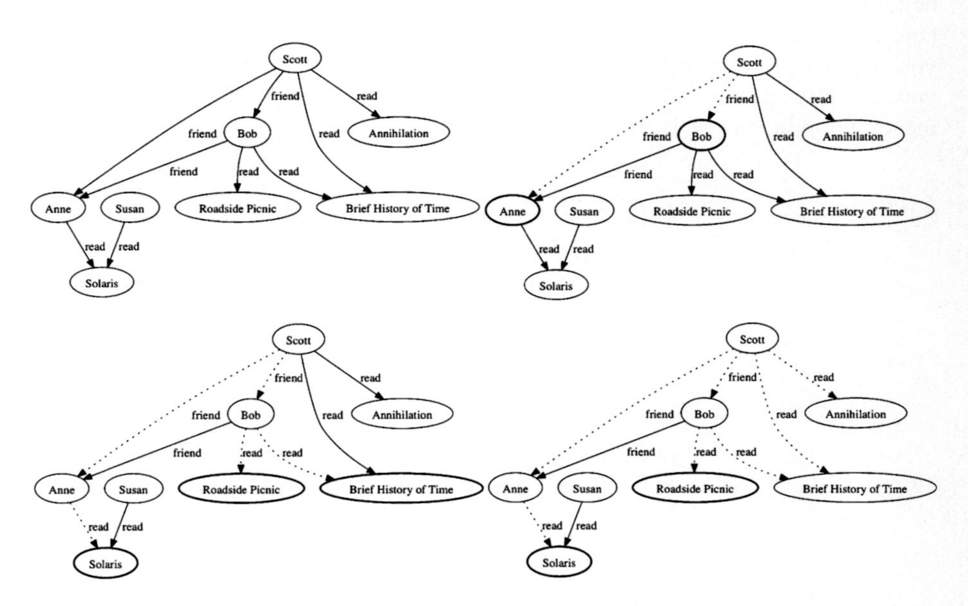

Figure 22.1 Generating recommendations by traversing a graph, starting at top left with original graph, paths to Scott's friends, paths to books that Scott's friends have read, and paths to all books read by all persons in the graph.

other ways and when you're modeling a graph that will be stored in a graph database, it's best to think about properties for nodes and edges when you start. The information contained within properties allows you to find particular vertices and to follow paths through the graph.

For the remainder of this chapter, we'll look at several graph databases. In each instance, we were going to start off by loading a toy graph. The toy graph is a property graph describing a small social network and the books its members have read. Nodes have properties that identify them as people or books. People nodes are connected via an edge that represents a friend relationship. People nodes are also connected to books when a person has read a given book. We'll use this graph to generate reading recommendations for a person in the graph. These recommendations will be based on based on their own reading list and those of their friends. So we'll have to traverse the graph and perform some very simple computations in order to output these recommendations (Figure 22.1).

HeliosJS

Let's start with a Javascript-based graph database called HeliosJS. HeliosJS runs entirely within a Web browser. So our graph program is embedded in a Web page. To run this example yourself, download HeliosJS from http://entrendipity.github.io/helios.js/ and create a Web page that contains the HTML and Javascript code below. The example also uses a Javascript programming library called Jquery, so you will need that as well. If you wish, you can put this code on a Web server, but you can also create the file locally and access it via the "Open File" or similar menu option in your web browser.

```
<html>
<head>
<title>Graph-based book recommender</title>
<script src = "helios/lib/q.min.js"></script>
<script src = "helios/lib/uuid.js"></script>
<script src = "helios/lib/q-comm.js"></script>
<script src = "helios/helios.js"></script>
<script src = "jquery/jquery-2.1.1.min.js"></script>

<script>
var graph = new Helios.GraphDatabase();

var json_graph = {
  "graph": {
    "mode":"NORMAL",
    "vertices":[
      {"name":"Scott","age":36,"_id":1,"_type":"vertex" },
      {"name":"Bob","age":47,"_id":2,"_type":"vertex"},
      {"name":"Anne","age":34,"_id":3,"_type":"vertex"},
      {"name":"Susan","age":45,"_id":4,"_type":"vertex"},
      {"title":"Solaris","category":"novel","_id":5,"_type":"vertex"},
```

```
        {"title":"Roadside Picnic","category":"novel","_id":6,"_type":"vertex"},
        {"title":"Annihilation","category":"novel","_id":7,"_type":"vertex"},
        {"title":"Brief History of Time","category":"nonfiction","_id":8,"_type":"vertex"}
      ],
      "edges":[
        {"_id":9,"_type":"edge","_outV":1,"_inV":7,"_label":"read"},
        {"_id":10,"_type":"edge","_outV":1,"_inV":8,"_label":"read"},
        {"_id":11,"_type":"edge","_outV":2,"_inV":6,"_label":"read"},
        {"_id":12,"_type":"edge","_outV":2,"_inV":7,"_label":"read"},
        {"_id":13,"_type":"edge","_outV":3,"_inV":5,"_label":"read"},
        {"_id":14,"_type":"edge","_outV":4,"_inV":5,"_label":"read"},
        {"_id":15,"_type":"edge","_outV":1,"_inV":2,"_label":"friend"},
        {"_id":16,"_type":"edge","_outV":1,"_inV":3,"_label":"friend"},
        {"_id":17,"_type":"edge","_outV":2,"_inV":3,"_label":"friend"}
      ]
    }
  }

  graph.loadGraphSON(json_graph)
    .then(function(g) {
     g.V({name:{$eq:'Scott'}}).out('read').then (
         function(hasRead) {
             g.V({name:{$eq:'Scott'}}).out('friend').out('read').except(hasRead).map('title').
               then (
                function(results) {
                    var readingListMessage = 'Recommended reading for Scott: ';
                    for (item in results) {
                        readingListMessage + = '"' + results[item].title+ '", ';
                    }
                    readingListMessage = readingListMessage.slice(0,-2);

                    $('#Gremlin_results').replaceWith('<div id = "Gremlin_results">' +
                      readingListMessage + '</div>');
                });
         });
    }, function(error) {
           console.error(error);
    });

  </script>
  </head>
  <body>
  <h2>Graph Book Recommender</h2>
  <div id = "Gremlin_results"></div>

  </body>
  </html>
```

The HTML file starts with the usual elements for a Web page. The script elements in the header load the necessary libraries for this example. The Javascript code is embedded in a script block in the header of the file. It includes a JSON object that represents the graph, and Javascript code that loads the graph, traverses it, and generates a list of recommendations. The graph is serialized using

GraphSON, which we reviewed in chapter 18. The first line of Javascript creates a Helios graph database. This is followed by a declaration which creates the GraphSON object and stores it in a variable called json_graph. Next, the statement graph.loadGraphSON(json_graph) loads the graph data into the graph database.

HeliosJS supports Gremlin-style queries and path traversals. Gremlin is a graph pattern matching and graph traversal language that is supported by several graph databases. It is at this point the closest thing to a standard graph query and traversal language in the world of graph databases. Several widely used property graph databases, including Titan and Neo4J, support Gremlin. The remainder of the Javascript executes a Gremlin path traversal and loops through the results to generate and output a reading recommendations list.

Titan

Titan is an open source scalable graph database implemented in Java. It is modular such that the underlying storage can be one of several noSQL big data databases, such as Hbase and Cassandra, as its storage backend. Cassandra works well for larger graphs, because it is faster at read and write transactions. Titan is bundled with a number of other technologies, including Gremlin and the rexster Web application server that exposes graph functionality through a REST interface. Titan also includes several Java libraries. Of note is Blueprints, which provides similar functionality to the JDBC (Java Database Connector) API for relational databases. With Blueprints, you can write Java or Groovy programs that connect to a graph database server, load a graph, and perform CRUD transactions on the graph. With Gremlin or Blueprints, you can interactively or programmatically add vertices and edges, build property key indexes, search by properties, and perform path traversals. The following Groovy program uses the Blueprints API and Gremlin to load a graph and traverse it for recommendations, and the Jung graph analysis library to generate degree metrics for book nodes:

```
import com.thinkaurelius.titan.core.TitanFactory
import com.tinkerpop.blueprints.Vertex
import com.tinkerpop.blueprints.oupls.jung.GraphJung

import edu.uci.ics.jung.graph.Graph
import edu.uci.ics.jung.algorithms.scoring.DegreeScorer;
import edu.uci.ics.jung.algorithms.scoring.*

    g = TitanFactory.open("recommender")
    g.loadGraphSON("recommender.json")

    scottRead = g.V.has('name','Scott')[1].out('read').toList()
    Iterator<Vertex> fI = g.V.has('name','Scott')[1].out('friend').out('read')

    System.out.println("Recommendations for Scott ... ");
```

```
for (Vertex book : fI) {
  if (!(scottRead.contains(book))) {
    System.out.println(book.title)
  }
}

GraphJung bookGraph = new GraphJung(g)
System.out.println("Computing degree centrality...")

DegreeScorer degreeRanker = new DegreeScorer(bookGraph);
for (java.lang.Object nodeVal : bookGraph.getVertices()) {
  Double nodeScore = degreeRanker.getVertexScore(nodeVal)
  if (nodeVal.title) {
    System.out.println("Degree Centrality for\t"+ nodeVal.title+ "\t"+ nodeScore);
  }
}
```

The Blueprints API is supported by a variety of graph databases, including Titan, Neo4J, and OrientDB. As a result, the code above can be used largely unchanged with any of these graph databases, by simply importing and using the database-specific class for creating and opening a graph.

Neo4J

Neo4J is an opensource high-performance graph database that runs on a server. It has a REST API, a Java API, and its own query language called Cypher, which is somewhat SPARQL-like. Neo4J provides a Web interface called the Neo4J browser. This tool provides query and administrative access to an instance of the graph database, so you can create and query triples. A side pane keeps track of the node labels and relationships in the current graph, so you can browse the graph by clicking on labels or relationships. The graph will be displayed as a visualization which you can interact with. You can inspect nodes or move them around to see other parts of the graph. This is really only practical for local sections or small graphs but a really handy aspect of the inspection pane is that when you click on a relationship or node type, it constructs and displays the cypher query that generated the resulting graph. You can edit and re-execute these queries and is a good way to learn how to construct your own cypher queries (Figure 22.2).

Here is a Cypher query that returns recommendations for Scott:

```
MATCH ({name:'Scott'})-[:FRIEND]-()-[:READ]-(read)
WHERE NOT ({name:'Scott'})-[:READ]-(read)
RETURN DISTINCT read
```

The first line specifies a simple graph pattern to match: the nodes representing what Scott's friends have read. Edges are represented by dashes, with an optional edge label contained within square brackets, preceded by a colon. The where clause

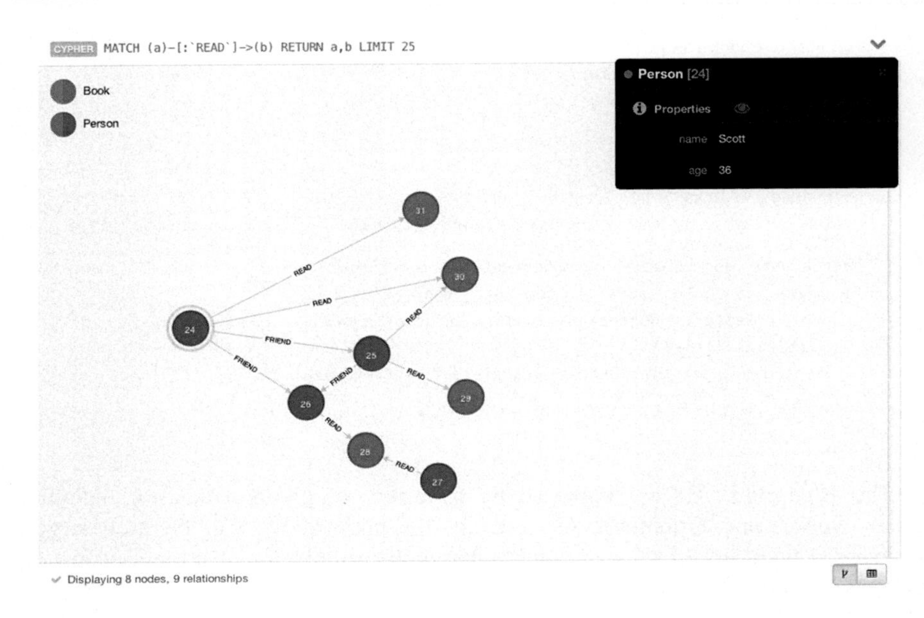

Figure 22.2 Neo4J Web interface with a visualization of the results of a Cypher query.

is a pattern that identifies nodes to exclude from the results: in this case, books that Scott read. Finally an aggregation of the results with duplicates removed is returned. As you may have noticed, this Cypher query resembles a SPARQL query. Like SPARQL, Cypher makes extensive use of graph patterns, such as node predicate node patterns, and variables which can be bound to, and thus contain, node values that are accumulated by executing the query. In this example, nodes pointed to by the "read" edge are stored in the variable "read."

TinkerPop3

TinkerPop3 is a newer graph software library that makes a distinction between graph transactional tasks (CRUD), and graph computational tasks (traversals), with a reference Java implementation. It groups these two types of functionality into separate libraries: a structural API and a process API. The structural API is used to create a graph database, to manage graph variables, which are key/value pairs that apply to the graph rather than to its elements, to create nodes and edges, and to manage properties for those graph elements. The process API is used to traverse the graph and to perform computation on data from the graph. The TinkerPop3 API can be used from several programming languages and with any TinkerPop3 enabled graph database. Neo4J and Titan are two such databases. These graph databases run on a dedicated server like a relational database or a triplestore, and can be managed interactively via Gremlin. Graph-based applications can use the TinkerPop3 API to perform CRUD tasks on a graph, and to perform graph computation functionality based on searches and graph traversals.

Like Blueprints, TinkerPop3 is intended to be a graph database agnostic programming library. In the following example, we will use the TinkerPop3 Gremlin console to demonstrate how to create a graph using the structural API. Then we will use the process API to perform the same recommender task we introduced with HeliosJS.

Gremlin, which is the name for a graph traversal language and an interactive tool that supports it, is part of a graph computing software library TinkerPop3. Gremlin is a graph centric query language that supports two primary means of discovery information in graphs: traversals and pattern matching queries against node and edge properties. These can be combined as needed so that you can formulate very sophisticated queries against property graph data. A traversal starts with a node or edge, identified by some criteria, and can continue along a path defined by some pattern, or a specific path identifying precisely which nodes and edges to follow. A pattern matching query attempts to locate a vertex or edge according to some property and, optionally, a specific value that property ought to have. Unlike SPARQL, Gremlin does not cling to awkward SQL-like metaphors. It was designed from the ground up as a graph query language. The Gremlin console also allows you to perform administrative tasks, such as loading and clearing a graph.

We're going to start by creating a new graph

```
gremlin> g = TinkerGraph.open()
```

This creates a new empty in-memory property graph. This graph can be accessed through the variable g. Now we'll use the addVertex and addEdge methods from the graph structure API to create a graph that looks exactly like the one we created with HeliosJS:

```
person1 = g.addVertex(Element.ID, 1, "name", "Scott", "age", 36)
person2 = g.addVertex(Element.ID, 2, "name", "Bob", "age", 47)
person3 = g.addVertex(Element.ID, 3, "name", "Anne", "age", 34)
person4 = g.addVertex(Element.ID, 4, "name", "Susan", "age", 45)
book1 = g.addVertex(Element.ID, 5, "title", "Solaris", "category", "novel")
book2 = g.addVertex(Element.ID, 6, "title", "Roadside Picnic", "category", "novel")
book3 = g.addVertex(Element.ID, 7, "title", "Annihilation", "category", "novel")
book4 = g.addVertex(Element.ID, 8, "title", "Brief History of Time", "category", "nonfiction")
person1.addEdge("read", book3, Element.ID, 9)
person1.addEdge("read", book4, Element.ID, 10)
person2.addEdge("read", book4, Element.ID, 11)
person2.addEdge("read", book2, Element.ID, 12)
person3.addEdge("read", book1, Element.ID, 13)
person4.addEdge("read", book1, Element.ID, 14)
person1.addEdge("friend", person2, Element.ID, 15)
person1.addEdge("friend", person3, Element.ID, 16)
person2.addEdge("friend", person3, Element.ID, 17)
```

It is also possible to set properties on a graph element after it is created, with that element's property method, for example,

```
book5 = g.addVertex(Element.ID, 5
book5.property('title', 'Complexity: A Guided Tour')
book5.property('category', 'nonfiction')
```

Now we'll look at some traversals through the graph, starting with the node that has the name property "Scott":

```
gremlin> scott.out()
==>v[7]
==>v[8]
==>v[3]
==>v[2]

This node has four outward pointing edges pointing to four nodes.
```

Here's a TinkerPop3 process call that prints out the names of Scott's friends:

```
scott = g.v(1)
scott.flatMap{it.get().out('friend')}.map{it.get().value('name')}

or more simply

gremlin> scott.out('friend').value('name')
==>Anne
==>Bob
```

The variable scott references a pointer to a vertex class, which is a process class that supports path traversals. The next two lines display books read by Scott and books read by Scott's friends:

```
gremlin> scott.flatMap{it.get().out('read')}.map{it.get().value('title')}
==>Annihilation
==>Brief History of Time

gremlin> scott.out('read').sideEffect({print(it.get())})
v[7]==>v[7]
v[8]==>v[3]

gremlin> scott.out('read').sideEffect({print it.get().toString() + " " + it.get().value ('title')})
v[7] Annihilation==>v[7]
v[8] Brief History of Time==>v[8]

gremlin> scott.out('friend').flatMap{it.get().out('read')}.value('title')
==>Solaris
==>Brief History of Time
==>Roadside Picnic
gremlin> scott.flatMap{it.get().out('friend').out('read').aggregate('x')}
==>[v[5], v[8], v[6]]
```

Finally, here's the TinkerPop3 traversal that will follow the graph to find what Scott's read, who his friends are, what they have read, and output a list of book recommendations that omits the books Scott has already read and eliminates duplicates:

```
gremlin> scott.as('start').out('read').aggregate('hasRead').back
  ('start').out('friend').out('read').except('hasRead').value
  ('title').dedup()
==>Solaris
==>Roadside Picnic
```

Now let's save our graph to the filesystem

```
g.saveGraphML("recommender.xml")
```

Although we executed all of these examples at the Gremlin console prompt, TinkerPop3 can be used in Java applications or in Groovy scripts. Groovy is based on Java but it is an interpreted language like Python, so there's no need to recompile a groovy script every time you make a change.

Before we close, it is worth noting some similarities and differences between relational databases and graph databases. The relational database model has always been focused on supporting interactive querying and real-time transactions. With a database you can perform a search or update a row in the database and the database responds while you wait. Large-scale updates are usually performed noninteractively with programs that run until they finish. The same is true of graph databases. Some actions cannot be performed in real time. The graph community recognized this bifurcation of tasks and formally embraced it. Thus graph transactions take one of two forms: interactive local transactions involving a starting point vertex and a portion of the graph (OnLine Transaction Processing or OLTP) and global transactions that utilize non-real-time strategies to examine all nodes in the graph (OnLine Analytical Processing or OLAP). There's a gray area between these two approaches. It is possible to use an OLAP approach to perform something that could conceivably be handled by OLTP (such as a path traversals that ultimately extend deep into the graph, touching many nodes), but it is essentially (and sometimes actually) impossible to do the reverse. In cases where the analysis involves less than the entire graph, it may require a bit of trial and error to determine the best approach. However if you want to calculate any sort of graph-wide metrics, where you look at all nodes and/or all edges, then OLAP is the only practical option for all but the smallest of graphs. Projects like Apache giraph and Faunus are examples of OLAP implementation. Faunus and giraph use the mapreduce paradigm to parallelize iterating over large graphs in what amounts to a divide, merge, and conquer strategy. Many systems modeled with graphs can be quite large, so being able to perform graph computation using the mapreduce paradigm brings big data technologies to big data system models.

Case studies

23

Case study 1 InfoSynth: a semantic web application for exploring integrated metadata collections

Purpose

To normalize, augment, and integrate bibliographic metadata in topical collections using Semantic Web technologies and to provide graph and semantic analysis tools for these collections.

Technologies used

OpenRDF, Sesame, Java, Cytoscape, GUESS, RDF, RDF/XML, various bibliographic and geographic ontologies, Linked Open Data, various graph serialization formats, JGraphT.

Overview

Many online library systems fail to provide sufficient opportunities for serendipitous information discovery. A narrow search will often aggressively weed out items that may be of interest. An excessively broad search will yield too many items many of which are likely unrelated to the user's actual information need. Even a well-constructed query can result in more results than a user is likely to be able to comprehend or efficiently review, and yet it could be the case that ultimately many of the items in the result set are of interest. Information scientists refer to this as the precision-recall problem. InfoSynth was an effort to target the serendipity sweet spot by (1) aggregating smaller sets of metadata into collections, (2) mapping this metadata to a common RDF model, (3) augmenting the RDF with content from Linked Open Data Web, and (4) providing specialized discovery tools that leverage this data model.

Example use cases

Use case 1

A team of biologists request information about papers related to the 2003 SARS outbreak.

A Librarian's Guide to Graphs, Data and the Semantic Web.

Use case 2

In a collection of papers about the geology of Mars, which authors have written about the topic of hematite?

Use case 3

In what locations in the American southwest have studies been conducted about the pine bark beetle?

Use case 4

What are some characteristics of the coauthorship network of papers on the topic of extracting uranium from seawater?

Technology

InfoSynth is implemented as a suite of tools that interact with a semantic repository via the OpenRDF API. The topic harvester component generates RDF/XML files for importing into a repository, or it can load triples into a triplestore as they are generated. The latter capability enables end users to generate their own collections in real time.

Because the interface layer interacts with REST-based Web services, InfoSynth can work with any semantic repository that supports the OpenRDF API. During the mapping process, in addition to generating triple representations of metadata elements and values, the process attempts to disambiguate author names. The process includes a step for identifying and including information from the Web of linked data. A single collection can contain data from multiple sources if needed.

Design and modeling

A topical metadata collection may contain metadata from one or many sources. Some content might be harvested from a search engine with a suitable API, downloaded in some machine processable format through a search engine's user interface, or harvested from OAI-PMH compliant repositories. Once the data is collected, it is normalized, linked, and aggregated into a repository which represents that collection. The harvesting process can accommodate XML formatted data from OAI-PMH repositories, metadata from SOLR results sets, MARC-XML, and CSV formatted data. This data is then normalized to a common Semantic Web representation (Figure 23.1). During the normalization process, some additional processing is optionally performed, including author name matching within the collection, identification of certain name entity types and searches using those elements to find

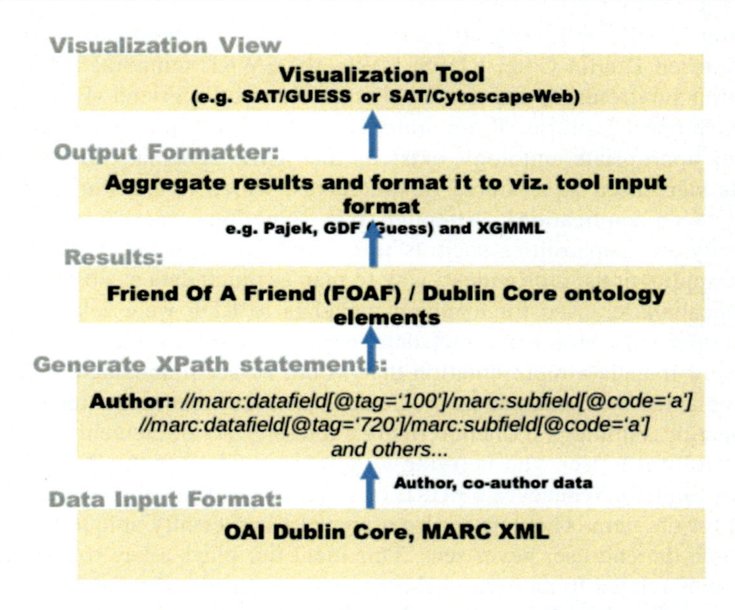

Figure 23.1 How data is transformed in InfoSynth to address various use cases.

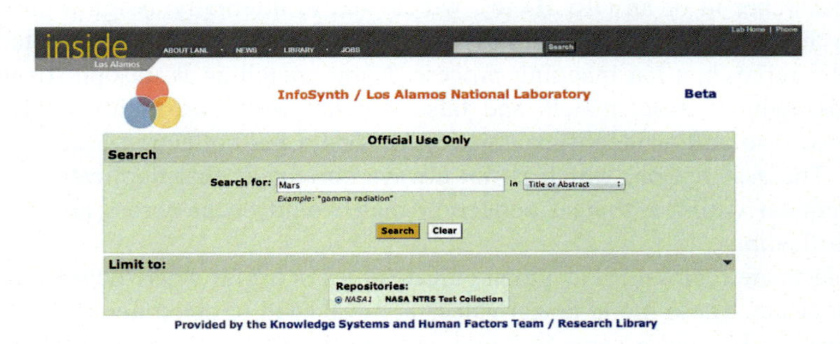

Figure 23.2 Start page for InfoSynth.

and create relationships with appropriate content in the Linked Data Web. Each collection is stored in its own repository in a triplestore.

The InfoSynth registry contains descriptions of collections (Figure 23.2). This description might include the original query used to assemble it, date information, a description of the collection, the source or sources of metadata that were mapped into the collection, the name of the semantic repository in which the triples are stored, and other metadata such as a collection title. The registry is a central component of the InfoSynth system. Registry entries support InfoSynth but they also ensure that it is possible to reconstruct the steps that were involved in creating a collection. Registry triples are based on predicates from Dublin Core, qualified Dublin Core, RDFS, OWL, the SWRL temporal ontology, JISC Information Environment Service Registry, Friend of a Friend (FOAF), and the Research Support Libraries Programme Collection Description schema. In cases where no appropriate ontology existed, the XML schemas for the specified standards were used as a source of predicates, which is a common practice in Semantic Web applications. Although this sometimes sacrifices some of the expressivity and capabilities such as inferencing when using XML schemas in semantic applications, it provides a way to map as much data as possible to RDF.

The vocabularies used for mapping metadata to RDF were selected based on several criteria. Dublin Core metadata was identified as the lowest common denominator metadata representation that would be accommodated, and so its 15 metadata elements are mapped as predicates when they are encountered in a metadata collection. Although it is not a richly expressive set of elements, it works sufficiently well for a user who is trying to determine whether the described item is of interest to them. Whenever a PURL or DOI exists, this is mapped to the identifier field for the item. The item is also assigned a universally unique internal identifier, which the end user never sees. This identifier plays a key role in retrieving all the triples related to an item as the system constructs views and visualizations of the data. People are represented with the FOAF ontology. An author is described using the foaf:Person class and has an identifier and a name property. Since it is only recently the case that people have public identifiers (in the form of a researcher id or an ORCID id), we elected to internally assign a universally unique identifier for each distinct name encountered during the metadata to semantic representation mapping process. Name matching is unsophisticated and depends upon an exact match, and false matches would be highly likely across collections, so author identifier assignment is on a per-collection basis, to reduce errors. The assumption, which is not always correct, is that duplicate names are less frequent within a topical collection than would occur across all disciplines and publications.

Subjects are represented as literal object values in triples where dc:subject served as a predicate. These literal object values are evaluated to determine if they contain place names. If a place name is found, it is resolved to an entry in Geonames and the latitude and longitude coordinates are incorporated into a pair of triples for that entry. These locally stored coordinates are used to generate a map representation of places associated with items in a topic collection. It would certainly be possible to simply add a triple that associated an item with a single link to triples about that place in a remote repository, but this is an instance where the system performance trumped linked data. It was determined that the map view of the content would be too slow if rendering it required repeated queries against a SPARQL query endpoint for Geonames. Since the coordinates of a place tend not to change over time, maintaining a local copy of the latitude and longitude coordinates in triples associated with an item in a collection seemed to be a safe compromise to make for the sake of system performance.

Implementation

While implementing InfoSynth, we looked for opportunities to augment its content with data from external sources. Some sources employed natural language processing and could identify named entities within text. These were used to analyze titles and abstracts for purposes of identifying named entities that corresponded to places. For example, Spotlight is a REST-based Web service that can analyze small segments of free text and can then identify the URI of one or more DBPedia entries related to that text. Another augmentation step would retrieve the RDF for each DBPedia entry and search for latitude and longitude coordinates.

The resulting triples from the harvest and augmentation process were then loaded into a distinct collection. Each topical collection is described by an entry in the InfoSynth registry. A registry entry contains triples which describe how the collection was constructed, what it contains, and what services are applicable to its contents. Although one of the goals of the normalization process is to ensure that the data can be explored in as many ways as possible, some capabilities of the InfoSynth system are not applicable for all collections. For example, a collection about "digital libraries and the Semantic Web" may not make much sense overlayed onto a map, and in any case will not contain much in the way of place resolvable data. So the InfoSynth registry description would not include statements about the geographic service.

InfoSynth has a Web interface that makes it possible to search many triple object literal values in a collection, such as titles and abstracts. The results sets returned in response to a query is an interactive text list, but filtered results can also be explored via interactive visualizations. Availability of visualization options is controlled by service entries in the InfoSynth registry on a per-collection basis.

When a user interacts with InfoSynth, the first thing they are presented with is a simple search form (Figure 23.2). This Web form identifies the repository that they are searching, provides a text input field for query text, and a pull-down menu which allows them to indicate whether the query should search title, abstract, or both (which is the default behavior). The interface also allows a blank search, which is handy for small collections, if the user prefers to review all the items for that topic. When the user submits the form, the data is submitted to a Java servlet which generates a SPARQL query. This is a parametric query, that is, a pre-created query with some values left undefined. The user's search text is inserted into this query string which is designed to target triples with the appropriate predicate (dc:title, or dc:description, or both), and find matching substrings within the literal (object) portion of those triples. Part of the SPARQL query specifies a pattern that corresponds to values that should be included in the result set returned when the query is processed. These values are used to construct a textual list view of the results set which is part of the results page. The following code illustrates how to use the OpenRDF API to connect and query a triplestore. It uses partially preconstructed SPARQL queries and combines them with the user's search string.

```
      String sesameServer = "http://someserver.org/openrdf-sesame";
      String repositoryID = repository;
      Repository crRepository = new HTTPRepository(sesameServer, repositoryID);
      crRepository.initialize();
      RepositoryConnection repoConnection = crRepository.getConnection();
...
        String sparql_query_base1 = "PREFIX dc: <http://purl.org/dc/elements/1.1/#>
PREFIX foaf: <http://xmlns.com/foaf/0.1/#> PREFIX rdf:
<http://www.w3.org/1999/02/22-rdf-syntax-ns#> PREFIX stb: <http://stbrl.lanl.gov/#>
SELECT DISTINCT ?docuuid ?title ?selfuuid ?knowsuuid ?name WHERE { { ?docuuid dc:title ?
title. ?docuuid dc:description ?description. ?docuuid dc:creator ?seq. ?seq rdf:_1 ?
selfuuid. ?selfuuid foaf:name ?name. ";

        String sparql_query_base2 = "} UNION { ?docuuid dc:title ?title. ?docuuid dc:
description ?description. ?docuuid dc:creator ?seq. ?seq rdf:_1 ?selfuuid. ?seq ?li ?
knowsuuid. FILTER (!(?knowsuuid = ?selfuuid)) ";
        String sparql_query_base3 = "?knowsuuid foaf:name ?name. } }";
        String filter_template_title = " FILTER regex (str(?title), \"_q_\", \"i\").";
        String paramPattern = "_q_";

        Pattern regExpPat = Pattern.compile(paramPattern);
        Matcher matcher = regExpPat.matcher(filter_template_title);
        String filter_title = matcher.replaceAll(query);
...
        if (field.equals("Title")) {
          System.out.println("Title only search");
          sparql_query = sparql_query_base1+ filter_title+ sparql_query_base2+
filter_title+ sparql_query_base3;
        }
...
      TupleQuery tupleQuery = repoConnection.prepareTupleQuery(QueryLanguage.SPARQL,
sparql_query);
      TupleQueryResult result = tupleQuery.evaluate();
      List<String> bindingNames = result.getBindingNames();
```

The results page includes the user's original query, a quick search form, and a two pane view of the results (Figure 23.3). Both panes are tabbed panes. On the left, a list of tabs corresponds to the visualization services available for this collection (Figure 23.4). Below these tabs is a list of results described with an abbreviated version of the item's metadata including at a minimum the item's title and author(s). When a user moves their cursor over an item in the result set, the right pane is dynamically updated with a full record view of the metadata for that item, which features the full abstract in addition to other metadata elements. This full record is displayed beneath a pair of tabs. The Text tab is the full record view, but there's also an optional Tags tab which, if the collection description allows it, provides access to user contributed data, including tags, comments, and a user ranking.

Tags, ratings, and comments are stored as triples which are associated with the contributor (any user who wishes to submit comments has to provide an employee identifier) and a universally unique internal identifier points to the item that is being

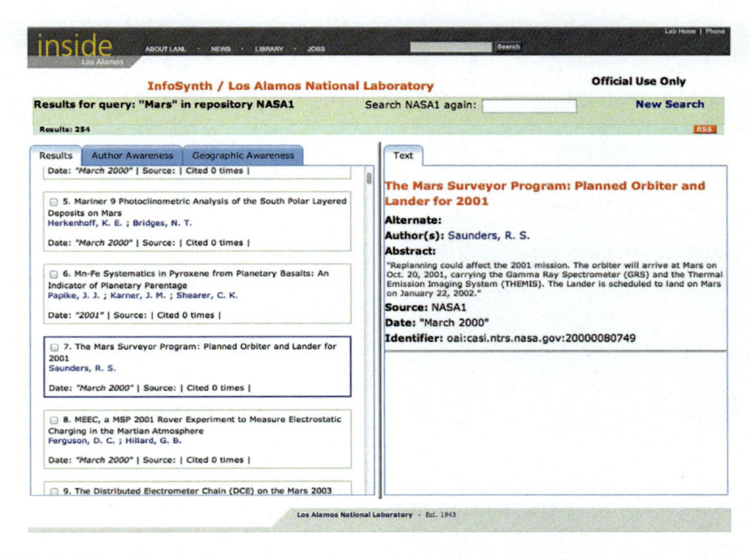

Figure 23.3 InfoSynth search results against a semantic repository containing triples describing NASA technical reports.

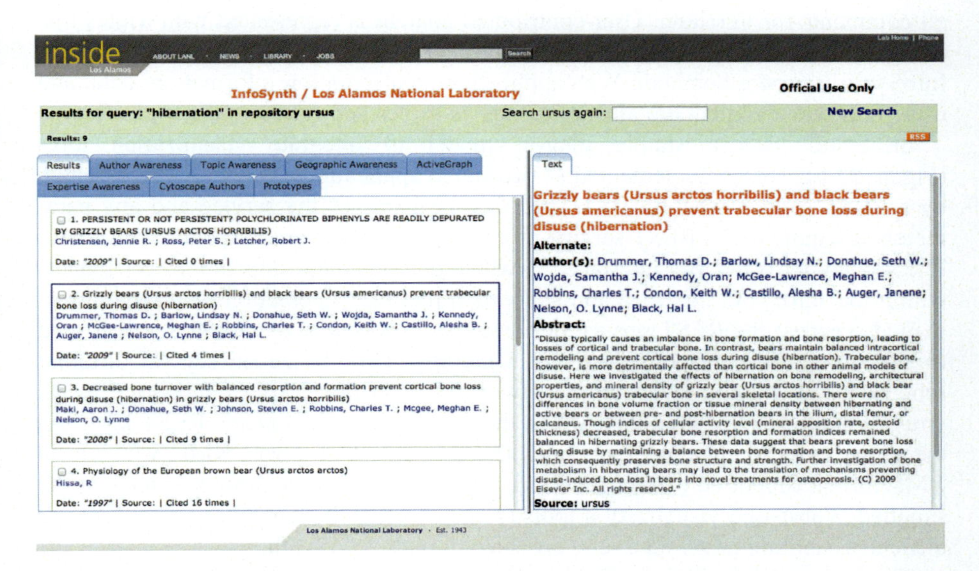

Figure 23.4 InfoSynth search results for a collection that supports additional visualization services.

annotated. End user contributions are inserted into a collection by a Java servlet that uses the OpenRDF API to dynamically update an RDF repository. An abbreviated summary of user comments, tags and ratings appears with the full record view, and users can click the Tags tab to see the emerging user-generated tag cloud and

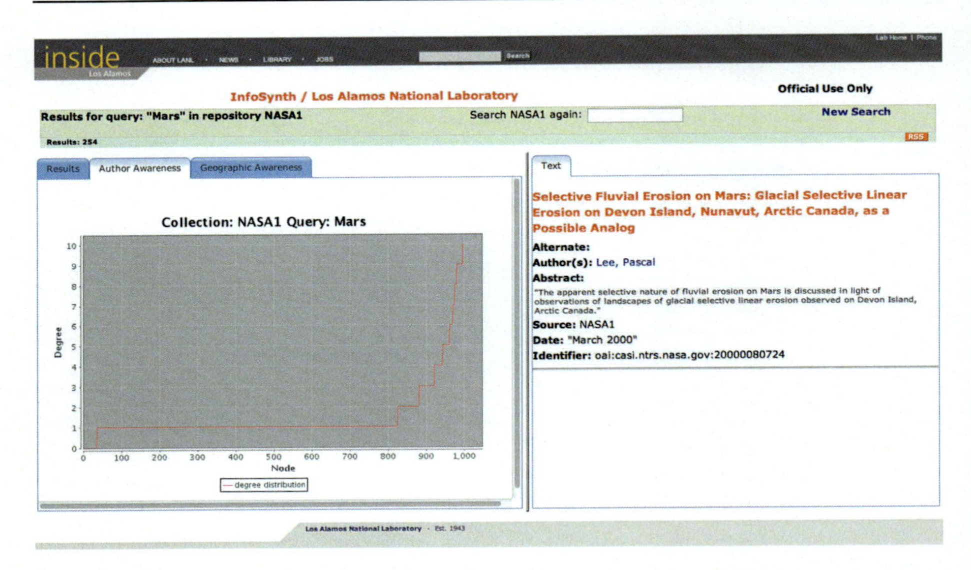

Figure 23.5 Plot of node frequency distribution for a coauthorship graph based on search results.

all comments for this item. User-contributed content is represented with triples that incorporate classes and properties from the FOAF and the SIOC ontologies. Thus InfoSynth is a pure Semantic Web application: configuration information, data, and user contributed content are all represented as triples and stored in the triplestore.

InfoSynth uses a simple plug-in model to integrate visualization tools (Figure 23.5). This is implemented as two-tiered applications. One tier is represented by a REST service where a URL specifies the name of the service and any parameters it requires. The REST service processes the request and responds with XML. The second tier is the user interface tier which presents the results of a REST request within the InfoSynth interface and supports direct user interaction. Advanced users may also access the REST service tier directly. This is why the REST services tend to support multiple response formats, including XML based on several different schemas, CSV output, and various network visualization formats supported by an array of graph visualization tools. Even the geographic component's REST layer has the ability to return data in a form suitable for Google Maps, or in KML, which is an XML format supported by Google Earth. In this way, the user is not restricted to the supplied Web-based visualization tools (some of which have memory limitations or difficulty handling larger data sets) provided through InfoSynth.

The Geographic Awareness Tool (GAT) overlays geographic metadata onto a map interface (Figure 23.6). The GAT REST service accepts a query parameter, a field parameter, and a format parameter. The query corresponds to text the user might have input in the initial search box, and the field parameter indicates whether the SPARQL query should search the object component of triples with dc:title, dc:description, or both. The format parameter indicates whether the results should be returned as a Javascript array object suitable for use with Google Maps, or a KML file which

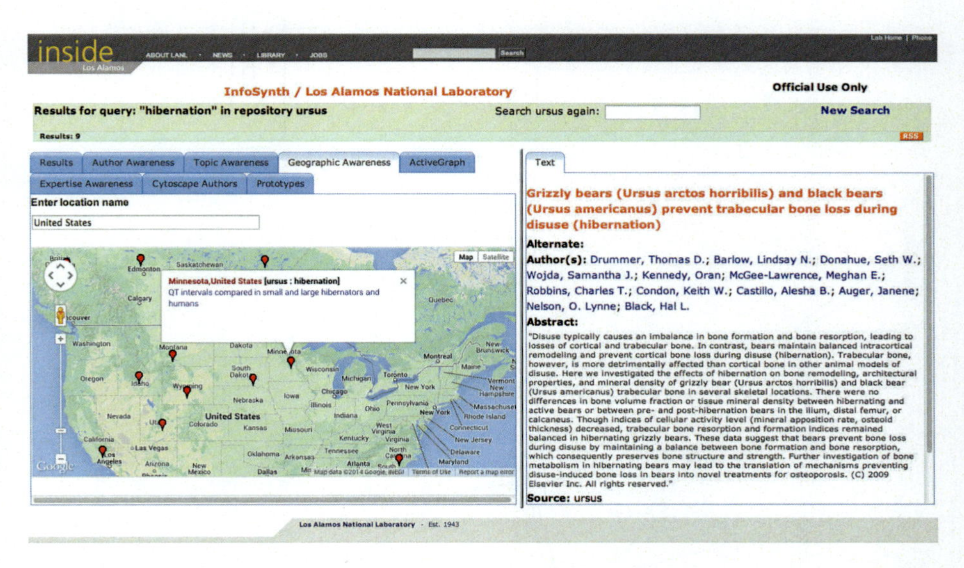

Figure 23.6 InfoSynth search results presented on a map using geospatial data and the GAT service.

specifies placemarkers and their coordinates, suitable for use with Google Earth. Since the GAT REST service can return KML, it is possible to use it with Google Earth.

The Social Awareness Tool (SAT) renders graph visualizations of coauthorship relationships in a collection. The user can view a coauthorship graph for items in an InfoSynth result set and specify several additional options. The user can select one of two graph visualization tools and optionally specify that the node with the highest degree or highest betweenness centrality be highlighted in the coauthorship graph. InfoSynth provides two graph visualization client options; one uses GUESS and the other uses Cytoscape Web. GUESS is a Java applet for rendering graphs. Cytoscape is implemented using Adobe's Flash technology. Cytoscape and the GUESS applet provide the user interface layer for the SAT. The SAT REST service supports several graph serialization formats including GEXF, GraphML, Pajek (a Windows graph analysis tool), and a CSV representation of an adjacency matrix for the coauthorship graph (Figure 23.7).

The Topic Awareness Tool (TAT) presents a subject-item view for an InfoSynth collection. The visualization is a bipartite graph with nodes for subjects and nodes for items in the result set. Subject nodes are labeled with their string value, and title nodes are labeled with the title string associated with that item. Users can then see the extent to which various subjects and keywords occur and link items in the result set. As with the SAT there are two layers modeled after the SAT service: a visualization layer which is a wrapper for GUESS and Cytoscape, and a REST service layer that returns the network data in various structured graph representation formats. Node centrality measures are not calculated for graphs generated by the TAT.

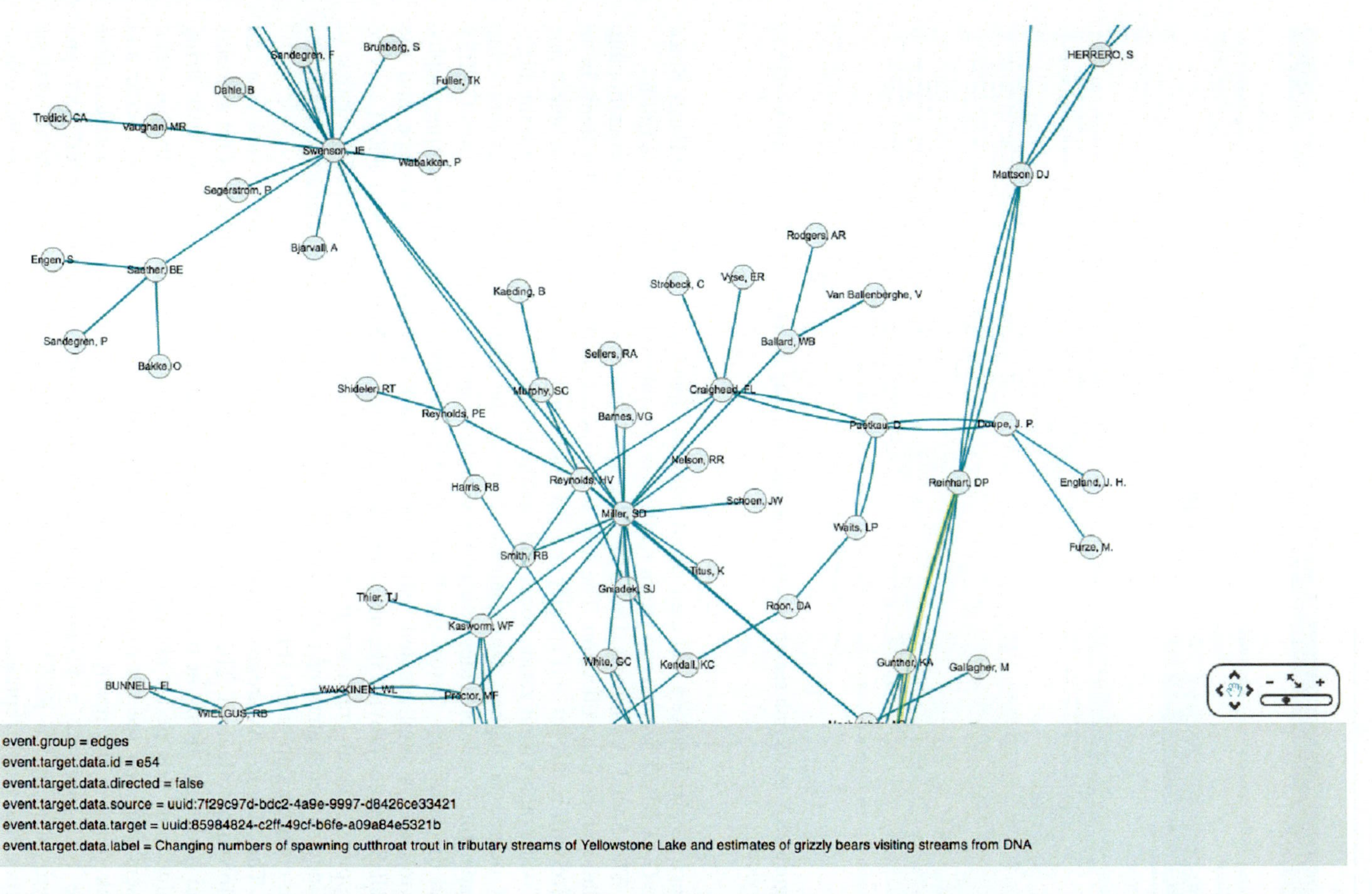

Figure 23.7 Co-authorship graph from InfoSynth rendered via Cytoscape Web service.

InfoSynth provides a couple of other ways of exploring coauthorship graphs. One is a linear plot which is a plot of the degree value for each node in a coauthorship graph, sorted from lowest to highest degree. Some graphs, as discussed in the previous chapters, exhibit a power law distribution, in which there are a few highly connected nodes and a large number of nodes with few connections. The node degree plot provides an at-a-glance overview of the connectedness of the coauthorship graph for a user's query. Such plots can reveal whether the coauthorship graph has characteristics of a small-world or scale-free network, for example. Another component of InfoSynth, called Expertise Awareness, provides a tabular report of various centrality measures by author for a result set. The centrality measures are by node measures of degree centrality, betweenness centrality, closeness centrality, and the node's cluster coefficient.

Graph visualizations and graph analytics require the programmatic generation of a projection of the semantic graph, where nodes and edges are derived from the semantic data but are not a direct representation of that underlying data. An RDF graph is good at representing data about facts, but the expressiveness and shared understanding about what a given subject or predicate means comes at the cost of adding a layer of abstraction to the semantic graph which can obscure other important aspects of the network. InfoSynth generates subgraphs for graph visualizations and graph analysis. Subgraphs are represented using the JGraphT software library, which is also used to calculate node centrality measures for the subgraph. The following code excerpt illustrates the use of JgraphT to calculate node centrality measures with a subgraph derived from collection metadata retrieved from a triplestore:

```
UndirectedGraph<String, DefaultEdge> g;
g = this.queryRepository();

CentralityComputer cc = new CentralityComputer(g);
Iterator nodeIterator = graphData.iterator();
while (nodeIterator.hasNext()) {
  currentNodeBetweenness = cc.findBetweennessOf(String.valueOf(count));
  currentNode.setBetweennessCentrality(currentNodeBetweenness);
  currentNodeDegree = cc.findDegreeOf(String.valueOf(count));
  currentNode.setDegreeCentrality(currentNodeDegree);
```

Conclusion

InfoSynth is an application designed for a population of users who are already comfortable with data visualizations and graphs. It offers enhanced search and analysis capabilities for topical metadata collections. These topical collections could serve as a compliment to finding aides such as LibGuides. RDF graphs and Semantic Web technologies offer new ways of integrating and analyzing information. InfoSynth demonstrates some of the novel ways in which RDF data can enhance the user experience.

Case Study 2 EgoSystem: a social network aggregation tool

Purpose

To discover, harvest, aggregate, and provide access to public social networks of alumni.

Technologies used

Java, Groovy, Titan, Blueprints, Frames, Rexster, Javascript, JSON, JQuery, D3

Overview

EgoSystem was developed to (re-)discover and help maintain relationships with former postdoctoral students employed at Los Alamos National Laboratory (LANL). In a university setting, a nearly identical use case exists which involves maintaining a relationship with former students. These populations are usually referred to as alumni. Since relationships were central to various proposed use cases, the system was built around a property graph.

At LANL, minimal information is retained about alumni. This consists primarily of data gathered during exit interviews. EgoSystem uses this exit interview data as seed data to discover the individual's public online identities. Identities and first-degree social networks are retrieved from public profiles hosted within various social networking and academic sites. These social networks are merged into a larger graph within EgoSystem. As the discovery process progresses, an individual's relationships to organizations and artifacts, such as publications and concepts, are added to the graph.

Example use cases

Use case 1

A manager is planning a trip to an area in proximity to universities from which many LANL postdocs originate.

Use case 2

LANL decides to recruit more students from colleges and universities that have been historically under-represented at the Lab. Are there alumni who have ties to some of those target universities?

Use case 3

The Lab would like to help early career researchers partner with researchers in their field who are located at other Labs. Who at LANL has connections with these researchers?

Use case 4

How many postdocs who came from the California university system went on to jobs in the pharmaceutical sector after they left LANL ?

Technology

Recall that a graph database is an information retrieval system that natively stores data as a graph. Many graph databases allow properties to be associated with nodes and edges. Properties are represented as key,value pairs, so there's a label (a key) and an actual string or numeric value that may be unique to that node or edge which is associated with that key. Graph databases support the standard create-read-update-delete (CRUD) transactions for data contained in the graph. A creation task can include creating a new graph or inserting a node or adding an edge between two nodes in an existing graph, or adding key, value pairs to a node or edge. A read task might use a pattern matching query against node property values, a search for nodes that share a certain type of relationship (edge), or a path traversal query to show the nodes that fall along the edges that connect two other nodes. An update task might involve changing properties of a node or edge, or changing the node to which a particular edge connects. Deletion removes nodes or edges. Property graph databases provide various ways of indexing property values for nodes and edges to support searching. Because graphs contain paths, graph databases also support path traversals.

Design and modeling

The task of designing a graph model involves deciding upon what things and relationships exist, as well as the characteristics of those elements. Consideration must be given to what data uniquely identifies a node or edge (e.g., a label or identifier) and what data would help characterize these graph elements (time stamp, type). Identifying properties for graph elements is at times a bit like designing a schema for a relational database. For example, you have to think about property names, property types, and data normalization within the graph. Normalization involves identifying and eliminating or minimizing duplicate data in the graph. One obvious way to normalize the contents of a property graph is to create multiple edges to existing nodes. However, certain data such as time points and time intervals can make normalization more challenging.

An alumni system is first and foremost concerned with people. People have relationships with one another through shared affiliations with an institution, connections within the context of an online social networking site, common interest in a field of research, or a coauthorship relationship with respect to a research paper. The simplest way to represent these relationships is to create edges between people for each occurrence of a given relationship. Each edge would have properties that convey the nature of the relationship. For example, if two former LANL employees went on to work for IBM, you could create a "shared affiliation" edge between them, with properties that include a company label, and a basic type such as "worked at." But this simplistic property graph model lacks sufficient granularity to model all the potential relationships of interest. For example, while two individuals may have worked at IBM they may have worked at different locations, they may not have had the same job, and they probably didn't start and end their affiliation with IBM at the same time. A good graph model tries to take into account all the possible use cases and all the available data that would be leveraged to address those use cases. In EgoSystem, we decided that in addition to people, artifacts (articles, papers, books), concepts (subjects, keywords), and institutions (businesses, universities) needed to be represented in the property graph as nodes, as well as things like affiliations and online identities.

The EgoSystem graph model is built around four primary node types: person, institution, artifact, and concept (Figure 23.8) . Each of these node types has a distinct collection of properties which serve to define it, but they also share some basic properties. These shared properties are defined in an abstract node type called Thing. Thing properties include a name label, platonic node type, temporal data, and a globally unique identifier. A name is an arbitrary string label for the node. A platonic type can be one of four values: person, institution, artifact, or concept. Temporal properties include startTime and endTime. Timepoints are encoded as UTC time stamps. The endTime property may also be zero or null depending on whether the endTime is valid to current time, or unknown. A unique node identifier is a generated UUID value conforming to RFC 4122 and is guaranteed to be unique within the graph.

The four primary node types are referred to as platonic nodes. A person node represents a LANL alumni. An institution represents an organization such as a university or business, with which a person had or has some type of relationship (e.g., worked for or studied at). An artifact is a distinct content entity, most often a publication, which a person had a role in creating. Finally, a concept is a term (keyword or phrase) which represents a fundamental unit of knowledge associated with an institution or artifact.

Platonic nodes aggregate multiple online and affiliation identities. These identities must be represented as discrete entities within the graph. A person has multiple online identities. A person might have had multiple affiliations with an institution over the course of their career. The same is true with regard to a person's relationship to artifacts such as publications. So these relationships are represented with another type of node, called an identity node. Platonic nodes are connected to identity nodes through edges that represent relationships such as "authored," "workedFor,""studiedAt," "hasConcept," "follows," and "hasIdentity."

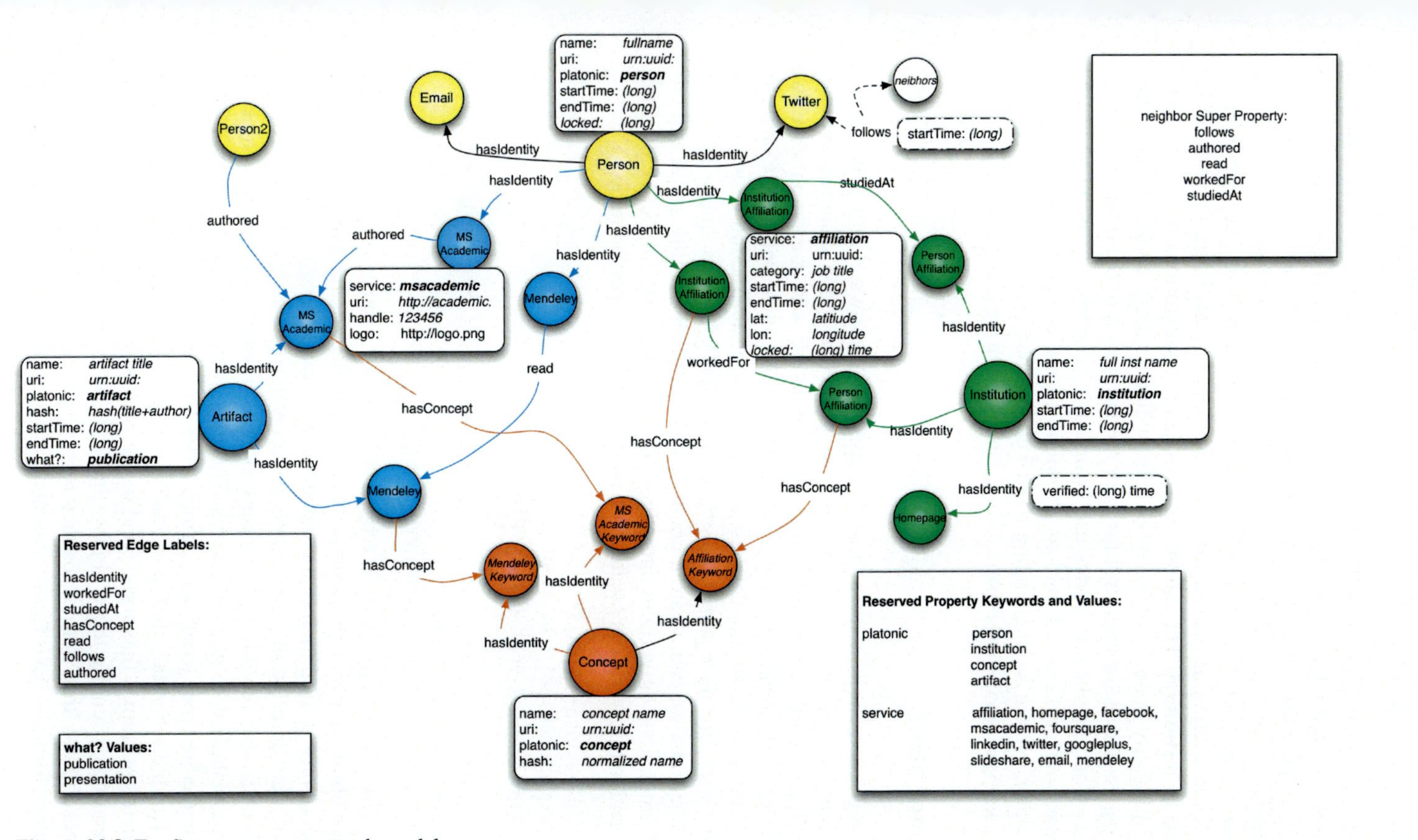

Figure 23.8 EgoSystem property graph model.

Every platonic node that has a direct connection with another node is connected via an edge with a hasIdentity property. Furthermore, this edge is always an outgoing edge, that is, it has a direction which points away from the platonic node to an intermediate identity node type. Identities can be thought of as instances of a platonic node in some other context. For example, a twitter id is a person's network identity in twitter. An institution affiliation identity represents a relationship that person has or had with an institution. This allows distinct temporal durations to be associated with a given identity node. Artifacts have intermediate identity nodes for hasAuthor relationships, as well as for identities for each representation of the object that might exist online. Concept platonic nodes use hasIdentity properties to point at institutions, people, and artifacts, as well as to online identities for a concept such as DBPedia content. It can be challenging to strike a balance between various requirements such as expressivity and traversability, when designing a graph model.

Implementation

Programmatic interactions with a graph happen at a software API layer which defines libraries for graphs, nodes, and edges. The Titan graph database included TinkerPop 2 graph APIs. For connecting and interacting with the graph store, we used Blueprints. Blueprints plays the same role as the Java Database Connector (JDBC) API does for relational databases: it is a layer of abstraction between communications with the data store, its storage primitives, and its query language. Through Blueprints, we can create a graph or connect to an existing graph and create or perform actions on vertices and edges. The Groovy code snippet below illustrates how an identity vertex is created and associated with a person node.

```
  public Boolean storeIdentities (String linkedInUrl, String platonicUri,
    Map<String, Object> discoveredInfo) {
    Person person = eg.getPlatonic(platonicUri)
...
     LinkedInPerson linkedInPerson = this.createIdentity(properties,
       LinkedInPerson.class)
     person.addIdentity(linkedInPerson)
```

In a property graph, any node or edge can have any number of properties. The Java Frames library allows a programmer to represent the graph model in Java code. The Frames library is used to define templates for nodes and edges. These templates are Java interface descriptions that enumerate allowable properties for a given graph element. Frames also provide a Java beans model for setting and getting values of properties associated with graph elements. The EgoSystem defines a number of distinct node and edge types to support various types of objects and for defining temporally distinct, bidirectional, and potentially repeating relationships among these objects. There are frames that correspond to the various node and edge types which enforce consistency among these objects and relationships. The following Groovy code defines frames that define abstract representations for Thing and Platonic, which together form the basis for all platonic node types in the Ego property graph.

```
public interface Thing extends VertexFrame {

  @Property("frame")
  public void setFrame(final String frameClass);

  @Property("frame")
  public String getFrame();

  @Property("alias")
  public String getAlias();

  @Property("alias")
  public void setAlias(final String alias);

  @Property("name")
  public String getName();

  @Property("name")
  public void setName(final String name)

  @Property("uri")
  public String getUri();

  @Property("startTime")
  public Long getStartTime();

  @Property("startTime")
  public void setStartTime(final Long
    startTime);

  @Property("endTime")
  public Long getEndTime();

  @Property("endTime")
  public void setEndTime(final Long endTime);

  @Property("locked")
  public Long getLocked();

  @Property("locked")
  public void setLocked(final Long time);
}
```

```
public abstract interface Platonic extends Thing
 {
 @Property("platonic")
 public String getPlatonic();

 @Condition("it.out('hasIdentity').hasNext()")
 @Adjacency(label = "hasIdentity")
 public Iterable<Identity> getIdentities();

 @Condition("it.out('hasIdentity').hasNext()")
 @GremlinGroovy("it.out('hasIdentity').has
   ('service',service)")
 public Iterable<Identity> getIdentities
   (@GremlinParam("service") final String
   service);

 @GremlinGroovy(value = """
   other = identity.asVertex()
   if(!it.out('hasIdentity').retain([other]).
     hasNext())
     it.addEdge('hasIdentity',other)
 """, frame = false)
 public void addIdentity(@GremlinParam
   ("identity") final Identity identity);

 @GremlinGroovy(value = "it.out('hasIdentity').
   has('service',service).hasNext()",
   frame = false)
 public Boolean hasIdentity(@GremlinParam
   ("service") final String service)

}
```

In Titan, Gremlin provides functionality similar to that provided by SQL for relational databases. Gremlin supports interactive CRUD transactions with a graph store. Graphs can be created, updated, destroyed, or imported and exported to/from the filesystem in various formats. Gremlin also supports the creation and execution of pattern matching and graph traversal queries. Pattern matching queries are searches against the values associated with a particular property of nodes or edges. Search results are returned as a list of node or edge identifiers. Graph traversals follow the links between nodes according to directional and pattern matching criteria. Here is a Gremlin example that locates all the people followed by a particular twitter identity. It first attempts to find a vertex with a 'uri' property assigned a value of 'http://twitter.com/twarko' and then traverses all the outgoing edges with the label 'follows.' It returns the name properties for all the vertices it finds.

gremlin> g.V('uri', 'http://twitter.com/twarko').out('follows').map('name').

EgoSystem uses Groovy-based extensions to provide REST interfaces for searching the graph database in various ways. These are hosted by a Web application tool called Rexster. The REST interface expects JSON objects as input parameters and returns results as JSON. These extensions support data requests that come from the EgoSystem user interface. Here are some of the REST requests supported by EgoSystem:

- getMethod
- getThingByLocation
- getThingByName
- getThingByUri
- getThingInTimeRange

Here is an example of a request to an EgoSystem Rexster extension and the response it returns:

service request:

```
http://localhost/graph/web/getThingByUri
```

JSON object posted to the service:


```
{"uri":"urn:uuid:e92925c5-91d1-4b26-a67b-48c561643edf"}
```


JSON object returned by the service (excerpt):


```
{
  "properties": {
    "platonic": "person",
    "alias": null,
    "name": "Rodriguez, Marko",
    "endTime": null,
    "startTime": null,
    "frame": "gov.lanl.egosystem.frames.platonic.Person",
    "locked": 1374698679437,
    "uri": "urn:uuid:e92925c5-91d1-4b26-a67b-48c561643edf"
  },
  "methods": [
    {
```

```
      "method": "discoverMendeley",
      "parameterTypes": "[EgoSystemGraph]",
      "returnType": "Boolean",
      "canExecute": true,
      "description": "Execute the Mendeley discovery algorithm for this
platonic"
    },
    {
      "method": "discoverTwitter",
      "parameterTypes": "[EgoSystemGraph]",
      "returnType": "Boolean",
      "canExecute": true,
      "description": "Execute the Twitter discovery algorithm for this
platonic"
    },
    {
...
  ],
  "identities": [
    {
      "properties": {
        "outDegree": null,
        "inDegree": null,
        "logo": null,
        "location": null,
        "handle": "slidarko",
        "service": "slideshare",
        "alias": null,
        "name": "Rodriguez, Marko",
        "endTime": null,
        "startTime": null,
        "frame": "gov.lanl.egosystem.frames.identities.slideshare.
SlideSharePerson",
        "locked": null,
        "uri": "http://www.slideshare.net/slidarko"
      },
      "methods": [
        {
          "method": "getFollows",
          "parameterTypes": "[Integer, Integer]",
          "returnType": "Iterable",
          "canExecute": true,
          "description": "No description is available"
        },
...
```


The getMethod is a special request type which returns the kinds of actions that can be performed with a particular node. Since nodes have properties that define what types of actions (services) they support, a call to getMethod for a given identity

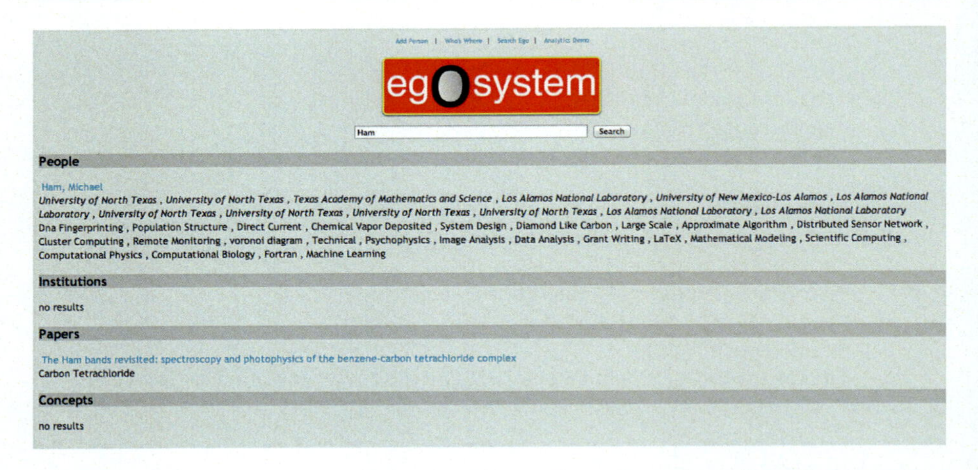

Figure 23.9 EgoSystem query with results from multiple platonic node types (people, artifacts).

UUID will retrieve a list of valid actions for that node. This allows the EgoSystem user interface to dynamically discovery what it can do with a given identity.

End users interact with EgoSystem through a Web interface. The user starts at a simple Google-like search page (Figure 23.9). Results are organized by platonic node type. A result set might include person, artifact, institution, and concept nodes. Any request from the EgoSystem Web interface targets an EgoSystem server-side REST request. The EgoSystem Web interface is implemented in Javascript. Javascript prototypes define object containers for REST API requests, nodes and their properties, search results, and path traversals. For example, any platonic node data returned by the graph database through a REST API call is mapped into an instance of an EgoPlatonic Javascript object that has appropriate fields and methods to allow other interface code to use this data.

```
function EgoPlatonic(jsonPlatonic) {
  this.uuid = jsonPlatonic.properties.uri;
  this.name = jsonPlatonic.properties.name;
  this.hash = jsonPlatonic.properties.hash;
  this.kind = jsonPlatonic.properties.platonic;
  this.locked = jsonPlatonic.properties.locked;
  this.rawJson = jsonPlatonic;
  this.queryTime = jsonPlatonic.queryTime;
...
EgoPlatonic.prototype.getUuid = function() {
    return this.uuid;
}
EgoPlatonic.prototype.getName = function() {
    return this.name;
}
EgoPlatonic.prototype.getKind = function() {
    return this.kind;
```

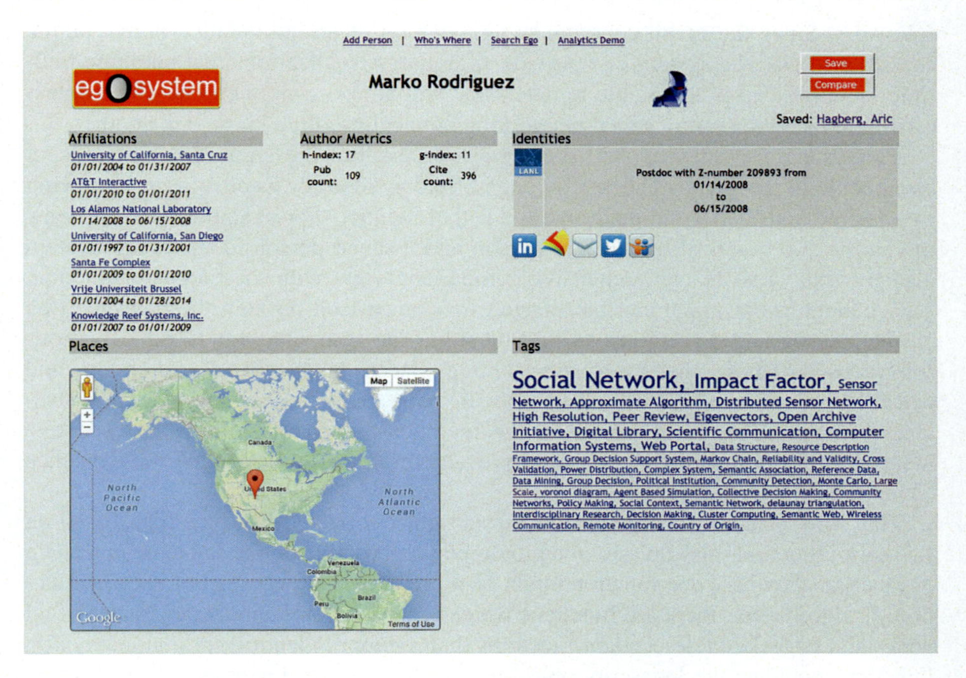

Figure 23.10 Person profile supports the main use case for EgoSystem: outreach.

```
}
EgoPlatonic.prototype.getServices = function() {
    return this.services;
}
```

Search results are returned grouped by platonic type. When a user selects an item in the result set, a getThingByUri call is issued. The data returned for this request is used by the Web interface code to create a platonic profile page. The profile page will include the properties for that node and information about nodes it is connected to, such as identities for a person node, or locations or concepts for an institution. There's also a location-based search, which uses ElasticSearch. Users can select a location such as a city and specify a radius for the search. For example, a user might chose San Francisco, CA, as a location and indicate that results within a 100 mile radius of that city should be returned.

A person profile is the heart of the Web interface (Figure 23.10). This profile includes demographic data about a person including affiliations, online social networking identities, publications, and keywords the person is associated with. It is from the person profile page that the EgoSystem user can explore various other aspects of the person's social and professional network. Many of the results of these sorts of queries are rendered as graph visualizations. Some are the results of Gremlin path traversals to locate connections between two specific individuals. Others are renderings of the first-degree network surrounding a person, such as all of the people they coauthored papers with, all of their Twitter or Slideshare followers. Since the graph contains an aggregation of an individual's online public social networks, the system can provide aggregate visualizations that combine multiple identities. So it is possible to determine who knows whom and in what context (affiliation, coauthorship, social networking connection) they know one another.

EgoSystem provides two different ways to explore the combined networks of two people in the graph. The profile page offers an identity specific way of viewing two people and their combined graphs for that identity. For example, you can view the authorship graph of the current person and a saved person identity. EgoSystem also provides a more comprehensive comparison view with the compare function. Two people in the graph can be selected for comparison through the interface (the current person and a previously saved person). The compare page retrieves various subgraphs for these two users representing places, keywords, coauthorship, and coaffiliation relationships if both individuals have the data necessary for each visualization type. This is indicated by the methods associated with their respective identities. The compare page is built by evaluating rules to determine the existence of identities (Figure 23.11).

The Web interface for EgoSystem uses an object-oriented-like paradigm based on Javascript functions and Javascript's prototype property. Functions can exist in a chain of inheritance, where one function might be a prototype (or ancestor) of another function. In EgoSystem, there are functions which represent common characteristics of all nodes and edges, and descendant functions that represent identities or platonic nodes. Functions populate the Javascript object using JSON returned in response to a request made to a Rexster extension. User interface code uses these objects to build Web pages. These Web pages often contain multiple iframes. Each iframe references an HTML wrapper page. The wrapper page interacts with one or more Javascript prototype objects to populate itself with data from the graph. For example, the tag cloud looks for an identity object that has a tagcloud method, such as a Microsoft Academic identity. It makes a getMethod request with the method name of tagcloud, together with the identity URI. This data is used to populate a Javascript ConceptMap object. A tagcloud ConceptMap has a field that contains tag names and a number that represents the number of occurrences of that tag. The tagcloud HTML wrapper page converts the contents of a ConceptMap object into an HTML representation of a tag cloud that is then displayed within an iframe (Figure 23.11).

The Javascript-based Web interface uses simple rules to determine how to construct various Web pages. Rules govern the layout and contents for person, concept, and institution profile pages (Figure 23.12), as well as the compare page. Central to the rules process is the "method" property associated with an identity node. When a request is made for a platonic person, all of the identity information, and all of the methods for each identity, is returned for that person. This information represents "conditions" which serve as input to the rules process. EgoSystem rules are expressed in JSON. Rules define conditions and actions that should be performed if a given condition is true. The interface uses a Condition object to process rules. The Condition object loads a JSON rules file and iterates through it. If a condition is met, the specified action (either a call to another Javascript page or a snippet of HTML that is to be incorporated into a page) is executed and the next

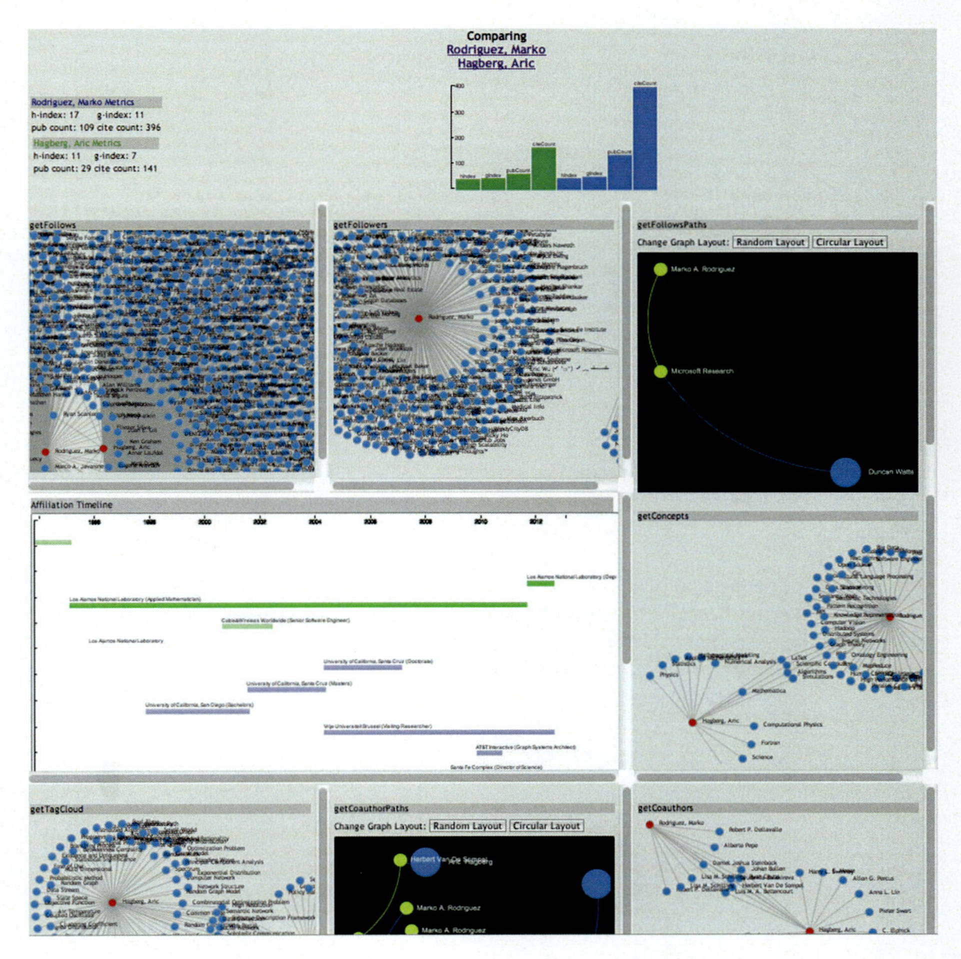

Figure 23.11 Comparing two people to look for connections between them is another EgoSystem use case, supported by the compare dash board.

method is evaluated for that identity until all methods are exhausted, then the process is repeated for other identities.

```
var ruleSet = [
  {
     "antecedent": {
       "methodName": "getPlatonic",
       "returnType": "Platonic",
       "parameterTypes": "[]",
       "canExecute": true,
       "uri": "http://academic.research",
       "service": [ "msacademic" ],
       "renderAs": "*",
```

```
      },
      "consequent": {
          "component": "author.html"
      }
  },
  {
      "antecedent": {
        "methodName": "getCoauthors",
        "returnType": "Iterable",
        "parameterTypes": "[]",
        "canExecute": true,
        "uri": "",
        "service": [ "msacademic" ],
        "renderAs": "*",
      },
      "consequent": {
          "component": "coauthors.html"
      }
  },
  {
      "antecedent": {
        "methodName": "getRankedCoauthors",
        "returnType": "Map",
        "parameterTypes": "[]",
        "canExecute": true,
        "uri": "",
        "service": [ "msacademic" ],
        "renderAs": "*",
      },
      "consequent": {
          "component": "../components/charts/basicBar.html"
      }
  },
  {
      "antecedent": {
        "methodName": "getTagCloud",
        "returnType": "Map",
        "parameterTypes": "[Integer]",
        "canExecute": true,
        "uri": "",
        "service": [ "msacademic", "linkedin" ],
        "renderAs": "*",
      },
      "consequent": {
          "params": "10",
          "component": "../components/tags/tagWords.html"
      }
  },
...
```

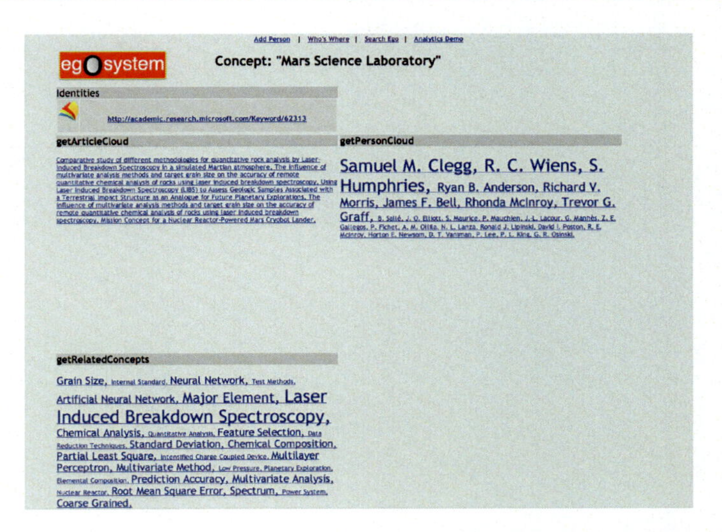

Figure 23.12 Institutions, Concepts, and Artifacts have profile pages based on the EgoSystem graph. Here is an example of a Concept page.

Conclusion

EgoSystem supports many different use cases for aggregate social networks. Users search the graph database to find profile pages. From a profile page, they might click through a user's tag cloud to a concept page for a given topic. From a topic page, they might click through to the page of an artifact associated with that keyword, and then locate other authors of that artifact. Another user may start at a person profile page and navigate to an institution page from which they can search for other people who may have been associated with that institution between some start and end date. Or they may start off with a location-based search and then navigate to a person profile page or institution page to find people or organizations located in that area. Another user, perhaps interested in second-degree identities to which a person is connected, might start at a person profile page and view their twitter social network, then click through to see who one of their followers is connected to. These interactions traverse the underlying EgoSystem graph. The EgoSystem's graph model can accommodate a large, complex aggregate social network. This same graph contains publications, concepts and organizations. The graph even knows how to populate itself. Identity nodes have discovery methods that search for public online identity and publication resources, given just a small amount of demographic starter information, so the whole system can bootstrap itself. Identities have other methods that ultimately control how the EgoSystem user interface works. Graph elements such as platonic and identity nodes are mirrored by Javascript objects in the user interface. The REST API defines methods that retrieve specific nodes, search nodes by property values, and perform path traversals to generate subgraphs that are subsequently rendered in the UI. These characteristics makes EgoSystem a pure graph-based application.

Index

Note: Page numbers followed by "*f*" refer to figures.

Printed in the United States
By Bookmasters